10/03

GAMBLING

Contemporary Issues

Series Editors: Robert M. Baird
Stuart E. Rosenbaum

Volumes edited by Robert M. Baird and Stuart E. Rosenbaum
unless otherwise noted.

GAMBLING

Who Wins? Who Loses?

EDITED BY GERDA REITH

 Prometheus Books

59 John Glenn Drive
Amherst, New York 14228-2197

Published 2003 by Prometheus Books

Inquiries should be addressed to
Prometheus Books
59 John Glenn Drive
Amherst, New York 14228–2197

716–691–0133 (x207). FAX: 716–564–2711.
WWW.PROMETHEUSBOOKS.COM

07 06 05 04 03   5 4 3 2 1

Library of Congress Cataloging-in-Publication Data

Gambling : who wins? who loses? / edited by Gerda Reith.
        p. cm. — (Contemporary issues series)
    Includes bibliographical references.
    ISBN 1–59102–073–5 (pbk. : alk. paper)
    1. Gambling—United States. 2. Gambling—Law and legislation—United
States 3. Gambling—Psychological aspects. 4. Gambling—Social aspects.
I. Reith, Gerda, 1969– II. Series.

GV1301.G33 2003
306.4'82—dc21   2002036618

Printed in the United States of America on acid-free paper

CONTENTS

SECTION THREE: LAW, CRIME, AND COMMERCIAL REGULATION

SECTION FOUR: THE "ADDICTION" DEBATE

SECTION FIVE: SOCIAL TRENDS, PROBLEM GAMBLING, AND THE CHALLENGE TO PUBLIC POLICY

SECTION SIX: PSYCHOLOGICAL AND ENVIRONMENTAL FACTORS

SECTION SEVEN: ETHICAL AND PHILOSOPHICAL ISSUES

Introduction

PATHOLOGY AND PROFIT

Controversies in the Expansion of Legal Gambling

Gerda Reith

n the past century, gambling has undergone a profound transformation. From being regarded as an economically marginal, politically corrupt, and often morally dubious activity, it has, at the start of the twenty-first century, become a global player in the economies of North America, Europe, and Australasia. Today, the gambling industry is a billion-dollar enterprise, creating vast profits for commercial organizations and contributing massive amounts of revenue to both state and federal governments.

This expansion has been particularly acute in the past decade, in which increasing liberalization has resulted in the massive growth of both the size of the industry and gambling expenditure throughout the world. In addition, the emergence of new media such as the Internet has revealed the potential of technology not only to dramatically increase existing gambling opportunities but also to introduce new ones of hitherto unimagined proportions.

Recently, wide-ranging, independent studies conducted in the United States, Australia, and Great Britain have provided a clear picture of the vast size of the gambling industry, and the immense influence of the activity—both beneficial and harmful—on the individuals and communities involved with it. In 1999 the National Gambling Impact Study Commission (NGISC) documented a seismic shift in American attitudes toward gambling over the past thirty years. In the mid-1970s, the United States had allowed gambling only in a few states, but at the beginning of the twenty-first century, gambling in some form is legal in all but three states. Over 60 percent of the population gambled in 1998, and government itself is increasingly involved in the gambling business, whether through involvement in state lotteries and Native American casinos, or through the taxation and regulation of private commercial operators. Revenues from legal gambling grew by almost 1,600 percent between 1976 and 1998, with the size of the industry growing tenfold. Actual expenditure (the amount wagered minus payouts for winnings, which are directly taxable) increased from $10.4 billion in 1982 to $50 billion in 1997, with the total amount wagered standing at approximately $551 billion. Among the adult population, annual per capita spending is approximately $238.

The gambling industry is a major economic force in the United States and one of the nation's largest employers. In 1996, more than half a million people were employed in it, earning over $15 billion. The casino industry alone directly employed 300,000 people, paying $7.3 billion in wages and indirectly supporting a further 400,000 jobs, with a payroll of $12.5 billion. Out of its revenues of around $25 billion, it paid $2.9 billion in taxes.[1]

Similar trends of proliferation, industry growth, and increased consumer expenditure were found in the studies conducted in Australia and Great Britain. In Australia, the Productivity Commission documented that gambling revenues had more than doubled in the last decade, with actual expenditure growing from AU$ 2.7 billion in the early 1970s to over AU$ 11 billion in 1997–98, and with over AU$ 95 billion wagered in 1997–98. Over 80 percent of the adult population had gambled within the year of the study, with an average per capita spend of approximately AU$ 760 (around U.S. $ 417).[2] Overall, the Australian gambling industry directly employs some 37,000 people, with another 120,000 in gambling-related work; and contributes AU$ 3.5 billion in taxation.[3]

According to statistics from a study conducted in 2000, in Great Britain approximately 70 percent of the population gamble in a given year, resulting in an annual expenditure of £7.3 billion and an annual per capita expense of around £155 (about U.S $ 226).[4] The industry itself has a turnover of £42 billion and contributes £1530 million in gambling duties and taxation to the government.[5] It is also a significant employer, with casinos, bingo, and slot machines alone providing jobs for over 55,000 people.[6]

ECONOMIC AND SOCIAL IMPACTS

There is ongoing debate about the economic benefits of gambling, with advocates of its expansion drawing attention to its potential for creating revenue and employment, and critics arguing that such claims are exaggerated and that the social costs of gambling outweigh any benefits it may offer.

At this point, a distinction should be made between different types of gambling, as not all segments of the industry produce the same effects. For instance, widely dispersed forms of "convenience" gambling, such as slot machines and games played over the Internet, create few jobs and have very little impact on the economy. As they tend to encourage repeated play and are relatively unregulated, they are also more likely to contribute to problem gambling.

The casino and pari-mutuel industries, in contrast, are highly concentrated and strictly regulated commercial ventures that create a significant number of direct and indirect jobs, increasing consumer expenditure and stimulating economic growth. Particularly in depressed communities, the economic effects of casinos can be dramatic, with newly created jobs reducing unemployment and welfare outlays, encouraging capital formations, and increasing social wealth. As the NGISC study shows, the benefits of increased tax revenues and recreational opportunities, as well as rising property values and better health care, training, and education for individuals and communities, are undeniable.[7] On a broad scale, states have used lotteries to raise revenue for various public services, while gambling on North American Indian reservations has created wealth among previously impoverished tribes.

However, a closer examination reveals that the overall economic impact of gambling is not as unambiguously positive as it may first appear. In fact, the net result of gambling expansion is not so much a dramatic *increase* in wealth as a *transfer* of existing wealth. Although the introduction of gambling facilities can generate jobs and income, these are likely to be at the expense of jobs and income in other areas. The resources that are utilized in the expansion of gambling would likely have been used by other leisure industries, with a similar overall result. Similarly, the money spent on gambling would have been spent on other forms of leisure or recreation. Many small businesses actually report a reduction in profits as a direct result of the competition from commercial gambling and for this reason their owners frequently oppose the expansion of new gambling outlets. In fact, although the gambling industry may create additional jobs or income (for example, in economically depressed areas), much of the apparent growth is simply a manifestation of resources diverted from other areas, and so the net effect is small.[8]

Nor are the enormous revenues generated by lotteries an unqualified social good. Although the revenue they create undoubtedly benefits the state, there is no evidence that the projects they pay for would not be funded were it not for lottery money. In fact, some states have reported a decrease in general funding for services for which lottery money was earmarked, and many more have become entirely dependent on lottery revenue for certain services and consequently suffer when playing declines and revenues fall. Furthermore, lotteries are played disproportionately by the poorest and most disadvantaged groups, with the unemployed, the low paid, the undereducated, the elderly, and minority groups spending far more than others. In real terms, the various projects and services funded by lotteries are paid for primarily by the poorest members of their communities, in effect making lotteries a highly regressive form of taxation.[9]

Although certain forms of gambling may benefit economically depressed communities, the NGISC concluded that an overall cost-benefit analysis of its impact was impossible to estimate. The Productivity Commission was more decisive, arguing that, as economic transfers cancel out net economic gains, the real benefit of gambling must be counted in terms of social factors and consumer satisfaction and offset with any social problems it may introduce.

Problem Gambling

These social factors are the most controversial aspect of the spread of gambling, as its growth is associated with a range of problems among individuals, families, and communities, including displacement of local residents, negative environmental effects, increased indebtedness and crime,[10] and the occurrence of problem and pathological gambling.[11]

The incidence of problem and pathological gambling is of particular concern, for although games of chance provide enjoyable recreation for the majority of those who engage in them, for a significant minority, they can initiate a spiral of problems from dependency, debt, and bankruptcy to crime, domestic violence, familial breakdown, and suicide.

Generally, the distinction between "problem" and "pathological" gambling is one of severity, with pathological gamblers less able to control their actions and more likely to suffer adverse effects than problem gamblers. Somewhat ironically, the definition and measurement of the extent of problem gambling in a population can itself be problematic. Generally, one of two measurement instruments is used to determine whether an individual is a problem gambler: the South Oaks Gambling Screen (SOGS)[12] and the fourth edition of the American Psychiatric Association's *Diagnostic and Statistical Manual of Mental Disorders* (DSM-IV).[13] Whereas the SOGS is concerned with behavior, such as chasing losses, controlling gambling, and feeling guilty about gambling more than intended, the DSM-IV emphasizes psychological factors such as preoccupation, tolerance, and gambling as a form of escape. Prevalence rates can also be measured in two ways: by counting those who meet the criteria for problem or pathological gambling only in the past twelve months ("past-year gamblers") or by including all those who have ever fulfilled the criteria ("lifetime gamblers"). There are problems with both approaches, as "lifetime" measures may overestimate the problem, whereas "past-year" measures may underestimate it.

The lack of standard, universal criteria leads to difficulties in estimating the extent of problem gambling, and the two scales give different results. However, based on the SOGS criteria, the Productivity Commission calculated that around 1 percent of Australia's adult population (130,000 people) experienced severe gambling problems, while a further

1.1 percent (163,000) suffered moderate problems.[14] The U.S study used the DSM-IV and commissioned two pieces of research—one by the National Opinion Research Council (NORC)[15] and one by the National Research Council (NRC) of the National Academy of Sciences.[16] These studies estimated the prevalence of pathological gambling in any given year to be between 0.9 percent and 0.6 percent of the population (1.8 to 1.2 million people) and the prevalence of problem gambling to be between 2 and 0.7 percent (4 to 1.4 million).[17] The British study used both screens to determine the prevalence of those who had experienced problems in the past year. The DSM-IV put the figure at 0.6 percent, or 275,000 people, while the SOGS estimated it to be 0.8 percent, or 370,000 people.[18]

Although it is difficult to compare these results accurately, all three reports make clear that a significant minority of the population suffers problems related to gambling. These problems are damaging to economic productivity, social stability, and familial cohesion, to say nothing of the personal misery suffered by the individuals affected. Furthermore, problem gamblers contribute disproportionately to overall gambling revenues: the Australian evidence shows that this group account for around one third of the gambling industries' market.[19]

Two things become abundantly clear from this research: one, that commercial gambling is a major economic force and mainstream leisure activity, and two, that it is at the same time a deeply problematic enterprise. As the gambling industry continues its relentless expansion into a global marketplace, the debate becomes increasingly polarized between those who regard it as a legitimate commercial business and those who see it as a harmful social activity.

At one extreme, advocates of the expansion of gambling emphasize its economic benefits to states, communities, and commercial enterprises, as well as its entertainment value to consumers, and argue that the gambling industry should be allowed the same freedoms as any other business. This view of gambling as an innocuous product was expressed by a spokesperson for Circus Circus Casino in Las Vegas who compared the casino to a store: "[The casino] is an entertainment merchant. It's just that we happen to merchandise playtime to our customers rather than goods."[20]

At the other end of the spectrum, many academic researchers and treatment professionals focus on the damaging nature of gambling and argue that its social and individual costs outweigh any (supposed) benefits it may bring. Vocal opposition can come from religious and temperance groups, as well as from problem gamblers themselves. The perspective of such groups, to varying degrees, is that gambling is a potentially harmful activity whose expansion should be restricted and regulated accordingly.

Such a conflict of opinion is not new. The relationship of most societies to gambling has always been ambivalent, vacillating between a climate of liberal promotion (usually based on economic grounds), and critical prohibition (usually based on ethical or moral or, more recently, medical grounds). The situation today is largely the result of centuries of tension between these opposing perspectives and the specific cultural, economic, and ideological assumptions that underlie them. Because these debates have shaped the way we view gambling today, it is instructive to briefly trace their historical development to better understand our current situation.

THE HISTORICAL LEGACY

The Critical Tradition

The history of gambling has been the history of attempts to outlaw, banish, and repress what was regarded as a disruptive and dangerous activity from civil society. The terms of the criticism have varied according to the social climate of the time,[21] but generally, the tone has been one of open hostility to what was considered to be a "deviant" activity—especially when the gamblers in question were members of economically marginal groups. From the Reformation onward, games of chance were seen to encapsulate an orientation to economic enterprise that opposed mainstream values of hard work, personal effort, and saving. Reliance on luck or pure chance to determine social position and wealth undermined the Protestant work ethic, with the result that gambling was strongly condemned by the Church as a sinful activity.[22]

During the more secular climate of the Enlightenment, criticism focused on the nonrational elements of gambling that tended to encourage superstitious beliefs in luck and predetermined fate. These elements were anathema to rational, modernizing societies that required individuals to work, save, and, crucially, take personal responsibility for their own future welfare and happiness. Gambling was regarded as an unproductive and potentially disruptive activity, and various laws and statutes were enforced in order to minimize its harmful effects.[23]

On the whole, this legislation was highly selective and managed to be both patrician and paternalistic at the same time. Its proponents focused mainly on the poor; reasoning that whereas the rich could take care of themselves, the poor needed protection from the poverty and destitution that would invariably follow if they were allowed to gamble. Particularly in Great Britain, although to a lesser extent throughout Europe and North America, legislation was drafted specifically to prevent lower social classes from participating in any form of gambling. In Australia, however, a smaller, less influential middle class and the reduced involvement of the Church in the regulation of gambling created a far more liberal climate in which individuals' desire to gamble was tolerated to a far greater degree than in Europe or North America.[24]

Despite widespread disapproval, European governments at this time were quite amenable to exploiting gambling for their own ends, which they did in the form of lotteries. As their potential to raise revenue became obvious, lotteries developed throughout Europe during the sixteenth century, with Britain exporting its model to the colonial States, where the money they raised helped to finance the building of the New World.

In a pattern that has been repeated throughout history, when gambling is economically expedient, it has been tolerated and even encouraged, and when it becomes superfluous, it is simply outlawed. During the Industrial Revolution, a resurgence of the evangelical movement and increased demands for industrial productivity saw a return to the emphasis on gambling's disruptive and undesirable qualities. Coincidentally, by this time lotteries no longer provided crucial revenue and so were speedily banned by the very governments that once had profited from them. Now, as the perception of gambling as a vice began to take hold in the public mind, lotteries began to be associated with political corruption, dishonesty and crime. However, instead of being criticized in religious terminology, gambling was now brought down to the level of human failing, and its ability to undermine the work ethic was increasingly linked to individual defects. During this period of social Darwinism, biomedical theories were used to "explain" perceived moral failings. Along with prostitution and alcoholism, the "vice" of gambling was incorporated into this model and was analyzed by Freud as a compulsive mania. Out of this psychoanalytical and biomedical climate, the notion of gambling as an illness or compulsion emerged, and the groundwork for its medicalization, which would reappear at the end of the twentieth century, was created.

Although the terminology has changed, elements of this critical discourse in which gambling was perceived as a sin and a vice can still be found today in the view of gambling as an essentially harmful activity capable of corroding the fabric of a healthy society. However, this is only one side of the story. To understand the complex position of modern gambling, we must also consider the contrary view.

LIBERALIZATION AND COMMERCIALIZATION

At the same time that gambling was being condemned as a vice, a trend was developing that would have a massive impact on the discourse of the previous centuries and ultimately revolutionize the position of gambling throughout the world.

This was the force of commercialization: the organization of games of chance for profit that ended attempts to ban and outlaw them and led to the view of gambling as a legitimate form of consumption—a leisure pursuit and a source of recreation that was, like any other product, a legitimate part of capitalist enterprise.

The shift in perception from deviance to leisure started at the beginning of the nineteenth century, although what would come to be known as the gambling industry did not begin to emerge in any recognizable form until the early 1970s. At the turn of the nineteenth century, individual entrepreneurs such as bookmakers and gambling house operators organized private, local games on a small scale. But toward the end of the century, the commercial potential of gambling activities other than lotteries began to emerge. As scientific understanding of probability developed, it became clear that there were profits to be made from organizing and overseeing games of chance. This recognition, together with increased demand, encouraged the development of large syndicates that, although illegal, were assured virtual monopoly status through political connections. These organizations, the forerunners of the modern gambling industry, made their profits from players' losses—otherwise known as the "house edge." Across Europe and North America, this commercialization gradually changed the way people gambled. Instead of wagering directly against each other, their bets were now mediated through a third party: the "house." Now they purchased a leisure experience, and price of that experience was paid in losing wagers.[25]

Over the course of the twentieth century, a range of factors combined to alter the status of gambling still further. In the first half-century, economic recession and fiscal deficits, together with the political unpopularity of taxation, encouraged states to consider alternative means of raising revenue. In the second half, increasing affluence and the declining influence of the work ethic led to a more libertarian, consumerist ethos in most industrialized countries. Together, these factors encouraged a more pragmatic approach to gambling, in which the needs of the state and the desires of the consumer were seen to come together. Efforts to prohibit gambling altogether were supplanted by attempts to regulate it. If it was all but impossible to prevent gambling, so the argument went, better for the state to ensure that it was run fairly and legally—and, as a bonus, share in the profits from its taxable revenue.

The process was most obvious in the case of lotteries, whose revenue-generating potential was once again recognized by states that wanted to increase revenue without resorting to the politically unpopular move of raising taxation. In a climate in which, as John Kenneth Galbraith noted, the increasingly affluent majority were unwilling to pay taxes to provide for the less fortunate minority, the economic utility of gambling to states was enormous. New Hampshire reintroduced its lottery in 1963, with other states following its example one by one. The same logic of revenue creation lay behind the gradual liberalization of other forms of commercial gambling, with the steady proliferation of pari-mutuel wagering and casinos on riverboats and Indian reservations, as well as the spread of convenience gambling from the 1970s onwards.

The post-war expansion took a slightly different form in Great Britain and Canada, where a more interventionist approach led to the enforcement of stricter regulatory legislation and the subsequent development of smaller commercial markets. In Britain in particular, a paternalistic approach led to laws that attempted to "protect" gamblers, especially those from the working class, from their own excesses and to limit gambling opportunities and availability.[26]

In Australia, a more tolerant culture and high levels of state involvement both legitimated gambling and gave it a central place in national life. From an early period, it was regarded as a social activity to be regulated by the government for the welfare of its citizens, in a similar way to health and education. In keeping with this generally more favorable climate, Australian federal policies did not prevent states from running lotteries, as they did for a time in the United States.[27]

However, despite their differences, these models are driven by the same simple motive—the extraction of commercial and state profit from games of chance. And, in the twenty-first century, commercial gambling does indeed generate huge revenues from a variety of sources: direct taxing of gross revenue; indirect contributions in the form of federal, state, and municipal income taxes; property and payroll taxes; and a variety of miscellaneous local taxes and license fees.[28]

The increasing involvement of states in commercial gambling has resulted in a degree of interdependence between the two. Although owned by the state, many lotteries are franchised to private enterprise where they generate revenue for government projects as well as profits for private companies. In such a situation the maximization of profit becomes the aim of both government and business. In a market in which sales of lottery tickets quickly reach saturation point, leading to stagnant or declining revenue, many states are involved in the aggressive promotion of their lotteries: advertising to target groups, introducing new games, and developing increasingly sophisticated technologies to promote their product.[29]

The gambling industry itself is increasingly owned by a limited number of multinational corporations, concentrated in an oligopolistic market. It is organized in a similar way to other major industries, with market research and advertising strategies designed to identify and target niche groups. Frequent innovations ensure a regular supply of new and specialized gambling opportunities, so that it is now possible to gamble on a wide range of occasions: from taking a day-trip to a casino or a family vacation in Las Vegas to passing a few hours on a slot machine or buying into the dream of a big win with a weekly lottery ticket. Modern consumers have a variety of products and experiences to choose from, and an ever-larger and more powerful industry to supply them.

The success of commercial gambling has resulted in an increasing perception of the gambling industry as a mainstream, legitimate business, selling a commodity—which in this case, happens to be chance—as if it were any other product. Likewise, gamblers appear now as ordinary consumers—as hedonists, escapists, or risk takers, perhaps, but certainly not immoral or criminal degenerates. The state-sponsored fantasy of the instant win actually reverses the Protestant ethic, leaving no trace of its troubled past as vice or sin.

Medicalization

In this era of consumerism and normalization, criticism of gambling still exists but tends to be expressed in language specific to the cultural climate of its time. In the period of increasing liberalization around the 1980s, the specter of "the gambling problem" reappeared. The medical-moral associations that gambling had assumed in the nineteenth century allowed it to be incorporated easily into a medical paradigm, which at the time was being extended to describe and explain increasingly disparate types of activity.[30] From substances that were seen as inherently "addictive," such as alcohol, illegal drugs, and nicotine to activities that compelled the individual to repeat them over and over again, such as sport, eating, sexual relations, and work, there seemed no limit to the variety of human behavior that could be explained by science.[32] Out of this discourse the figure of the "pathological gambler" emerged.

The increasing medicalization of gambling throughout the 1980s was reflected in its changing classification in the American Psychological Association's *Diagnostic and Statistical Manual* (DSM). In 1980, gambling was included for the first time under the heading of an impulse control disorder—as "compulsive gambling."[32] By 1987, an increased emphasis on its physiological characteristics such as tolerance and withdrawal caused it to be reclassified as a pathology similar to substance dependence.[33] This emphasis pointed to the possibility of a physiological basis for excessive gambling, and various scientific studies were conducted to investigate the relation.[34] Substances such as endorphins, nonadrenaline, and serotonin have been associated with altered levels of arousal and impulsive mood disorders, and brain-imaging techniques have been used to uncover the physical mechanisms underlying pathological gambling. More controversially, researchers have postulated that certain receptor genes associated with substance abuse, alcoholism, and compulsive overeating may also be responsible for gambling disorders.[35] Besides diagnosing the problem, medicine holds out the hope of a cure. Various therapeutic options exist, from attempts to modify the gambler's behavior and thought processes to treatment with lithium and antidepressants.

Whatever the exact cause of the problem, all these medical models assume the fundamental abnormality of the gambler in some way. Terms such as "pathology" and "compulsion" describe behavior that is out of control, unwilled by its owner, and not amenable to rational volition. If this is the case, individuals suffering from such afflictions cannot legally be held responsible for their actions and should not be found guilty for criminal acts committed while in this state.[36]

Whether this position is justified is a moot point: indeed, there is considerable disagreement over the application of the medical model to gambling.[37] However, this view of the gambler as a victim of his or her own compulsions is the logical conclusion of the more extreme medical and behaviorist models, and the utility of these models must be situated in their specific sociohistorical and cultural climate. Today, the language of "problem" gambling is part of a secular medical and scientific discourse that seeks to absolve and cure the individual, rather than a specifically religious or rationalist view that, in previous eras, sought to condemn and punish them for their actions. Although elements of earlier attitudes linger—the idea that gambling is problematic because it is wasteful, immoral, or irrational—today's discussion of the "problem" is couched primarily in medical terms.

DEBATING THE ISSUES

The historical development of both critical and commercial perspectives has established the groundwork for our modern gambling discourse and has outlined the parameters of the contemporary debate. The former approach is mainly ideological and is related to gambling's denial of the work ethic and its disruptive effects on individuals and society, while the latter is mainly pragmatic and is concerned with the commercial possibilities of gambling. Today, the legacy of these two perspectives is a debate in which opinion is sharply divided between two very different camps.

On the one hand, in what can be called the "medical model" that emerged from the critical tradition, gambling is viewed primarily in terms of its potential for pathology; as something that can ruin the lives of individuals, their families, and their communities. As the "illness" involves a progressive loss of control, legally the consumer—the gambler—cannot be held responsible for his or her actions, and therefore responsibility for harm caused must lie with the producer—the industry. In this view, regulation and organization of this industry cannot be left to those who profit from it but should be overseen by higher authority at the state level. In addition, the industry has a duty to act responsibly: to regulate itself, limit potential harm, and ameliorate any negative side effects caused by its product. In this model, the interventionist role of the state is regarded as both desirable and necessary.

On the other hand, the emergence of what can be called the "commercial model" out of the more liberal perspective has created a climate in which the gambling industry is viewed as a legitimate entertainment provider that should be allowed the same freedoms as any other business; most obviously, the right to promote its product without interference from the state. In this view, any problems individuals encounter with that product are primarily the responsibility of those individuals, who should seek their own personal solutions. One industry leader expressed this view of minimal responsibility when he asked himself: "Do problem gamblers exist? I am yet to be convinced of this: however, I fully acknowledge that there are people with problems who gamble."[38] In such a model, state intervention is a hindrance to the operation of the free market.

♥ ♦ ♠ ♣

Due to the constraints of space, this discussion is necessarily simplified, aiming only to provide a general outline of the main trends and issues surrounding the gambling debate. The reality, as always, is far more complex, and most positions fall somewhere between the two extremes set out here. The task of exploring these subtleties is given over to the essays collected in this volume which attempt to provide a detailed and comprehensive analysis of the issues surrounding the expansion of commercial gambling. The difficult and pressing questions addressed here include:

- How can the economic benefits and the enjoyment that gambling brings to millions of consumers be balanced against the need to protect the vulnerable from potential harm?
- Is "pathological gambling" an illness similar to drug dependency? If so, what is the best way to identify and treat problem gamblers?
- To what extent should commercial gambling be regulated, and what type of organization is best suited to implementing such regulations?
- To what extent should states become involved in the gambling business? Should they rely on lottery revenues to pay for public services?
- What is the best way to deal with the growing impact of new gambling technologies?

The essays in this volume are arranged into seven sections, each dealing with a particular aspect of the debate from legal, economic, and political issues to psychological, social, and ethical ones. The collection begins by examining current trends in commercial gambling. William R. Eadington provides an overview of ongoing international trends and analyzes the controversial and often problematic decisions to liberalize gambling law. Jan McMillen looks at regulatory challenges as gambling moves from a small-scale community activity to a hi-tech, global one, focusing on the role of new technologies such as the Internet in this shift.

The second section analyzes the economic and social costs and benefits of gambling. Earl L. Grinols begins by correcting common misconceptions about the economic value of gambling, conducting a rigorous cost-benefit analysis of casino gambling that demonstrates negligible net benefits. Robert Goodman criticizes what he calls the "grand illusion" of gambling as a viable strategy for economic development and counts the cost to communities when commercial gambling fails to deliver on this promise. From another angle, B. Grant Stitt, Mark Nichols, and David Giacopassi examine the subjective response to the spread of gambling by conducting an empirical study of residents' responses to the adoption of casinos in their communities.

Section three discusses issues of law, crime, and commercial regulation. I. Nelson Rose begins by outlining how historical "waves" of prohibition and legalization have been transformed into the current "explosion" of legal gambling in the United States today. New technologies such as the Internet are a significant force in this expansion, and the complex regulatory issues they raise are the focus of Michael E. Hammond's essay on the legal status of Internet gambling. Jay Albanese assesses the relation between casino gambling and crime and emphasizes the need for the continued close regulation and monitoring of gambling to keep the risk of crime low. Regulation in the interests of player protection is also advocated by David Miers, who draws attention to the equally important need to balance such regulations against the protection of consumer sovereignty and the encouragement of competition among suppliers.

The controversies surrounding the notion of "addictive" or pathological gambling are the focus of the fourth section. Howard J. Shaffer begins by outlining the difficulties in defining gambling—and, in fact, any behavior—as "addictive," and examines the existence of other, related disorders alongside the problem of gambling behavior. His argument is ultimately pragmatic and makes the point that the value of the concept of pathological gambling rests with the treatment benefits sufferers receive from its application. Mark Dickerson's critical piece takes a more extreme position, suggesting the redundancy of the term *pathological* and pointing to differences between the political, research, and academic climates in the United States and Australia to demonstrate the expediency—or otherwise—of its application in those countries. Stanton Peele argues that while gambling is addictive, it is not a disease and should therefore be understood in behavioral and experiential, not biological, terms.

Recent trends in gambling behavior, especially in problem gambling, and the challenge these trends pose to public policy, are the subject of the fifth section. Rachel A. Volberg outlines the contemporary situation, documenting the increase in gambling behavior in America in terms of the age, sex, ethnicity, and attitudes of participants, and further analyzes this in terms of problem gambling by group and by type of gambling activity. Jeffrey Derevensky et al. examine trends among youth—the group most vulnerable to developing problems with gambling—and discuss the implications of these trends for policy making, while, at the other end of the age range Dennis P. McNeilly and William J. Burke focus on the impact of gambling among the often overlooked older generation. In the final essay in this section, Keith Whyte highlights the impact of problem gambling as a serious public health issue and calls for a national policy response that incorporates prevention, education, treatment, enforcement, and research.

The influence of psychological and environmental factors on gambling behavior is the subject of section six. Mark Griffiths and Jonathan Parke analyze the way in which a range of environmental features, such as music, light, and color, can induce gamblers to play for longer periods or, conversely, make them stop early. From another angle, Neil A. Manson examines how gamblers' subjective (and often erroneous) beliefs concerning probability affect their playing strategy—and the amounts of money they stand to lose.

The widely debated moral and ethical aspects of gambling are the subject of the final section. Jerome H. Skolnick looks at relativistic and shifting definitions of "vice" throughout history, examining gambling in relation to other "wicked pleasures" and arguing that public policy must find a regulatory mean somewhere between criminalization and exploitation in order to regulate it. Peter Collins's essay draws on the political philosophy of Hobbes, Locke, and Mill to argue that, in a liberal democracy, the outlawing of gambling is a morally illegitimate abuse of power. Kathryn Gabriel's wide-ranging study examines the role of gambling, both as a metaphor and as a practice, throughout world mythology. She concludes that the dynamic behind all gambling behavior is fundamentally spiritual, and as such, it should be understood in terms of religious belief, rather than as a sin or a vice. Finally, John Scanlan provides a philosophical and literary reflection on the wider role of chance in life and its implications for issues of rationality and knowledge.

All of these essays, in their various ways, bring a critical perspective to bear on the complex social, individual, legal, political, and economic issues brought about by the spread of commercial gambling. Although they may not provide straightforward solutions to all the problems they identify, they do begin to establish the parameters for further research and, in so doing, provide the impetus for informed and ongoing debate of this complex and rapidly growing phenomenon.

NOTES

1. National Gambling Impact Study Commission (NGISC), *Final Report* (Washington, D.C., Government Printing Office, 1999).

2. Based on an exchange rate where AU$ 1 is equivalent to U.S.$ 0.54 and £0.38.

3. Productivity Commission, *Australia's Gambling Industries: Final Report* (Canberra: Commonwealth Government, 1999).

4. Based on an exchange rate where £1 is equivalent to US$ 1.45 and AU$ 2.65.

5. Kerry Sproston, Bob Erens, and Jim Orford, *Gambling Behaviour in Britain: Results from the British Gambling Prevalence Survey* (London: National Center for Social Research, 2000); Department for Culture, Media, and Sport (DCMS), *Gambling Review Report* (London: Stationery Office, 2001).

6. Gambling Board for Great Britain, *Report of the Gambling Board for Great Britain, 2000–01* (London: Stationery Office, 2001).

7. NGISC, *Final Report*, p. 7–10.

8. Robert Goodman, *The Luck Business* (New York: Free Press, 1995); Productivity Commission, *Australia's Gambling Industries*, pp.16–17.

9. Charles Clotfelter and Philip Cook, *Selling Hope: State Lotteries in America.* (Cambridge: Harvard University Press, 1989); NGISC, *Final Report*, chap. 7.

10. However, the NGISC cautions that there is insufficient evidence to establish this connection with crime conclusively.

11. National Research Council (NRC), *Pathological Gambling: A Critical Review* (Washington, D.C.: National Academy Press, 1999), p. 157.

12. Henry R. Lesieur and Sheila B. Blume, "The South Oaks Gambling Screen (SOGS): A New Instrument for the Identification of Pathological Gamblers," *American Journal of Psychiatry* 144 (1987): 1184–88.

13. American Psychiatric Association, *Diagnostic and Statistical Manual of Mental Disorders*, (DSM-IV) 4th ed. (Washington D.C.: American Psychiatric Association, 1994)

14. Productivity Commission, *Australia's Gambling Industries*.

15. This survey used a new screening instrument known as NODS (*NORC DSM SCREEN* for Gambling Problems), based on DSM-IV criteria.

16. NRC, *Pathological Gambling.*

17. The NRC estimated that at some time in their lives, 1.5 percent of the population (3 million people) had been pathological gamblers and 3.9 percent (7.8 million) problem gamblers, while the NORC estimated that 1.2 percent (2.5 million) had been pathological gamblers and 1.5 percent (3 million) problem gamblers some time in their lives.

18. Kevin Sproston, Bob Erens, and Jim Orford, *Gambling Behaviour in Britain.*

19. Productivity Commission, *Australia's Gambling Industries.*

20. Circus Circus, *Circus Circus Annual Report, 1989.*

21. See I. Nelson Rose "Compulsive Gambling and the Law: From Sin to Vice to Disease," *Journal of Gambling Behavior* 4 (1988): 240–60, and Gerda Reith, *The Age of Chance: Gambling in Western Culture* (London: Routledge, 1999).

22. Roger Munting, *An Economic and Social History of Gambling in Britain and the U.S.A* (Manchester: Manchester University Press, 1996), p. 29; Reith, *The Age of Chance.*

23. David Dixon, *From Prohibition to Regulation: Bookmaking, Anti-Gambling, and the Law* (Oxford: Clarendon Press, 1991); Munting, *An Economic and Social History of Gambling*; John Findlay, *People of Chance: Gambling in American Society from Jamestown to Las Vegas* (Oxford: Oxford University Press, 1986).

24. Geoff Caldwell et al., *Gambling in Australia* (Sydney: Croom Helm, 1985); W. Selby "Social Evil or Social good? Lotteries and State Regulation in Australia and the United States" in *Gambling Cultures: Studies in History and Interpretation*, ed. Jan McMillen (London: Routledge, 1996).

25. Findlay, *People of Chance*; Vicki Abt, "The Role of the State in the Expansion and Growth of Commercial Gambling in the United States," in *Gambling Cultures.*

26. Dixon, *From Prohibition to Regulation*

27. Jan McMillen, ed. "Understanding Gambling: History, Concepts, and Theories" in *Gambling Cultures.*

28. Vicki Abt, James F. Smith, and Eugene M. Christiansen, *The Business of Risk: Commercial Gambling in Mainstream America* (Lawrence: University Press of Kansas, 1985); Abt, "The Role of the State in the Expansion and Growth of Commercial Gambling," p. 183.

29. Clotfelter and Cook, *Selling Hope.*

30. Peter Conrad, *Deviance and Medicalization: From Badness to Sickness* (Philadelphia: Temple University Press, 1992).

31. Richard L. Solomon and J. D. Corbit, "An Opponent-Process Theory of Motivation," *Psychological Review* 81 (1974): 119–45; Jim Orford, *Excessive Appetites* (London: John Wiley & Sons, 1985).

32. American Psychiatric Association, *DSM-III, Diagnostic and Statistical Manual of Mental Disorders*, 3d ed. (Washington, D.C.: American Psychiatric Association, 1980).

33. American Psychiatric Association, *DSM-III-R, Diagnostic and Statistical Manual of Mental Disorders*, 3d ed., rev. (Washington, D.C.: American Psychiatric Association, 1987).

34. David E. Comings, "The Molecular Genetics of Pathological Gambling," *CNS Spectrums* 3, no. 6 (1998): 20–37; M. J. Koep et al., "Evidence for Striatal Dopamine Release during a Video Game," *Nature* 393 (1998): 266–68.

35. See NRC, *Pathological Gambling*, chap. 4, for an overview of this research.

36. Rose, "Compulsive Gambling and the Law," pp. 240–60.

37. Michael Walker, "The Medicalization of Gambling as an Addiction," in McMillen, ed., *Gambling Cultures*; Stanton Peele, *The Meaning of Addiction: Compulsive Experience and Its Interpretation* (Lexington, Mass.: Lexington Books, 1985); Orford, *Excessive Appetites*.

38. Quoted in Productivity Commission, *Australia's Gambling Industries*, p. 26.

CURRENT TRENDS IN COMMERCIAL GAMBLING

I

VALUES AND CHOICES

The Struggle to Find Balance with Permitted Gambling in Modern Society

William R. Eadington

I n country after country, gambling laws are in flux. From strict prohibitions only a generation or two ago, laws governing permitted gambling, ranging from lotteries to casinos to electronic gaming devices to betting shops, have been steadily liberalized by governments interested in new sources of tax revenues, new catalysts for job creation and capital investment, new attractions for tourism or foreign spending, and—occasionally—in response to citizens' desires to participate in such permitted gambling for the fun of it.

This essay examines the major political, social, and economic dynamics that have resulted in the rapid proliferation of permitted gambling—especially casinos and casino-style gambling—in the United States and various other countries over the past quarter century. This process of legalization and deregulation has created gaming industries of increasing size, sophistication, and presence, which have become or are becoming part of the mainstream of modern commercial entertainment, leisure, and tourism industries in many parts of the world.

Economic benefits notwithstanding, permitted gambling and especially casino-style gaming remains a highly charged political issue. In the minds of many people, casino gaming is still an essentially unhealthy activity that has not wholly lost its previous status as a pernicious vice. Most jurisdictions that have authorized casino gaming have done so with limited competitive or monopoly-franchised structures, which create economic rents or monopoly profits as a byproduct of efforts to control the social impacts of gambling through regulatory constraints, government ownership, or under-supply. Nonetheless, pressures to expand the scope of permitted gaming can be found in many jurisdictions, especially when needs for tax revenue generation or job creation are substantial.

This essay discusses parallels between gambling and other vices—such as illegal drugs, alcohol, tobacco, and commercial sex—and presents a framework for evaluating costs and benefits associated with changing gambling's legal status. Within this context, the various arguments in favor of or in opposition to permitted gambling can be evaluated. It is difficult to make an unambiguous case either in favor of, or in opposition to, permitting commercial gambling into any community that previously did not have such activities. Nonetheless, in the first years of the twenty-first century, it appears that state-sanctioned commercial gaming industries will be expanding in new and diverse ways in many jurisdictions on various continents.

These debates on the merits and demerits of gambling continue a process that dates back at least to the 1960s and 1970s, when governments in various countries, states, and provinces took the gamble to authorize casinos and casino-style gaming for a wide variety of reasons. This decision began a fundamental change away from the long-standing prohibitions against such gaming that had characterized virtually every society through much of history. We find ourselves still debating these issues, but in the early twenty-first century, we have considerably more evidence than ever before as to what really happens when permitted commercial gaming is widely available. However, it remains difficult to fully comprehend what the evidence is telling us.

TRENDS IN GAMING IN DIFFERENT PARTS OF THE WORLD

Events of recent years are a continuation of processes toward legalization and a greater presence of permitted gaming that began in America with Nevada's casino legislation in 1931 and New Hampshire's lottery legalization in 1963. In the United States, the main spread of legal commercial casinos occurred in the first half of the 1990s. Before 1988, casinos had been authorized only in Nevada and in Atlantic City, New Jersey. Atlantic City itself was a relatively new addition, with its casinos opening their doors for the first time in 1978. Between 1988 and 1996, nine states[1] authorized new casino industries, some as riverboat casinos, some as limited-wager casinos in former mining towns, and some as urban casinos. Indian tribal casinos were effectively legalized by a Supreme Court decision in 1987[2] and were provided a statutory framework with the passage of the Indian Gaming Regulatory Act in 1988.[3] Indian casinos spread to nearly thirty states by the early twenty-first century, with the most significant tribal casinos found in such states as Connecticut, Minnesota, Michigan, New York, and California.

The proliferation of permitted commercial casinos in the United States slowed down after 1993, coinciding with improvements in the American economy. However, another trend soon emerged: the authorization of gaming devices at race tracks in various states, purportedly to provide the racing industry with a level playing field against newly authorized forms of gaming and a competitive edge over tracks in other states in attracting purses and high-quality race horses. The effect of this development was to create a number of "racinos," where the presence of slot machines would transform race tracks into de facto casinos and typically lead to a high proportion of total revenues for such operations being generated by the gaming devices rather than by wagering on racing. Such race track casinos developed in Iowa, Delaware, West Virginia, New Mexico, and Louisiana in the 1990s.

Canada also experienced a rapid spread of casinos and casino-style gaming in the 1990s, although it followed a path somewhat different than that of the United States. Because of Canadian law and philosophy, casinos are not owned by private sector organizations but by the government through Crown corporations. In the 1990s, the provinces of Manitoba, Saskatchewan, Ontario, and Quebec all introduced government-owned casinos, though in some cases—notably in Ontario—the government used a competitive bidding system to select casino companies that would operate the provincial casinos and build permanent gaming facilities on behalf of the province. This model was followed for the Windsor Casino, the Rama Casino (north of Toronto), and the Niagara Casino at Niagara Falls. Canadian casinos are generally located in urban centers and are typically monopoly casinos.

Many of the Canadian provinces also expanded their lottery offerings in the 1990s to include not only traditional lottery products such as scratch tickets and lotto games but also Video Lottery Terminals (VLTs), a form of electronic gaming device available in age-restricted areas, such as bars and taverns. With the exception of British Columbia, VLT gaming was authorized throughout the country between 1990 and 2000. In comparison, only two states in the United States had adopted the lottery model of VLTs in bars and taverns: South Dakota and Oregon. Generally speaking, VLTs—or gaming devices, however called—operated in age-restricted locations, such as bars and taverns, create considerably greater political controversy than casinos alone. Reasons for this reaction are discussed below.

In Europe—where gambling laws have historically changed more slowly than in the New World—most of the casino industries are characterized by high tax rates, regional monopoly status, and sometimes direct government ownership. However, a number of recent developments are expanding the presence of casinos and casino-style gaming in various European nations, with the potential of spreading into neighboring countries. The main catalysts for this change can be seen in the dynamics for legal and institutional changes in gaming industries in such countries as the United Kingdom, Switzerland, and Sweden. In 2001, the Home Office of the United Kingdom released a major review of its gambling policy that sets the stage for substantial liberalization of commercial gaming industries in the first decade of the twenty-first century.[4] The accompanying debate will probably center on such questions as whether the United Kingdom should authorize destination resort casinos in only a few locations, mimicking the American strategy in such venues as Atlantic City, Biloxi, Tunica County, and Las Vegas, or authorize urban casinos similar to those in Australia and Canada.

The United Kingdom will confront other questions as well. For example, how can the existing gaming and wagering industries be protected from new competition and, indeed, should they even be protected? How far should the government go in permitting Internet gaming opportunities to develop? And what regulatory protections and taxing provisions should be implemented to address this new technological world of gaming opportunities? As will be the case in many countries, the British will have to evaluate the pros and cons of other new technologies, such as interactive television gambling and the use of electronic money to place bets or make wagers from a wide variety of venues such as modular telephones and wireless compact computers.

Substantial changes can also be found in other European countries. In 2001, Switzerland completed a bidding process that had begun with the passage of a 1992 law. The primary intent of this change which will ultimately create twenty-one casinos in cities and tourist areas throughout the country, is to allow the Swiss to better exploit their existing foreign tourist base and to stimulate additional foreign visitation. New casinos will also assist in reversing monetary flows from cross-border casino customers; in the past, Swiss gaming patrons had to travel abroad to make wagers in excess of SFr5 (approximately US $3.66). In the future, French, Italian, German, and Austrian gaming customers will cross the Swiss frontier in pursuit of more favorable gaming environs—unless, of course, their own governments change gaming laws even more liberally at home.

Sweden is another European country that was late in coming to the casino gaming tables. The government is in the process of opening four casinos, to be operated through the Swedish Lottery Company (Svenska Spel). The first two opened in 2001, in the rural northern town of Sundsfeld and in the city of Malmo, near the Danish border. The next two will be located in the major cities of Stockholm and Gotenberg and are scheduled to open in 2002 or 2003.

The dynamic underlying the spread of casinos throughout North America, Europe, Australia, New Zealand, and South Africa has recently reached Asia, which has long been a part of the world with only limited casino offerings characterized by monopoly or franchises in such places as Macau, Malaysia, the Philippines, and South Korea. Now there are increasing signs that the movement toward liberalization of gambling laws is well underway.

Macau came under Chinese rule in 1999, and with its annexation, many questions were raised regarding the fate of its existing gaming industry. After years of economic domination by a casino industry monopolized by a single private owner—an industry carrying a reputation that no one could admire— Macau was allowed by China to solicit bids from some of the most reputable and professional casino companies in the world. The hope in Macau, and apparently in Beijing, is that the former Portugese colony will be successful in transforming its casino industry into one that looks more like the gaming venues of Las Vegas and Atlantic City than the seedy reality that prevailed in Macau since the early 1960s.

Other Asian countries have either entered into new casino ventures since 1990 or have opened the doors of discussion as to whether it would be wise for them to do so. New or expanded casino industries can now be found in South Korea and the Philippines. Thailand and Taiwan are both assessing the wisdom of authorizing casinos within their borders, knowing full well that many of their citizens cross international borders or go on cruises into international waters so that they can fulfill their personal desires to gamble, casino-style. It is unlikely these discussions will abate soon, and they may very well result in increases in the availability of casino gaming outlets to greater numbers of Asian citizens.

Changing economic circumstances may also contribute to the casino debate in various parts of the world. In the first decade of the twenty-first century, the United States seems to be going through another round of discussion on whether to legalize and expand casinos and casino-style gaming. Economic circumstances in many ways parallel the period from 1988 to 1993, when the national economy slowed and then moved into recession, and when many states found themselves financially strapped and desperate for job-creating strategies. With the economic slowdown and recession beginning in 2000, an increasing number of jurisdictions in the United States have found themselves in financial difficulty. As slowdowns have occurred, commercial gaming has often been one of the strategies put forth for raising government revenues and stimulating local and regional economies. Thus, debates on casinos, slot machines at race tracks, and even slot machines in bars and taverns have taken place in state legislatures and among political leaders in Hawaii, Kentucky, Pennsylvania, New Hampshire, and Minnesota, among others.

Other events can also affect the debates over whether to expand the presence of casinos. In October 2001, shortly after the September 11 terrorist attacks, the state of New York authorized six new tribal casinos and slot machine gaming at eight race tracks in the state. This decision was motivated in no small measure by the need to close the gap against large impending state deficits, related both to the economic slowdown and to the anticipated economic consequences of the terrorist actions and the subsequent war on terrorism. The debate was hastened by the reality that New York has been increasingly surrounded by successful casino gaming venues, in Atlantic City, eastern Connecticut, and Ontario, Canada.

COMMERCIAL GAMING AND CONTROVERSY

Between 1982 and 2000, total gaming revenues of commercial gaming industries in the United States alone expanded from $10.2 billion to $61.5 billion, with more than half of the 2000 total coming from commercial and tribal casinos. Lotteries, pari-mutuel wagering on racing, and charitable gambling, including bingo, all lost market share as casinos and electronic gaming devices increased their presence and popularity over the last two decades of the twentieth century. However, in spite of rapid economic expansions, general attitudes toward the acceptance of gambling remain at best lukewarm in most political jurisdictions. There is growing sentiment in a number of states, provinces, and countries that—at least in some situations—governments have authorized too much gaming. In such locales, there are pressures to reverse some of the trends that have characterized commercial gaming industries in the past two decades.

In some situations, substantial commercial gaming industries have seen their legal status revoked in the United States and elsewhere. Authorization for video poker machines in South Carolina was allowed to expire in 2000, eliminating an industry that was generating gross gaming revenues in excess of $500 million per annum. In 1996, local elections reversed the legal status of video poker machines in thirty-four of the sixty-six parishes in Louisiana. Similarly, the government of Turkey allowed its once thriving casino industry to become illegal in 1998.

Following publication of a Productivity Commission Report on Gambling,[5] Australia declared problem gambling to be a public health issue and adopted a number of restrictions on electronic gaming devices under a strategy of harm minimization. This legislation followed a decade when the number of electronic gaming devices expanded from about 70,000 to approximately 190,000, 90 percent of which were located outside of casinos.[6] The Productivity Commission Report claimed, among other findings, that the 2.1 percent of adult Australians who were problem gamblers made up 10 percent of regular players on gaming machines and generated 42 percent of spending on gaming machines in Australia.

New technological developments in the gaming industries have also been part of the political controversy. Perhaps the most dramatic of these is Internet gambling, whose legal status has been actively debated in many countries throughout the world, with no clear resolution in the early twenty-first century in general trends and directions. Internet gambling has a very large potential market, and has the capability of bringing highly sophisticated gaming products into households everywhere. Based on the spotty evidence that exists on this still largely "gray area" activity, the size of the global Internet gambling market is already measured in the billions of dollars.[7]

In contrast, Internet gambling raises social concerns about the potential adverse impacts such ubiquitous gaming opportunities might bring about, especially in the areas of underage gambling and problem and pathological gambling. Internet gambling also poses interesting challenges regarding regulation and taxation, creating a dilemma for governments that permit gaming primarily because they can extract economic rents from excise taxes on it (see p. xx). Because Internet gambling operates with little concern for national borders and because some jurisdictions have decided to encourage Internet gaming sites to locate within their borders by offering low tax rates, other jurisdictions will have to match or come close to those tax rates to remain competitive. As soon as some of the more respected nations (e.g., so-called Tier 1 countries such as the United States, Canada, the United Kingdom, Germany, and Australia), pursue this strategy then all other countries will be forced to follow because of the "commodity" nature of Internet gaming products. In their first few years of development, most Internet gaming companies were licensed and operating in developing countries (Antigua, Belize, the Dominican Republic, Vanuatu), though some Tier 2 countries, for example the Isle of Man, increased their efforts at licensing, regulating, and taxing Internet gaming operations.

It is possible that the Internet gambling industry is just the tip of the technological iceberg. Interactive television betting and the use of various handheld computer devices for playing games and making wagers are perhaps the next major developments in commercial gaming. However, these forms of gambling will continue to be politically controversial because of the difficulties in exercising social controls over them and because of the ability of new technologies to outstrip legislative attempts to constrain the presence or availability of gambling in general. Regardless of the wishes and desires of legislative and parliamentary bodies, gambling activities that take place through the Internet and other low-cost, virtually instantaneous communications will be difficult to constrain.

EVALUATING THE BENEFITS AND COSTS OF EXPANDED GAMBLING

One aspect of legalizing new forms of permitted gambling is that such actions create economic benefits—especially for local or regional economies—that are generally tangible and measurable. But an expanded presence of permitted gambling also generates social costs that affect individuals and households in ways that are far less tangible, measurable, and visible. It is extremely challenging to policy makers and social scientists to conceptualize, identify, and measure the social costs that accompany gambling in any meaningful way.[8] Furthermore, because of the relative lack of attention to the costs and benefits of gambling before the mid-1990s, little serious effort was undertaken to address these problems.[9] It is likely that the benefits and costs associated with gambling will remain at the heart of the debate over the wisdom of expanding or contracting the availability of permitted gambling for some time to come.

Nonetheless, a number of observations can be made about the benefits and costs of permitted gambling in comparison. For those jurisdictions that are still debating the status of gaming within their control, such observations should prove useful.

The primary benefit associated with permitted gambling is the creation of *consumer surplus*, the incremental value to consumers of being able to participate in a previously prohibited activity. Consumer surplus is generally defined as the difference between what consumers would be willing and able to pay for an activity versus what they actually have to pay for that activity. Such gains accrue predominantly to the consumers of gambling services rather than to the producers or the governments that authorize the activity.

However, when permitted gambling is authorized in a manner that prevents the market from expanding to its demand potential, or when the market structure is designed to result in monopoly or otherwise restricted competition, the price of the activity increases. As a result, a portion of potential consumer surplus becomes value for someone else; referred to as *economic rents*. Economic rents can be captured by a government through the implementation of excise taxes on gambling or by outright ownership of the gaming franchise. Other economic rents might be captured by companies or organizations that offer gambling services through exclusive or limited franchises. Only when the market is allowed to expand to its demand potential or when competition from related substitute activities bids down the price of the primary activity to competitive levels are the economic rents bid away.[10]

As with other activities, most of the costs and benefits associated with permitted gambling are internal to its consumers and producers. Consumers choose to spend money on gambling because they derive greater value from participation than from the expected or realized cost. Producers provide gambling services because they provide a greater economic return than the next best alternatives. Consequently, there is little reason for public policy considerations to affect the decision processes that generate these private benefits and costs.

Public policy is typically justified when *negative externalities* are associated with an activity.[11] With gambling, the primary negative externalities are linked to problem and pathological gambling. Generally speaking, two major driving forces have influenced societal decisions to liberalize gambling laws and regulations. They are (1) a desire on the part of governments to capture economic rents through permitting a previously prohibited activity, and (2) a desire to mitigate the negative side effects (real or perceived negative externalities) associated with the activity by constraining it to allow for greater control of the adverse side effects. The combination of these two somewhat conflicting forces has led to a variety of eccentric laws passed in various jurisdictions throughout the world. In the United States, riverboat gambling with mandatory sailing, or mining town casinos with loss limits and restrictions to historic buildings only, reflect the combination of efforts by states to capture economic rents for some particular interests and, at the same time, to provide protections against people who might overindulge in gambling activities. In Great Britain, the Gaming Act 1968 was initially justified as an attempt to mitigate the negative social costs associated with the demands for gambling. Thus, the primary principle was to permit gambling that would cater to the "unstimulated demand" that existed in British society, but not beyond that. It was only later that governments turned more and more to permitted gambling as a tax revenue source. In Canada, provincial governments turned first to lotteries and later to casinos and video lottery machines—owned and operated by the provincial governments—primarily as a means to capture economic rents for an activity that had considerable public appeal. Only recently has greater attention been paid to the adverse social impacts from provincially owned and operated gambling in Canada.[12]

As with the other vices of tobacco, alcohol, illicit drugs, and commercial sex, gambling is perceived as an activity that has a strong realized and latent demand that emanates from a portion of the population. Like the other so-called vices, it produces a variety of negative side effects—perceived or real—that are viewed as immoral or otherwise socially damaging by (typically) another subset of the population. Such side effects have served as the impetus for constraints on permitted gambling services. As with the other "vices", there is no clear consensus on the best approach to regulating and constraining the availability of gambling, and as a result, the manner in which legal gambling has been permitted and constrained has been inconsistent from one political jurisdiction to another.

The extent of demand for gambling that is realized—as opposed to remaining latent—is partly a function of gambling's legal status. If casino gaming, through the process of legalization or deregulation, is made more attractive and available to a society's population centers, then the demand for gambling in general, and the total amount of income spent on gambling, will increase. The greater the availability of gambling and the fewer the constraints applied to gaming activities, the larger the realized demand will be. Furthermore, the more that permitted gambling is offered in a competitive market context, the more that demand for gambling will increase. Increased competition will result in lower prices to consumers for gambling, and competition will enhance the price and availability of complementary nongaming activities as well. The recent experience of competitive venues such as Las Vegas and Mississippi riverboat casinos—in contrast to more supply-constrained or monopolistic jurisdictions such as the urban casinos in Australia, Canada, or Europe—clearly demonstrate these effects.

In trying to evaluate the social benefits and costs associated with gambling, it is important to consider the alternatives to the status of permitted gambling under consideration. If a society currently prohibits gambling but has a substantial amount of illegal gambling taking place within its borders, removal of the prohibitions will likely diminish the adverse economic impacts of the illegal industry, and—quite possibly—diminish the severity of some of the social costs associated with such illegal activities as well.

This was clearly the case with the Republic of South Africa when legislation was passed to authorize casinos in 1996. Most of the major urban areas in the country—especially Durban, Johannesburg, and Cape Town—were plagued with illegal gambling casinos following the end of apartheid in 1990. The ability or motivation of existing authorities to enforce the laws against such facilities was extremely limited, so a large number of illegal gambling houses were allowed to operate in the open and with no consumer protections, with only token efforts to diminish their presence. When the government implemented a legal and regulated alternative, a number of adverse social consequences, such as loan sharking, political kickbacks, corruption of local law enforcement, and links to other illegal vices, were substantially diminished. Furthermore, the channeling of previously illegal spending on gambling into legal—and taxed—casino venues increased the benefits accruing to the government.

On the other hand, one could argue that legalized gambling increased the appeal of gambling as entertainment to South Africans. This increased attractiveness has resulted in greater spending on gambling among the population at large and probably in an increased incidence of problem and pathological gambling. Legalization substantially changed the benefits and costs, both economic and social, associated with gambling in South Africa. Determining whether legal gambling has created net benefits for the country, as well as for specific regions within the country, would require a careful economic and social analysis taking into account the consumer surplus implications of increased spending on gambling by South Africans as well as by foreign nationals, the reductions in social costs attributable to a diminished importance of illegal gambling in the country, and an evaluation of the social costs associated with increases (if any) in problem and pathological gambling.

It is also useful to look at the general locational structure under which casino and casino-style gambling is offered, in terms of its potential for delivering benefits and costs. Though it is argued elsewhere that benefits and costs of permitted gambling should be done at the national level,[13] most policy analysis concentrates on local and regional economic benefits associated with permitted casinos and casino-style gaming. Using the regional level as a starting point, one can create the following categories of casinos and near-casinos:

- Resort casinos located away from population centers (such as Las Vegas; Biloxi, Mississippi; or the Gold Coast of Queensland, Australia);
- Rural casinos located away from population centers (such as Foxwood's in Connecticut and many other tribal casinos in the United States; Sun City in South Africa; and the casinos in Deadwood, South Dakota, and in Central City, Blackhawk, and Cripple Creek, Colorado);
- Urban or suburban casinos located in or near major metropolitan areas (such as those in Detroit, or in and around St. Louis, Kansas City, and Cincinnati; and most U.K. casinos); and
- Neighborhood casino-style gaming (such as gaming devices found in bars and taverns throughout much of Australia and Canada; in rugby and ex-servicemen's clubs in Australia; and in arcades in the United Kingdom).

If we compute benefits and costs for gambling in the traditional manner and discount the importance of consumer surplus,[14] we find that jurisdictions that export gambling to citizens of other jurisdictions tend to capture a substantial amount of economic benefit in the form of economic rents and value added by producers and owners of local resources (e.g., the benefits of increased local employment), whereas the social costs associated with problem gambling in particular tend to be exported to the jurisdictions where the gambling consumers reside. In such cases, the ratio of benefits to costs within the jurisdiction is relatively high. Benefit/cost ratios for rural casinos are also fairly high, especially if the region for which the impacts are being evaluated includes only the rural area. This is often the case with Indian tribal casinos in the United States, where the primary group of interest is the tribe itself, and most of the casino customers are not tribal members.

If urban or suburban casinos are evaluated in this manner, however, the benefit/cost ratio is considerably lower. Most of the gaming activities provided by such casinos cater to demand in the local market. In such a case, spending on gambling does not stimulate the local economy in the same manner as it would if gambling activities were exported. Furthermore, social costs typically remain within the community where the gaming facilities are located. Thus, measured benefits will be lower and social costs will be higher than in either of the first two cases. Nonetheless, such urban/suburban casinos can create significant regional investment and may serve as efficient mechanisms for tax revenue generation. Furthermore, they may encourage local residents who otherwise might travel out of the region to pursue gambling activities to spend their gambling budgets in local casinos instead.

If we consider the situation of *convenience gambling*—gaming devices in bars and taverns, or in arcades located in neighborhoods—the general tendency is for benefits to be lower and social costs to be higher than in any of the previous situations. Since such facilities generate little in the way of new investment or job creation associated with the gambling activities, economic benefits tend to be lower.[15] Because casino-style gaming is offered in more accessible surroundings than is typical for site-specific casinos, there may be a greater incidence of impulsive gambling and, as a result, of problem and pathological gambling.

The ratio of benefits to costs for a region or jurisdiction is a bellwether to the extent of controversy associated with the various types of permitted gambling. For this reason, especially when consumer surplus is given relatively little standing, it is not surprising to see convenience gambling as the most politically vulnerable of the alternatives considered, as evidenced by the recent experiences of Australia, Canada, South Carolina, and Louisiana with convenience gambling and the political backlash associated with it.

This analysis also carries implications for the new forms of gambling. Internet gambling and interactive television gambling, for example, will likely prove to be very low on perceived economic benefits and very high on social costs. The competitive and global dimensions of Internet gambling make it very difficult for governments to capture economic rents, especially in the form of taxes on gross gaming revenues. Furthermore, the regulatory challenges of permitted gambling in the home, especially gambling by youth or by those prone to overindulge, imply that the social costs associated with such activities will be both socially dangerous and very hard to control without violating other dimensions of personal privacy. Thus, the newest forms of gambling may prove to be the most controversial of all.

CONCLUSIONS

In summary, the ongoing dynamics of the economic and social impacts of gambling and of permitted gaming industries point out a number of important characteristics of the activity, the industry, and public policy processes regarding gambling. The most important considerations follow:

- Gambling is one of the largest industries whose fundamental economic characteristics are substantially determined by political decisions;
- Political decisions regarding gambling are largely influenced by the ability to capture economic rents associated with liberalizing permitted gaming activities. This tendency is often countered by perceived or real social costs associated with problem and pathological gambling and with an increased availability of gambling in society;
- A strong latent demand for casino-style gaming (including gaming within casinos and with electronic gaming devices outside of casinos) is manifested when the legal status of gambling is liberalized;

- Technologies developed over the past two decades have broadened the appeal of, and the market for, commercial gaming. The same technologies have raised concerns over some adverse social impacts that such an increased presence of gambling in society might bring about, notably those related to problem and pathological gambling behavior;
- Benefit/cost analysis applied to permitted gaming activities is still a relatively primitive science, primarily because of the difficulties in conceptualizing, observing, and measuring social costs. Because gambling is still often perceived as a vice, consumer surplus associated with gambling consumption is often discounted in policy discussions;
- Some types of permitted gambling raise greater social concerns over their impacts than do others. For this reason, some types of venues for casinos and casino-style gambling are more vulnerable to political controversy and possibly to reversal of liberalization of permitted activities than are others. The types of gambling with the greatest potential for controversy include convenience gambling, Internet gambling, and interactive television gambling.

The debate over the proper role of permitted gambling is far from over, though there are some clear long-term trends—visible for much of the past half century—that have supported increased legalization and deregulation in many jurisdictions. In many respects, these trends reflect society's increased acceptance of gambling as a proper form of (adult) leisure and entertainment.

However, as has been demonstrated in various situations, public attitudes toward gambling can be fickle. Should significant problems arise—such as corruption scandals, the presence of organized crime, or even sensational incidents involving pathological gamblers—gambling can once again come under fire. If the perceptions of social costs associated with gambling become substantial relative to the economic rents that it is creating, then the political winds can quickly shift against its permitted status. Unless and until respect for gambling achieves a level comparable with other legal consumption activities, newer types of permitted gambling will continue to raise public policy debates and remain at the center of political controversies.

NOTES

1. The states were South Dakota, Iowa, Illinois, Colorado, Louisiana, Mississippi, Missouri, Indiana, and Michigan. Of these nine only Michigan, where voters authorized three casinos in Detroit in 1996, was added to this list between 1994 and 2001.

2. *California et al. v. Cabazon Band of Mission Indians et al.*, No. 85-1708, February 25, 1987, reprinted in William R. Eadington, ed., *Indian Gaming and the Law* (Reno: University of Nevada Press, 1990), pp. 227–54.

3. P.L. 100-497, 100th Congress, reprinted in *Indian Gaming and the Law*, pp. 255–90.

4. *Gambling Policy Review* (London: Stationery Office, 2001).

5. Productivity Commission *Australia's Gambling Industries* (Canberra 1999), [online] http://www.indcom.gov.au/inquiry/gambling/index.html

6. Sean Monaghan, "Australian Gaming Machine Review: Assessing the Pace and Cost of Harm Minimization," Burdett Buckeridge Young, analyst report (Sydney, 2000).

7. See, for example, Anthony Cabot, ed., *The Internet Gambling Report*, 4th ed. (Las Vegas: Trace Publishing, 2000).

8. See, for example, Douglas M. Walker and A. H. Barnett, "The Social Costs of Gambling: An Economic Perspective," *Journal of Gambling Studies* 15, no. 3 (1999): 181–212; and William R. Eadington, "Measuring Costs from Permitted Gaming: Concepts and Categories in Evaluating Gambling's Consequences," *Journal of Gambling Studies* 19, no. 2 (2002): 185–212.

9. Until casinos spread beyond Nevada and Atlantic City in the United States, there was little institutionally funded research on gambling. Similar circumstances prevailed in other countries. Since the 1990s, a number of major national studies have been undertaken in various countries, including the National Gambling Impact Study Commission, *Final Report* (Washington, D.C.: Government Printing Office, 1999) [online], http://(www.ngisc.gov); Britain's *Gambling Review Report* (London: Stationery Office, 2001); and Austalia's *Productivity Commission Report* (Canberra, 1999).

10. It should also be noted that the idea of consumer surplus has seldom been an important factor in deliberations regarding legalizing or deregulating gambling, probably because of long-standing prejudices that gambling is a tainted activity and that people who gamble are exercising poor judgment in their consumption choices, and should therefore not be given much consideration in deliberations. As a result, most policy deliberation relies primarily on the magnitude and distribution of the economic rents.

11. Negative externalities arise when the market transactions between two parties create costs for third parties not involved in the transactions. Without policy intervention, this shifting of costs results in overproduction of the activity that creates negative externalities.

12. See, for example, Jason Azmer and Garry Smith, *The State of Gambling in Canada: An Interprovincial Roadmap of Gambling and Its Impact* (Calgary, Alberta: Canada West Foundation, 1998).

13. Earl L. Grinols and David B. Mustard, "Business Profitability versus Social Profitability: Evaluating Industries with Externalities: The Case of Casinos," *Managerial and Decision Economics* 22, (2001): 143–62.

14. See note 10.

15. It should be noted however, that such gaming devices can be extremely efficient tax collectors.

♥♠♣

2
FROM LOCAL TO GLOBAL GAMBLING CULTURES

Jan McMillen

ambling is a crucial component of contemporary popular culture, traversing societies to captivate and entertain participants, both as a pastime and as an increasingly global business. Unlike other aspects of popular culture that have a strong spectator component, such as sports and television, gambling is intensely participatory. To watch others gambling is not enough; by definition, gambling involves active play. Moreover, more people are now gambling than ever before. An expanding range of readily accessible gambling opportunities is being promoted as legitimate entertainment, resulting in a dramatic rise in gambling expenditure and participation.

However, we are now less likely to play games instilled with local meanings and practices than were our parents and grandparents. Whereas

This paper is based on a SPIRT Grant from the Australian Research Council to investigate sportsbetting and Internet gambling. My special thanks to Richard Woolley and Richard Martino for their research assistance and thoughtful contributions.

gambling in the past was shaped by the cultural values of localized communities, contemporary gambling is increasingly commercialized, standardized, and global. It has become big business, central to the activities, values, and commercial imperatives of national and transnational organizations.

In most developed countries, such as Great Britain, Australia, and the United States, early forms of gambling developed around community activity in cities and rural areas. The community-based nature of, for example, horseracing, card playing, and bingo (or numbers games in the United States) was emphasized and shaped by the local social infrastructure. Although often illegal, gaming has thrived in the suburbs of major cities that had a high concentration of migrants from southern Europe, Asia, and the Middle East. Charitable gambling also has been an important feature of many societies and, like other forms of gambling, has been organized and experienced in ways determined by the particular sociocultural environment.

Contemporary forms of gambling are more commercial, individualistic, and urban. The increasing urbanization of society during the twentieth century and the shift in economic power from small, local institutions to large conglomerates has tended to undermine traditional forms of gambling, such as country racing and culturally specific games, and encourage new international forms, such as urban casinos and the concentration of gambling ownership in large corporations.

This essay argues that gambling has been transformed from a diverse and localized activity to a transnational industry that embodies the complex intermeshing of global and local values and practices. Gambling is assuredly a source of pleasure and entertainment to many, and commercialization and contemporary technology have increased its availability worldwide. But this is a contradictory relationship. Globalized commercial sportsbetting, for example, has the capacity to both unify and divide contemporary society.

BEYOND LOCALIZED GAMBLING CULTURES

Gambling has always been a crucial component everyday life, whether through cockfights in Bali, the formalized display of power and privilege by European aristocrats gambling at European casinos in the eighteenth and nineteenth centuries, or sportsbetting today by fans betting on their national heroes in global competitions, such as World Cup soccer, Test Cricket, professional golf, tournaments, and the Olympics. Many accounts of gambling situate it at the center of national culture and national identity, either in a celebratory or a critical way. Resolute risk-taking poker players in Western gambling saloons and the elegant, self-possessed British spy, James Bond, are examples of the mythical gamblers often depicted by the media to embody the character of a period or a nation. In Australia, historians and sociologists have gone further to argue that gambling itself is a reflection of the national character.[1]

Through commercialization, the cultural and national aspects of gambling have acquired value that enables them to be exchanged for profit. Popular forms of gambling that were previously not part of market logic have been offered "for sale" on the market by private entrepreneurs and corporations. The growth in the number and influence of commercial gambling corporations, particularly in their global form, has provided additional opportunities for private entities to invest in new localities and new gambling products.

Many scholars have noted the homogenizing forces of globalization: economic dominance of transnational corporations, often American; the acceptance of certain governing rules and economic tendencies; and standardization of products and consumer behavior. Behind these formulations is the notion that this new globalization is a largely cultural phenomenon, whatever its economic base. Nowhere is this better seen than in the transformation of gambling into one of the world's most rapidly expanding consumer activities.

Commercialization

The overall consequences of the commercial transformation of gambling are enormous. In many respects, gambling has become an industry much like any other. Since governments began to progressively liberalize gambling legislation in the 1980s, private investors have been attracted by the prospect of large profits, providing enough impetus to pump-prime an entirely new economic sector before public concerns about the social consequences forced governments to rethink their policies. The proliferation of gambling entrepreneurs and corporations has implied a profound reorganization of the way gambling functions. As is the practice of most productive, competitive firms, the entire gambling organization conforms to the profit motive as it relates to customers and suppliers.

The experience of commercial gambling is one of almost universal regularity. Games have been standardized so that every casino offers similar games, with only minor variation of house rules. Blackjack, roulette, and gaming machines are ubiquitous; the marketing symbols and social rituals are the same worldwide. A casino gambler would feel at home in any casino around the world. Globalization applies as much to equipment as to the games. Manufacturers of gaming machines compete vigorously for a share of the global market, dominated by a small number of internationalized companies. For over a decade, International Gaming Technology (IGT), an American firm and the world's largest gambling machine manufacturer, has fought a running battle to keep Aristocrat, Australia's largest manufacturer, out of the lucrative U.S. market.

But commercial gambling also has noneconomic, cultural aspects. As gambling has been internationalized, its commercialization and bureaucratization have effected profound changes in national cultures and traditional practices. Racing, for example, has been transformed from a small-scale local social activity to a transnational industry driven by the search for profits. Rationalization of "uneconomic" horse race meetings has been achieved through reduction in the number of small country meetings and through strategic neglect. Many race clubs that previously conducted regular meetings have been squeezed out of business or compelled to introduce night racing or gaming machines to generate sufficient income. There has been a concerted drive to attract new clientele through the promotion of racing as a "tourist event" or international contest rather than a community experience. Races such as the Japan Cup, Kentucky Derby, Melbourne Cup, and Dubai Cup have become major global events with huge prize money provided by corporate sponsorship. These races are telecast around the world and have often been accompanied with the heavy promotion of particular horses and jockeys as national racing stars. Individual races have been rescheduled to maximize betting opportunities across national and international time zones. Telephone and online betting allows gamblers around the globe to place their bets while watching the races on cable or satellite television.

Role of Technology

Technology has had a marked influence on gambling. Over the last century, technological development has influenced the extent and character of gambling by aiding the introduction of new gambling products as an alternative leisure pursuit. The development of transport and communication networks, the mechanical totalisator, radio and television, the telephone, and microchip technology and computers have made gambling progressively more accessible and facilitated commercial operations and regulation. Among all the technological factors of gambling commercialization and globalization, a particularly significant role has been played by computerization and, more recently, the emergence of the Internet and global telecommunications.

Internet Gambling

Innovative telecommunications technology has propelled the development of Internet gambling across state and national boundaries. Information technology makes gambling a truly global activity, linking home gambling with international operators. Although this technology is currently in the early stages of development, the potential for new interactive gambling products using digital television is now widely recognized. BSkyB, a British satellite television company, has offered interactive betting services to subscribers since 2000.

Conflicting claims about new patterns of social interaction have been associated with the emergence of the Internet as a new gambling medium. Advocates argue that online communication liberates gamblers from territorially bound forms of gambling, overcoming the limitations of locality and politics. Critics argue that the spread of Internet gambling will lead to social isolation, problem gambling, and the exploitation of communities on the economic periphery by powerful groups who own and control the new global gambling economy. Both arguments have been made in the absence of a substantial body of reliable empirical research on the actual uses of the Internet by different groups of gamblers. They seem to be built around simplistic assumptions, such as an ideological opposition between harmonious local communities of an idealized past and the dominance of global forces on contemporary social life.

Besides oversimplifying the issues, the questions that dominate the public debate about Internet gambling make an understanding of the new global patterns of gambling interaction difficult. It is important to base our interpretation on scholarly evidence and analysis and to try to make sense of this knowledge in order to propose hypotheses about the relationships associated with globalized gambling in our societies.

SPORTSBETTING: THE GLOBAL-LOCAL NEXUS

A brief account of the trajectory of the most rapidly growing form of global gambling—sportsbetting—may illustrate the analysis presented here. The experience of sportsbetting has radiated beyond its community origins to become the vanguard of a new international gambling culture, a burgeoning form of globalized gambling that combines local sports institutions, grassroots identity, and commercial computer networks in the development of cultural expression and participation.

As with gambling, globalization and commercialization has transformed many sports into international commodities, marketed, sponsored, and owned by large corporations and media enterprises. In parallel development, the global market for sportsbetting has expanded, facilitated by emerging technologies such as the Internet and digital television. Online sportsbetting operators, including gambling industry newcomers as well as long-established companies such as Ladbrokes, William Hill, and Coral, offer their betting services to sports fans around the world.

Sports as a betting commodity is extremely well-suited to Internet delivery for several reasons. First, the sheer diversity of contingencies within a game allows for multiple and simultaneous bets with expanding betting types. Second, sports is a global phenomenon, with numerous sports and particular games on matches watched on television by millions of people around the globe.[2] Taken in this context, there are still many jurisdictions where sportsbetting is not legally offered, and as a consequence citizens have the convenience of placing bets over the Internet with providers who are licensed to do so in other jurisdictions, such as Australia. Centrebet, an Internet sports bookmaker licensed in the Northern Territory, is reported to attract 80 percent of its clientele from overseas, with 20 percent residing in the United States.[3] Canbet, operating out of Canberra, derives almost all its income from betting on college football in the United States, where such betting is illegal.

From the perspective of the host government and the betting operators, this form of gambling brings considerable economic benefit. It is in effect a new form of export income. On the other side of the equation, the losses incurred by gamblers in other countries are a cost that favors global corporate profits borne in favor of global corporate interests. But there are also risks to the commercial providers and to society as a whole.

THE RISKS

While the benefits of modern sports as both recreation and entertainment are undeniable, an expanding sportsbetting market also brings risks that have yet to be adequately addressed. These potential risks include:

- social impacts and problem gambling,
- regulatory inconsistencies and the potential for regulatory failure,
- the potential for sports corruption, and
- erosion of national sovereignty and cultural identity in the sports arena.

Social Impacts and Problem Gambling

The internationalization of sports and gambling provides fertile ground for legalization and commercial market growth. Indications are that an increasing number of people around the world are embracing online sportsbetting, whether it is legalized in their own country or not. While those countries, such as Australia, that decide to legalize and regulate sportsbetting stand to achieve a comparative advantage in a lucrative global market, a crucial issue for policy makers is to assess the potential community benefit against the potential social costs.

Regulatory innovations to date have failed to resolve the social and political risks of problem gambling. However, in debates about policy reform it is often argued that wagering poses less of a risk than other accessible forms of popular gambling such as gaming machines. For example, the Australian government was persuaded by arguments from the wagering industry that Internet wagering would be unlikely to result in an increase in problem gambling.[4] While scholarly research in this field does not match the importance of the topic, in many respects these claims have been supported by available evidence.[5] Hence, problem gambling legislation and policy innovations tend to concentrate on gaming venues (clubs, hotels, casinos). When wagering is included in such programs, it tends to implicitly have a lower priority than gaming. However, there is emerging evidence that wagering and sportsbetting may be creating increased problems for certain sectors of the community, such as young males.

It would be shortsighted to assume that the incidence of problem gambling related to sportsbetting will not increase as participation continues to rise and new gamblers are attracted to this activity. There is also the unanswered moral question of who is responsible for addressing any social harm that might result.

Regulatory Inconsistencies and the Potential for Regulatory Failure

The dynamic and politically sensitive environment of contemporary gambling and the diversity of jurisdictional controls highlight the complex and risky nature of the relationship between legal/illegal sportsbetting and popular sports. In Australia, for example, the Commonwealth government has used its telecommunications papers to ban Australian Internet gaming operators from providing a service to Australian residents (the Interactive Gambling Bill 2001). Following intense lobbying by the Totalisator Agency Boards (TAB) and the racing industry, Internet wagering and sportsbetting have been exempted from the Internet ban. Importantly, however, the Act also prohibits "real time" interactive sports betting on a contingency event within a match or game.

Spokesmen for the racing industry and TABs successfully argued that there are material differences between gaming and wagering. A key argument was that, unlike gaming operators, who conduct the gambling (provide the service) and also control the outcome of the game (the product), licensed bookmakers and TABs are required to be totally isolated from the outcome of the event. While the spokesmen acknowledged that the Internet offers a convenient alternative to existing access methods for wagering and sportsbetting, they argued that Internet delivery is merely an extension of telephone betting, which has functioned for decades without adverse social impacts.[6] However, the current sportsbetting legislation in many of Australia's jurisdictions fails to address the distinctive nature of this form of betting or the particular characteristics of the widely diverse sports involved.[7]

Most analysts predict that sportsbetting will increase with Internet usage, although the size of the predicted increase varies. Projected growth in this market begs the question as to what governments are doing to ensure that sports wagering is conducted under a regulated environment with the highest standards of integrity and in the best interests of both consumers and the wider community.

Potential for Sports Corruption

However, any commercial and entertainment benefits are offset by the potential hazards associated with exposure of sports participants to bribery and dishonesty. Internationally, sportsbetting has long been a feature of the gambling scene. During the twentieth century, betting on baseball and college football in the United States, although illegal, was at the center of headline corruption controversies. Other sports, in particular soccer, have also been the target of concentrated sportsbetting.

The impact of sportsbetting and the potential risks to sports associations, players, and gambling providers have been exacerbated by the commercialization and global televising of sports, and the impact of digital technology. Sportsbetting is now a highly technological industry promoting an enthralling product to an expanding global market.

The result of these changes and the growing globalization and commercialization of sports have meant that parts of the sportsbetting industry are becoming more like the gaming sector, with the same organization providing (or sponsoring) both the event and the opportunity to bet on it. The close association between contemporary sports and betting also presents greater opportunities for corrupt and unethical behavior and greater risks to sports players and officials. Substantial growth and change in the products and modes of delivery in the sportsbetting market in recent years have coincided with increasing occurrences of match fixing, bribery, and corruption in international sports.

The most problematic forms of sportsbetting, contingency and margins (spread) betting, are testing the capacity of legislative and regulative frameworks in every country. Contingency and spread betting, which have become increasingly popular in several countries, including the United States,[8] provide a ready means for the corruption of sports. A team member needs to shave only a few points off the potential score for the outcome of the spread to change dramatically. For example, there may be a spread of betting options for the number of three-point shots a basketball team may score over another. It would not be difficult for the team (or an individual player) to fix the game through decreasing the number of three-point shots they would usually shoot. This form of game-fixing is very difficult to detect, and concern about whether it is happening has undermined consumer confidence in sports, especially in the United States. When a team even slightly underperforms, there is doubt among consumers as to whether the game was fixed.

As a recent inquiry in the United Kingdom notes, "because [of] the opportunities to bet not only on the outcome of a sporting event but upon individual events within it, there are increased temptations for participants to fix the outcome of those events. Fixing an event within an event is much easier than fixing the overall result, which it need not affect"[9] The U.K. report found that "fixing the outcome of a match may require a considerable degree of collusion, possibly involving players on both sides, but some events may be in the hands of an individual player (for instance, the number of wides in an over)."[10]

In an effort to protect sports and its players, a number of sporting bodies (for example, the U.S. National Basketball League, Australian Cricket Board, and Australian Football League) have attempted to introduce new internal policy frameworks to prevent betting corruption and ensure the integrity of their own individual sports. But the risks from sportsbetting—to players, officials, supporters, and the game itself—have received little, if any, attention from analysts or government regulators.

In Australia for example, there are few mechanisms within gambling regulations to dissuade betting-related corruption in sports. Existing legislation is outdated and incapable of dealing with present and ongoing changes and growth in sportsbetting products, the range of betting options, the modes of delivery, or sponsorship of sports and players by companies with sportsbetting interests.[11] Criminal sanctions are presently limited to common law and, occasionally, to vague statutory provisions of criminal law. Because Australian betting legislation does not specifically address the potential for corruption or bribery in sports, it is difficult if not impossible to obtain a criminal prosecution for such actions—even if they are perpetrated by a licensed sportsbetting provider.

The potential risks that can occur with contingency betting warrant immediate attention and reform. The commercialization of sports and sportsbetting also requires an urgent assessment of the ethical dimensions of sportsbetting and the sponsorship of sports. As yet there has been no public debate about the ethics or acceptability of sportsbetting providers sponsoring sports clubs and sports on which they accept bets, or of the potential for sponsorship to mask concealed payments to teams or players.

National Sovereignty and Cultural Identity

At a global level, it seems unlikely that gambling regulation based on the traditional authority of a single government will be effective in the digital world. Online gambling is aimed at cross-border and global markets; it is not confined to a physical location subject to the laws of a nation-state. The convergence of gambling, telecommunications media, entertainment, and sports, facilitated by powerful alliances of transnational commercial interests, could be beyond the capacity of any one government to control.[12]

Yet nations are making varied and often contradictory responses to the global sportsbetting phenomenon, creating a complex and uncertain political-legal environment. While some governments continue to be wary of providing a legal environment for sportsbetting operators, others seem eager to capitalize on the new global market, particularly through Internet services.

- After a lengthy and comprehensive gambling review, the United Kingdom's Budd Report has recommended liberalization of sports-betting, along with most other forms of gambling, including Internet gaming.[13] Indeed, the government has already shown that it will support expansion of the sportsbetting market. After established British Internet bookmakers moved their operations to Gibraltar to avoid paying taxes, the U.K. government promptly indicated its willingness to offer tax concessions to attract them back onshore. U.K. sportsbetting providers are rapidly claiming a large share of the international market.

- South Africa also has an official policy of legalization but currently lacks the legislative and regulatory framework for implementation.
- The majority of U.S. governments, in contrast, have maintained their opposition to legalized sportsbetting, which continues to be legal only in Nevada casinos despite widespread illegal betting on college football and consistent reports of game-fixing in many sports.[14]
- A recent review of gambling in New Zealand has recommended an approach similar to that taken by the Australian government, with Internet sportsbetting being legalized but not Internet gaming.
- Hong Kong seems to be moving toward a similar strategy although it is possible that Internet lotteries will be approved.

Despite the fragmented and inconsistent national regulations, sports followers wishing to bet on their favorite team or player have no difficulty finding an operator willing and able to accept their wager. Europeans can place an Internet or telephone bet on a World Cup soccer match between Brazil and Iran with bookmakers in London, Alice Springs, or Vanuatu. Denied legal sportsbetting outlets in their own countries, sports fans in the United States and Asia are wagering large amounts with online operators in Australia, Great Britain, and Macau.

However, the transformation of sportsbetting from a localized, community-based activity to a globally shared cultural phenomenon and transnational industry has yet to be investigated or understood. Since the emergence of the Internet in the 1980s, several scholars have interpreted available evidence on the relationship between the Internet and society. But even the most basic questions about the use of the Internet for sportsbetting have not been addressed. We do not know, for example, who uses this medium for betting or the extent of cross-border sportsbetting.

Some evidence and analysis is beginning to emerge to base interpretation on firmer ground than the speculation and economic estimates that currently dominate public debate. But there are more substantive socio-logical questions about the role of sportsbetting and the Internet in struc-turing social relationships. What are the nature and scope of the global cultural and economic forces affecting local culture and process? Do the diverse set of consequences that result when global forces and local con-texts meet result in accommodation and acceptance or in ambivalence, or do they provoke incongruence and resistance? Is the expansion of Internet sportsbetting contributing to a globally shared, universalized gambling culture or is it a source of renewed community? Rather than causing the dissolution of local identities through the establishment of a homogeneous global gambling culture, to what extent is sportsbetting leading to the rearticulation or reinvention of national and local commu-nities?

The cultural importance of sports in establishing national identities and global communities has only recently received attention from ana-lysts.[15] To date there has been no systematic analysis of the effects of global sports, such as soccer and cricket, and their attendant corporate and intertextual alliances on local contexts and cultural practices such as sportsbetting. Such analysis must begin with the premise that the global and local manifestations of sportsbetting can be understood only in rela-tion to each other. Any discussion of the relationships posed by the glob-alization of sportsbetting needs to recognize the transforming nature of interdependent global forces with respect to both economic and cultural power. Yet it must also consider that sportsbetting may actually play a role in revitalizing multiple localized cultures. In different locations and to differing degrees, sportsbetting could result in the rearticulation and celebration of national and local cultural identities.

CONCLUSIONS

Caution is indicated in both overstating and understating the asymmet-rical effects of global gambling processes on local cultures and social contexts. We cannot assume that the globalization of gambling is a uni-form process that interacts with and influences all local cultures equally. Nor can we assume that resistance, accommodation, and agency are equal among every particular local culture. Several cultural theorists have called for a more dynamic, multidimensional approach to understanding the global-local nexus, one that refutes a deterministic view of globalization to recognize the diverse set of consequences that result when global and local forces meet. These questions are just as relevant to the study of gambling as they are to other cultural and economic phenomena.

Understanding the processes and effects of sportsbetting may provide valuable insights into the debates surrounding globalism and localism. It may be that the recent accelerated growth of sportsbetting is contributing not only to the flow of global gambling products and practices, but also to the rearticulation, or reinvention, of particular community identities built around notions of difference. Gambling, like many other cultural activities, can become contested terrain through which an authentic "imagined community" is constructed. Benedict Anderson has shown the significance of the international order in the construction of national identities: "Our nation is 'the best'—in a competitive, comparative field."[16] Any analysis of the opportunities and risks posed by globalized sportsbetting should recognize the politics and power relations associated with inventing a particular image of community in juxtaposition to the hegemonic global culture and economy.

In this regard, the Internet offers potential for global networks and new patterns of sociability and citizen participation to transform the categories of contemporary gambling.[17] The Internet provides the material base for expression of consumer rights by bringing gamblers into contact to share information, to voice their concerns and aspirations, and to propose alternative views on the political debate. The challenge for gambling studies is to better understand the apparent worldwide fascination with contemporary commercial gambling despite the fact that most gamblers must inevitably lose in economic terms. This apparent contradiction highlights the complexity of globalized gambling and its relationship with localized social life.

NOTES

1. See Jan McMillen et al., *Australian Gambling: Comparative History and Analysis* (Melbourne: Victorian Casino and Gaming Authority, 2000), pp. 196–98.

2. David Rowe, Geoffrey Lawrence, Tony Miller, and Jim McKay, "Global Sport? Core Concern and Peripheral Vision," *Media, Culture, and Society* 16 (1994): 661–75.

3. Jan McMillen, "On-Line Gambling," in *Electronic Commerce and the Law*, ed. Jay Forder and Patrick Quirk (Brisbane: Jacaranda Press, 2001), pp. 331–66.

4. Parliament of the Commonwealth of Australia, *Interactive Gambling Bill 2001: Report of the Senate Environment, Communications, Information Technology, and the Arts Legislation Committee* (Canbera: Commonwealth Government, 2001).

5. See, for example, The Parliament of the Commonwealth of Australia. 2001. *Interactive Gambling Bill 2001*; Department of Culture, Media, and Sport, *Gambling Review Report* (London: Stationery Office, 2001).

6. A similar argument was made to the recent Gambling Review board in Britain.

7. Jan McMillen. and Richard Martino, *Analysis of Sportsbetting Legislation and Regulations: Final Report*, report to the Australian Cricket Board (Australian Institute for Gambling Research, UWS, 2001).

8. See, for example, Benje Bailey "Gambling on College Sports," *Gaming Law Review* 4, no. 4 (2000): 339–47, and Daniel E. Ginsburg, *The Fix Is In: A History of Baseball Gambling and Game Fixing Scandals* (London: McFarland, 1994).

9. Department of Culture, Media and Sport, *Gambling Review Report*, p. 152.

10. Ibid., p.83.

11. McMillen and Martino, *Analysis of Sportsbetting Legislation and Regulations*.

12. Jan McMillen, "Online Gambling: Challenges to Regulation and National Sovereignty," *Prometheus* 18, no. 4 (2000): 391–401.

13. Department of Culture, Media, and Sport, p. xx.

14. Ironically, there are signs that some U.S. gambling operators are seeking to invest in sportsbetting operations licensed in other countries.

15. See, for example, David Rowe, *Sport, Culture, and the Media* (Buckingham: Open University Press, 1999).

16. Benedict Anderson, *Imagined Communities: Reflections on the Origins and Spread of Nationalism* (Verso: London, 1991), p. 17.

17. For analysis of the globalization of social movements, see Robin Cohen and Shirin Rai, eds., *Global Social Movements* (London: Althone Press, 2000).

Section 2

ECONOMIC AND SOCIAL COSTS AND BENEFITS

♥ ♠ ♣

3

CUTTING THE CARDS AND CRAPS

Right Thinking about Gambling Economics

Earl L. Grinols

For most of the twentieth century, the American gambling industry could be described as no more than a footnote to the national scene. Attention to the industry, when it occurred at all, was regional or episodic. Only after casinos spread from fourteen counties, all but one in Nevada, to hundreds of counties in dozens of states in the 1990s did the industry become nationally significant and the question of whether casinos were desirable a serious policy matter. This essay deals with the notional issues surrounding the social value of gambling. The emphasis is on correcting common misconceptions about the meaning of economic development and on applying logic to the valid cost-benefit evaluation of casino gambling.

HISTORICAL CONTEXT

During its rise to national attention in the early 1990s, the gambling industry and its spokesmen espoused the view that opposition to the spread of modern gambling should be puzzling to any sensible observer and perhaps could be understood only as the emotional outpourings of moralists or religious zealots. It was not to their advantage to acknowledge the possibility that opposition was the reasonable response to social costs that exceeded social benefits. Those in the news media at first took their lead from the industry. To provide balance to their news coverage, they unenthusiastically but dutifully included in their reports the misgivings of gambling opponents. Questioning the opposition to gambling gradually lessened, however, as newsworthy and often spectacular suicides (such as losers throwing themselves from the tops of tall casinos), bankruptcies, embezzlements, murders, robberies, government corruption, and other crimes began to surface. Reporters needed less education about the harmful effects of gambling when they knew a family member or acquaintance whose life was seriously injured by gambling. Interest in the reasons why gambling might differ from other forms of entertainment grew among the media and in government. Three questions of the time were (1) Did the gambling industry deliver on its often extravagant promises of economic development? (2) What were the social costs that opponents seemed to assert so vehemently? (3) How did problem and pathological gamblers enter into the evaluation of gambling?

The answers to these questions required serious research, of which there was little. Meaningful academic interest in gambling did not exist in most parts of the country because commercial casino gambling had been criminalized for most of the century, often specifically prohibited in state constitutions. A handful of respected scholars outside Nevada and New Jersey had paid some attention to lotteries, which were becoming more widespread by the 1980s, but answers to most questions were unavailable.

Research from states with the most experience with casinos—New Jersey and Nevada—provided little that could be used in the social evaluation of gambling. Even though casinos had been operating in Nevada since 1931, research from Nevada had not identified, let alone quantified, the social costs of casino gambling. No measures of the benefits of casinos had been estimated and the effect of casinos on causing problem and pathological gambling was unknown. In fact, the gambling industry initially denied that the spread of casinos affected the number of problem and pathological gamblers until the June 1999 publication of the research from the National Gambling Impact Study Commission made that position untenable. The industry's public position was that people would gamble regardless of the access to casinos and so access did not matter. Nevada experts did not know what the prevalence rate of pathological gambling was in Nevada because they had not studied it.

Pioneering research by Politzer, Morrow, and Leavey at Johns Hopkins University did quantify large costs associated with pathological gamblers.[1] For a number of years this research was left undisturbed and unchallenged by the gambling industry, which began to understand its significance only when its implications about the damage that gambling did to society were pointed out by later researchers such as Kindt.[2] Thereafter, the American Gaming Association endeavored to harm the reputation of this work by questioning its methodology.[3] The industry did not conduct research of its own on this topic however.

As data about problem and pathological (P&P) gamblers became more widely available, often from the studies of treatment specialists, they suggested that P&Ps lost far more in casinos than the average adult. Grinols and Omorov were among the first to raise this issue,[4] but other research soon followed. Combining loss figures with prevalence numbers for problem and pathological gamblers implied that this tiny group of individuals (problem and pathological gamblers generally constitute fewer than 4.5 percent of the population)[5] was responsible for a large share of casino revenues, as much as one third, or even in some studies one half.[6] Not surprisingly, research in Nevada had not investigated what share of casino revenues came from problem and pathological gamblers nor had it questioned what share of revenues came from the small portion of the population that gambled most. One Nevada academic testified that he had been involved in gambling research for twenty-five years but that it was "surprising how little we definitely know about the social and economic impacts of this $40 billion a year industry."[7]

THE ISSUES

Whereas in the early 1990s there were almost no studies with firm numbers, by the late 1990s a growing number of scholars had begun to ask tougher questions about problem and pathological gambling, its social costs, how much of casino industry revenues depended on the losses of problem and pathological gamblers, and whether the economic development claims of the gambling industry were credible. During the past decade, the public debate over gambling has matured. We now understand, for example, that gambling creates certain social costs that other entertainment industries do not. These costs have direct impact on other businesses and households and do not operate through prices and markets. They therefore fall into the classification that economists call *negative externalities*. The social costs of gambling can be identified, in principle, and compared with its social benefits.

In spite of the improvement in our quantitative knowledge about the effects of gambling, however, misconceptions persist. Gambling opponents emphasize social costs that outweigh social benefits; proponents emphasize "increased" numbers of jobs and "economic development." It is not uncommon for industry-financed studies to report the effect of a casino on jobs yet never compute the value to residents of these jobs or incorporate them into a cost-benefit assessment of casinos.

The situation is often not much more enlightened in government circles. Legislators still believe against logic that taxes raised from casinos are "free" because they are "voluntary." They commission reports to estimate how many tax dollars a casino project may provide but never incorporate these numbers into an applicable cost-benefit study. They ask for information about jobs and taxes but not about social welfare. What they hear of costs often must come from the citizen groups that appear before their committees.

An outside observer of the way in which casino expansion has been analyzed can rightfully be excused for being appalled at the lack of rigor. There is not even agreement on what constitutes a review. Industry apologists sell casino projects by counting jobs, government evaluates projects by looking at tax revenues, and the citizens split according to their status: Those who benefit personally—the casino owners and those with a direct stake in selling casino games to the public or who think that their taxes will be paid for them by the casino—are in favor. Those who are indifferent to gambling and ignorant of its social costs are neutral to mildly in favor because they believe they have no reason to prevent others from exercising their freedom of choice. Few are knowledgeable enough to understand what constitutes a theoretically valid cost-benefit review and sufficiently unprejudiced to pursue it.

JOBS ARE NOT BENEFITS

The most common misconception about the social evaluation of gambling is the belief that counting jobs created by casinos is the way to measure benefits. Jobs are not a benefit, and more jobs in an area may even be harmful to existing residents. In other cases, more jobs may be the means to benefits. In this section I discuss the connections between job creation and correctly counted costs and benefits. The concepts discussed are general; they apply to the evaluation of other businesses as well as casinos.

Economic Development and the Creation of Wealth

A faulty emphasis on jobs derives from an incomplete understanding of economic development. To answer the question, "What is economic development?" recall what the creation of wealth is. When individuals undertake productive activity, they produce goods and services that provide greater welfare or satisfaction than the inputs used. Paint and canvas, for example, are rearranged in the hands of a master painter into a work of art that has more value than the components had previously. A barber provides grooming that is more valuable to the customer than the value to the barber of the time given up. Consumer utility rises when activities are pursued and productive assets used in better ways. If society can reorganize so that someone is made better off without harming anyone in the process, the welfare of society is enhanced. Money and prices provide a convenient measure of the value of productive activity. When paint and canvas worth $100 dollars become a painting worth $10,000 a month later, the painter has generated income of $9,900 over that month.

Income is a flow per unit time, while wealth is a stock. Wealth is the claim to something of value. Income that has not been used for consumption can be used to acquire wealth. Claims to some assets have value to buyers because of expectations about how the assets will produce a flow of income in the future. When these expectations change, the value of the assets may change up or down, leading to capital gains or losses. With proper accounting for capital gains and losses, wealth is the accumulation of past unused (unconsumed) income.

Economic development is the creation of greater value by society. Greater value can result from a greater quantity of activity, activity that is more valuable, or both. Economic development means greater income and wealth, which lead to greater utility for members of society. The following constructed examples show that job creation is neither necessary nor sufficient for economic development.

In the first example, let casinos be introduced into a community of 10,000 employed individuals. The casino causes the demise of a nearby racetrack and takes business from neighboring restaurants. The casino hires one hundred employees, but these are matched by the loss of one hundred jobs at other businesses, and casino revenues are matched by reduced revenues at these other businesses. The net effect is the enlargement of the casino sector matched by an equal shrinkage of the rest of the economy. In this example, no economic development takes place because greater value is not created. Casinos in this example act much as another restaurant might in a town with many existing restaurants. The new entrant takes business from others, shifting the location of activity but not increasing it.

From the first example one might conjecture that hiring by a new business need not indicate an increase in jobs and that the failure to create jobs means there is no economic development. It is true that hiring by a firm may not represent job creation. However, the next two examples show that economic development is not linked to job creation: Development may occur with or without a net increase in jobs.

In the second example, assume that casinos attract clientele from the surrounding areas. Local residents do not gamble. Casinos hire 100 new employees who move in from surrounding regions, paying them out of casino revenues earned from outside clientele. In this example, the non-casino local economy continues to employ 10,000 people, whose earnings are unchanged and who buy and sell as before at unchanged prices.

In this case, regional net new jobs are created, but there is no economic development. The local economy is enlarged and employment rises 10 percent, but this enlargement provides no benefits to residents. Casinos operate like a toll house that uses the town as a platform for conducting its business. Money enters and money leaves. While total economic activity *in the vicinity of the town* rises, shifting the location of jobs without an increase in well-being is not economic development, even though the local economy is enlarged. Viewed from the national perspective, this example could be consistent with casinos operating like the restaurants of the first example: Increased employment in the casino sector is matched by reduced employment in other sectors. It is generally accepted, for example, that employment in Nevada is larger at the expense of lower employment in California, where many Las Vegas clients formerly lived.

The third example shows that economic development can occur without job creation. Assume that casinos begin operation, hire 100 employees, but cause the number of jobs in other sectors to shrink to 9,900. Because gambling is so desirable to residents and outsiders alike, the casinos earn higher profits than other businesses in town and bid up the prevailing wage rate. Housing prices also rise due to the willingness of casino owners to pay higher prices. Residents are better off because they can gamble nearer to home than before and they receive higher wages for their labor, which also makes them better off, and their housing experiences capital gains. Because the work of the 100 casino sector employees generates greater profit than the profit lost from the businesses whose employment shrank, the total of wages and profits of all area business is higher. Casinos have brought economic development without new jobs.

In the first example, casinos did not increase jobs or provide economic development. In the second, casinos provided jobs but no economic development, while in the third, casinos provided economic development but no increase in jobs. What principle explains the different outcomes? Anything that increases the value of social product leading to greater welfare of residents is economic development, and anything that does not is not. Job creation is immaterial unless it happens to be a vehicle for increase in social value.

The increase in social value gets distributed to society in different forms. It can appear as direct consumer benefits to households, such as closer access to an activity that was already available. It can appear in the form of better prices for consumers. We will call the former benefit *distance consumer surplus*, the latter, *price consumer surplus*. For example, a new firm that is located closer to the consumer provides distance consumer surplus. A firm whose entry into the market causes the price for its product to fall provides consumers with greater price consumer surplus. A new firm may cause wage rates to rise, also providing households with greater price consumer surplus, even though the consumer acts in the role of labor supplier. Economic development can appear in other forms as well, including higher profits to firm owners, greater taxes collected by government, and even improved functioning of markets. For example, the introduction of Internet auctions such as eBay links markets, giving buyers lower prices and sellers higher prices for their goods. This situation also creates welfare.

Nowhere in the preceding description of economic development was the creation of jobs part of the discussion. Jobs matter only in the sense that they proxy for one or more direct effects that benefit residents. Additional jobs in an area may not be associated with any benefits to residents and can even be associated with loss of benefits. The point is that the benefit of an additional job to residents depends on specifics of the region and the case at hand. Using jobs as a proxy requires that the value of a job to residents be identified.

There is a close analogy between the construction of major league sports stadiums and the social costs of gambling. In the case of major league teams, a community is usually told that a sports team will generate jobs, but the community must pay to build a sports stadium. In the case of gambling, a community is told that a casino will generate jobs, but the community must pay the social costs of casino gambling. Commenting on major league sports teams, Rappaport and Wilkerson write:

> The large public spending on sports facilities has been controversial. Usually these costly projects are justified by claims that hosting a sports franchise spurs local economic development by creating numerous new jobs and boosting local tax revenue. However, independent economic studies suggest that taxpayers may not be getting such a good deal.[8]

They continue:

> [T]he impact studies almost always fail to measure benefits in a form that can be compared with public outlays . . . Correctly measuring the benefit from job creation requires both accurately accounting for the net number of new jobs associated with a team's presence along with *valuing the benefit of these jobs to the host metro area.* [Emphasis added.][9]

Based on their review of the available research literature, Rappaport and Wilkerson conclude that the value of a job to the host area could be nothing at all. Or, it could be as much as $1,500 per job created, depending on circumstances. Or, jobs could provide *negative* value to the host area because housing is made less affordable or because traffic and other forms of congestion increase:

> For some existing residents, the net result may be that they are hurt rather than helped by net job creation. . . . The ambiguity of whether a metro area benefits from net job creation sharply contrasts with the common perception that local net job creation is a benefit in and of itself."[10]

WHAT COUNTS AND HOW TO COUNT IT RIGHT

The previous section tackled the prevalent confusion about job creation and economic development. This section provides a rigorously grounded formulation of the costs and benefits associated with the introduction of an industry such as casino gambling that imposes costs on society in the form of real-resource-using harmful externalities.

I base my approach to cost and benefits on the change in individual consumer utility, $u^1 - u^0$. Superscripts 0 and 1 identify pre- and post-change variables. Thus, u^0 refers to utility "before" (e.g., before casinos) and u^1 refers to utility "after." We assume that the individual's utility is a continuous function of the consumption of goods and services. With respect to casino gambling, utility also depends on the distance that the consumer has to travel to the nearest casino, the number of visits made, and the amount of money gambled per visit. The number of visits and the amount gambled are under the individual's control, but distance is taken as a given feature of the consuming environment, as are prices. Consumption is quantified in the vector $x \in R^n$. The quantity of goods and services consumed appear as positive components of x, while the provision of a good or service such as labor supplied by the consumer, is shown by a negative component. Consumption is assumed to be locally nonsatiable. That is, for any x there exists another vector near to x that is strictly preferred by the consumer.

Define $e(d, p, u)$ as the minimum expenditure needed to achieve utility u when distance to the nearest casino is d and prices are p. For fixed d and p, $e(d, p, u)$ rises and falls with u. In other words, $e(d, p, u^1) > e(d, p, u^1)$ if and only if $u^1 > u^0$. The welfare increase of individual i is therefore, $e^i(d_i, p, u_0^1) - e_i(d_i, p, u_i^0)$, measured in dollars, where the subscript i reminds us which variables are specific to individual i. For all consumers, welfare change is

$$\Delta W = \Sigma_i \, [e_i(d_i^1, p^1, u_i^1) - e_i(d_i^1, p^1, u_i^0)]. \tag{1}$$

Equation (1) treats a dollar of utility gain to one household as equal to a dollar of utility gain to another. This is a natural assumption and has a number of important implications, including that firm profits are equally important regardless of which firm generates them, and to whom they ultimately go. We assume that household i owns share θ_{ij} of firm j, where $\theta_{iij} = 1$.

The economy's available consumption goods come from one of three sources: endowments Ω, current production y, or international trade z. Endowments are goods inherited from nature or the past. Without loss of generality, assume that households own the endowments, $\omega_i \in R_+^n$, where $\Sigma_i \omega_i = \Omega$, the economy endowment vector. The current production of firms y_j adds to the economy total $\Sigma_j y_j = y$. An input, say labor time or the services of physical capital, appear as elements of y_j with a negative sign, while outputs are positive elements of y_j. International trade is a form of production where exports, entering z as negative numbers, play the role of inputs, and imports, entering z as positive numbers, play the role of outputs.

Government is also an agent in the economy. Government collects tax revenues and spends them for the benefit of consumers. Although the accounting framework can be made to accommodate as detailed treatment of government as needed, we make the standard simplifying assumption that government returns to the household in lump-sum fashion tax dollars used for the purchase of goods and services that enter household utility. Households spend these transfers. The remaining government tax revenues pay for resources to deal with costly externalities. For example, if casinos increase crime, government might need to hire more police. If casinos create pathological gamblers, government might need to provide more treatment counselors. Goods and services, g, used to counter externalities do not directly affect household utility, but because they divert available resources from productive activity, their removal represents a drain on the economy. Tangible resources used is the social cost of externalities. Accounting in real terms requires

$$x + g = y + \Omega + z$$

where $x \neq \Sigma_i x_i$ is aggregate consumption.

We assume that households are unconstrained in the long run in their purchase of goods and services. This implies that $p_i^1 \bullet x_i^1 = e_i(d_i^1, p_i^1, u_i^1)$ because an unconstrained consumer selects the least costly bundle for attaining a given utility u_i^1. In the initial situation, however, we allow for the possibility that the consumer may be constrained. If constraints are present, $p_i^0 \bullet x_i^0 > e_i(d_i^0, p_i^0, u_i^0)$. The most prominent example of a constraint is unemployment. If the consumer wants to work at the going wage, but is prevented, he is unemployed. We will return to unemployment as it relates to the effect of casinos later in this section.

The following identity rewrites (1) as a telescoping sum where each term cancels part of the preceding term. It decomposes the change in welfare into interpretable components.

$$\Sigma_i[e_i(d_i^1, p_i^1, u_i^1) - e_i(d_i^1, p_i^1, u_i^0)] = {}_i[\, p_i^1 \bullet x_i^1 - p_i^0 \bullet x_i^0 \,] \qquad (2.1)$$
$$\text{Income Effects}$$

$$+ \Sigma_i [\, p_i^0 \bullet x_i^0 - e_i(d_i^0, p_i^0, u_i^0) \,] \qquad (2.2)$$
$$\text{Consumption Constraint Gains}$$

$$+ \Sigma_i [\, e_i(d_i^0, p_i^0, u_i^0) - e_i(d_i^1, p_i^0, u_i^0)] \qquad (2.3)$$
$$\text{Distance Consumer Surplus}$$

$$+ \Sigma_i \, [\, e_i(d_i^1, p_i^0, u_i^0) - e_i(d_i^1, p_i^1, u_i^0) \,]. \qquad (2.4)$$

Price Consumer Surplus

To explain (2.1), make use of the budget identity

$$p_i \bullet x_i = \Sigma_j \, \theta_{ij} \Pi_j + p_\Omega \bullet \Omega_i + T_i - E_I \qquad (3)$$

where Π_j is the profit of firm j, $p_\Omega \bullet \Omega_i$ is earnings from the consumer's endowment, T_i is household taxes, and E_i is the household's share of the cost of gambling-induced externality expenditures. Summing (3) over consumers and differencing between the initial and final situations breaks (2.1) into the following terms:

$$\Sigma_i \, [\, p_i^1 \bullet x_i^1 - p_i^0 \bullet x_i^0 \,] = \Sigma_j \, \Delta \, \Pi_j \; + \; \Delta \, p_\Omega \bullet \Omega + \; \Delta T - \Delta E \qquad (4)$$

The change in firm profits, taxes, and social costs is self-explanatory. $\Delta \, p_\Omega \bullet \Omega$ is the value to the consumer of induced price changes—increases or decreases in the price of something the consumer owns, such as housing—that affects consumer welfare. We characterize these values as capital gains because they represent pure price effects.

The next component, (2.2), is the amount of money the individual would be willing to pay to remove the consumption constraints, if any. If the constraint is unemployment, for example, this component is the value of reducing unemployment. Expression (2.3) gives the value of having the nearest casino d_i^1 miles away compared to d_i^0 miles. Assuming that the consumer values gambling, the income needed to maintain original utility, $e_i(d_i^1, p_i^0, u_i^0)$, is smaller when $d_i^1 < d_i^0$. Expression (2.3) represents the surplus accruing to the consumer when the nearest casino is closer. It is proper to interpret (2.3) as the amount of money the consumer would be willing to pay each year to have the nearest casino closer. Expression (2.4) is a conventional consumer surplus term. It is the amount of money that the consumer would be willing to pay each year for the opportunity to trade at prices p_i^1 instead of p_i^0. For example, if casinos cause the wage rate to rise, the consumer is better off by this price change and would be willing to pay amount (2.4) to have the higher wage prevail.

Using equation (4) with equations (1) and (2) gives:

$\Delta W = \Delta$ Profits $+ \Delta$ Taxes

$+$ Distance Consumer Surplus $+$ Price Consumer Surplus

Capital Gains $+$ Consumption Constraint Gains

$- \Delta$ Social Costs.

(5)

Equation (5) is the form we want. It lists all cost-benefit components, and, with equations (1)–(4), specifies how each term should be constructed. Nothing is left out and there is no double counting.

Economic development is synonymous with greater creation of social value. The decomposition in (5) identifies the ways in which this increased value is captured by agents in the economy. An increase in profits is the share of economic development that goes to the owners of firms. Since profits are summed over all firms, it is the net profit increase that matters to (5). The increase in taxes captures the portion of economic development that citizens collectively capture through government. Taxes are used for the public good, so higher tax collection summed over all payers, not just casinos, represent a public benefit. Better access to casinos is captured in the distance consumer surplus term, while the possibility that casinos cause prices to change in ways that favor residents is captured in the price consumer surplus and capital gains terms.

If the economy exhibits consumption constraints and casinos are the cause of their elimination, then this also represents a benefit of casinos. It is theoretically possible that introducing casinos into the economy might reduce unemployment. The difficulty in propounding such a claim in practice, however, is that unemployment is generally understood to be a transitory phenomenon. The economy would eventually move to full employment without casinos. Comparing the final position of the economy with casinos to the final position of the economy without casinos would reveal no unemployment in either. Term (2.2) would then be zero. If one believes that casinos caused the *swifter* return to full employment, then during the period of transition this would be a temporary benefit of casinos. I am unaware of this argument being made and documented in practice.

The social costs of casinos are the cost of resources removed from other productive uses to deal with the social problems caused by casinos.

Nowhere in equation (5) do casino jobs or jobs created appear. Jobs matter only to the extent that they might be inputs to the creation of some other benefit identified in (5). Although the number of jobs sometimes is a good indicator of economic development, it is not always an accurate predictor. The value of an additional job to an area may be zero, as documented in the literature on the job effects of major league sports teams, already discussed.

THE BOTTOM LINE

The primary purpose of this essay is to correct misconceptions surrounding the evaluation of socially costly industries like gambling. A full-scale treatment of the literature estimating the costs and benefits of gambling would require more space than can be devoted here. Nevertheless, I would be remiss to close without summarizing the essential numbers in a short precis. Details can be found in the growing body of research that addresses the costs, benefits, and social implications of gambling.[11]

There are two main ways in which the social costs of gambling have been estimated. One is by identifying the costs of problem and pathological gamblers and combining these numbers with estimates of problem and pathological gambler prevalence in the general population to infer the size of total costs. The second is through direct observations of the impact of casinos on selected variables such as crime rates. The approach based on problem and pathological gamblers is the more widely employed. Its advantage is that the required inputs are more readily accessible through sampling and survey techniques. Its disadvantage is that it understates social costs by failing to count costs that do not operate through problem and pathological gamblers.

Direct Crime-Cost Estimates

Direct estimates of the crime costs due to casinos, for example, have led to numbers similar to the crime-cost estimates derived from the criminal activity of problem and pathological gamblers but slightly higher. Many experts believe that the primary cause of increased crime observed in counties with casinos is the problem and pathological gamblers them-selves. However, crimes could result in other ways, and tallying only crime committed by P&P gamblers would understate the true amount of crime due to casinos. To directly estimate this amount Grinols and Mus-tard compiled data for every county in the United States for the twenty-year period from 1977–96.[12] Based on statistical analysis, they reported that 8 percent of observed crime in casino counties was due to the pres-ence of the casino. They found that it generally takes three or four years after casino introduction before crime rates begin to rise. The cost of this crime was $63 per adult per year in casino counties. This figure is com-parable to the results of a study by Thompson, Gazel, and Rickman con-ducted in Wisconsin.[13] They reported that crime costs per additional problem gambler were $4,225, or 42 percent of the total costs found. On a per capita basis, crime cost $57 per adult. Both figures are higher than the $46 estimate used in Table 1 derived from the crimes of problem and pathological gamblers alone.

Costs Estimated from Problem and Pathological Gamblers

Pathological gambling is recognized as an impulse control disorder in the *Diagnostic and Statistical Manual* (DSM-IV) of the American Psychi-atric Association. Pathological gamblers experience repeated failures to resist the urge to gamble; lose control over their gambling, personal lives, and employment; rely on others to relieve a desperate financial situation caused by gambling; and commit illegal acts to finance gambling. Problem gamblers have similar characteristics but to a lesser degree.

According to a 1990 Maryland Department of Health and Mental Hygiene survey, 62 percent of problem gamblers in treatment had com-mitted illegal acts as a result of their gambling, 80 percent had committed civil offenses, and 23 percent were charged with criminal offenses.[14] A similar study of nearly 400 members of Gamblers Anonymous showed that 57 percent admitted stealing to finance their gambling. On average they stole $135,000 each. Total theft was over $30 million.[15] The National Gambling Impact Study Commission's final report, issued in June 1999, reported that among those who did not gamble (had not gambled in the past year), only 7 percent had ever been incarcerated. In contrast, more than three times this number (21.4 percent) of individuals who had been pathological gamblers at any point during their lifetime had been incarcerated.

By studying problem and pathological gamblers, the resource burden to society of an additional pathological or problem gambler (some studies lump the two groups together) can be determined. At least nine distinct types of gambling social costs that have been identified:

1. **Crime** (apprehension, adjudication, incarceration, and police costs),
2. **Business and employment** (lost productivity on the job, lost employment time, other costs to firms),
3. **Bankruptcy** (lawsuits and legal costs, bill collection costs),
4. **Suicide,**
5. **Illness** (costs associated with depression, stress-related illness, anxiety, cognitive distortions, cardiovascular disorders, chronic or severe headaches, etc.),
6. **Social services** (treatment/therapy costs, welfare, food stamps, costs associated with unemployment),
7. **Government direct regulation,**
8. **Family problems** (costs associated with divorce, separation, spousal abuse, child neglect),
9. **Abused dollars** (resources acquired from family, friends, employers under false pretenses).

Averaging the results of eight studies conducted between 1994 and 1999 that contain original research on one or more of the nine social costs resulted in the following estimates of the costs to society per additional pathological gambler[16]: crime, $3998; business and employment costs, $3995; bankruptcy, $316; suicide, not estimated; illness, $700; social service costs, $631; government regulatory costs, not estimated; family costs, $111; abused dollars, $3834. The total was $13,586.[17] The comparable totals for problem gamblers based on two studies are business and employment costs, $200; social service costs, $712. No other cost categories are available. The total for those costs that were estimated was $912.[18]

Based on a meta-study of others' field research, Shaffer et al. estimated that pathological gamblers were 1.4 percent of the population and problem gamblers 2.8 percent. Ninety-five percent confidence intervals for the percentage of pathological gamblers in the population were 0.90–1.38 percent, and for problem gamblers 1.95–3.65 percent. For an average 100 adults, these numbers imply social costs of $14,006 to $22,077, depending whether one uses both lower bounds or both higher bounds. On a per capita basis, the range is $140 to $221. For the nation as a whole, social costs for 197.5 million adults would be $27.6 to $43.7 billion.[19] These estimates place gambling among the handful of social problems, such as illegal drugs and alcohol, that impose substantial costs on society, including on those who do not engage in the activity.

Table 1: Summary of Per Capita Casino Costs and Benefits

BENEFITS	
Net Increase in Business Profits	$ 0
Net Increase in Tax Collections	$ 0
Distance Consumer Surplus for Non-problem, Non-pathological Gamblers	$ 34
	$ 34

COSTS	
Crime	$ 46
Business and Employment	$ 51
Bankruptcy	$ 4
Suicide	$??
Illness	$ 8
Social Services	$ 27
Direct Regulatory	$ 10
Family	$ 1
Abused Dollars	$ 44
	$190
NET SOCIAL COST	**–$156**

Fewer estimates of the benefits of casinos exist. Grinols reports distance consumer surplus as between $34 and $50 per adult, depending on whether one adjusts for the demand of problem and pathological gamblers or not.[20] How the other benefits of casinos are distributed depends on the market structure and the casino tax rate. In places where entry is free to any casino firm meeting the licensing standards, as in Nevada and the Gulf Coast of Mississippi, casinos exert no monopoly power, and profits, through competition, are driven down to the ordinary business level. Where casinos are taxed at the same rates as other businesses, the increase in casino taxes is matched by a comparable drop in taxes collected from businesses competing for the same dollars. In this case, the benefits of casinos in society accrue entirely to consumers in the form of distance surplus. The net change in profits plus taxes measured over all business is zero. These gains are conceptually easiest to identify and estimate. They are reported in Table 1 using cost figures in the middle of the estimated range. Where casinos are granted regional monopoly licenses, as in Illinois, some of the benefits of casinos are captured by the casinos themselves in the form of monopoly profits. The increase in profits to business reduces the benefits that end up in the hands of consumers. The net increase in profits to all businesses are harder to estimate for a number of reasons, including the fact that American Indian casinos are not required to report their profits. Similarly, if the government levies heavier taxes on casinos than on other businesses, some of the benefits of casinos are captured by government at the expense of benefits that would have accrued to the casinos and consumers directly.

Based on the costs and benefits in Table 1, the social costs outweigh the benefits by a factor of $190 to $34 or 5.6 to 1. An economy that includes casino gambling is worse off by $156 per capita compared with the same economy when casino gambling is prohibited. These figures do not yet include any capital gains or price-related benefits of casinos. Following the literature on the benefits of major league sports teams, let us assume that additional jobs due to casinos are associated with $750 in capital gains and price-related benefits to residents. Seven hundred fifty dollars is the mid-point of the $0–1,500 range identified earlier. Would these benefits change the unfavorable cost-to-benefit ratio?

The answer is probably not. To overcome the benefit-cost deficit in Table 1 through job creation would require twenty-one new jobs for every 100 adults in the population. Since labor force participation in the United States is 67 percent, casinos would have to cause the labor force to increase by 31 percent. Such a large increase is extremely unlikely.

The conclusion is inescapable: Based on the numbers currently available, casino gambling fails a theoretically grounded, theoretically valid cost-benefit analysis.

NOTES

1. Robert M. Politzer, James S. Morrow, and Sandra B. Leavey, "Report on the Societal Cost of Pathological Gambling and the Cost-Benefit/Effectiveness of Treatment" (presented at the Fifth National Conference on Gambling and Risk-Taking, Johns Hopkins Compulsive Gambling Counseling Center, 1981).

2. John W. Kindt, "Increased Crime and Legalized Gambling Operations: The Impact on the Socio-economics of Business and Government," *Criminal Law Bulletin* 30 (1994): 538–55; Kindt. "Legalized Gambling Activities as Subsidized by Taxpayers," *Arkansas Law Review* 48 (1995): 889–931.

3. Statement by Frank Fahrenkopf, CEO and President, at the National Gambling Impact Study Commission, at a press conference held by the American Gaming Association in Chicago, Illinois, May 21, 1998. (The AGA is a lobbying organization of the gambling industry. Although the national press was well represented at the NGISC hearings, none of the press except the Las Vegas papers carried the story or any of Fahrenkopf's criticisms.)

4. E. L. Grinols and J. Omorov, "Development or Dreamfield Delusions? Assessing Casino Gambling's Costs and Benefits," *Journal of Law and Commerce* 16, no. 1 (1996): 49–87.

5. Howard J. Shaffer et al., *Estimating the Prevalence of Disordered Gambling Behavior in the United States and Canada: A Meta-analysis* (Boston: Harvard Medical School, 1997).

6. Henry Lesieur, "Costs and Treatment of Pathological Gambling," *Annals of the American Academy of Political and Social Science* 556 (1998): 153–71; Productivity Commission, *Australia's Gambling Industries: Final Report, Summary* (Canberra, 1999); Rachel A. Volberg et al., "Assessing Self-Reported Expenditures on Gambling," *Managerial and Decision Economics* 22 (2001): 1–3, 77–96.

7. Committee on Governmental Affairs, *Testimony before the Senate Committee on Governmental Affairs on the Bill to Create the National Gambling Impact Study Commission* (Washington, D.C.: Government Printing Office, 1995), pp.156–57, 162.

8. Jordan Rappaport and Chad Wilkerson, "What Are the Benefits of Hosting a Major League Sports Franchise?" *Economic Review, Federal Reserve Bank of Kansas City* 86, no. 1 (2001): 55.

9. Ibid., pp. 60–61.

10. Ibid., p. 64 and footnote 5.

11. Politzer, Morrow, and Leavey, *Report on the Societal Cost of Pathological Gambling*; Kindt "Increased Crime and Legalized Gambling Operations" and "The Costs of Addicted Gamblers: Should the States Initiate Mega-lawsuits Similar to the Tobacco Cases?" *Managerial and Decision Economics* 22, nos. 1–3 (2001): 117–64; Ricardo Gazel, Dan S. Rickman, and William N. Thompson, "Casino Gambling and Crime: A Panel Study of Wisconsin Counties," *Managerial and Decision Economics* 22, nos. 1–3 (2001): 65–76; Lesieur, "Costs and Treatment of Pathological Gambling"; Productivity Commission, *Australia's Gambling Industries*; Dean Gerstein et al., *Gambling Impact and Behavior Study: Report to the National Gambling Impact Study Commission* (National Gambling Impact Study Commission, 1999); Earl L. Grinols, "Distance Effects in Consumption," *Review of Regional Studies* 29, no. 1 (1999): 63–76; Earl L. Grinols and David B. Mustard, "Business Profitabity versus Social Profitability: Evaluating Industries with Externalities—The Case of Casinos," *Managerial and Decision Economics* 22, nos. 1–3 (2001): 143–62; National Gambling Impact Study Commission, *National Gambling Impact Study Commission: Final Report* (18 June 1999); South Dakota Legislative Research Council, *Economic and Fiscal Impacts of the South Dakota Gaming Industry* (Pierre: South Dakota State Publication, 1998), pp. 1–146, with attachment: Letter of 7 January 1999 to Terry Anderson, Director, SD Leg. Res. Council, and table: "South Dakota Total Estimated Incremental Social Costs"; Timothy P. Ryan et al., "Gambling in Louisiana: A Benefit-Cost Analysis" (paper prepared for the Louisiana Gaming Control Board, Louisiana State University Medical Center, April 1999); Grinols and Omorov, "Development or Dreamfield Delusions?"; Grinols, "Incentives Explain Gambling's Growth." *Forum for Applied Research and Public Policy* 11, no. 2 (1996): 119–24.

12. Grinols and Mustard, "Business Profitabity versus Social Profitability," pp. 143–62.

13. William N. Thompson, Ricardo Gazel, and Dan Rickman, "Social Costs of Gambling: A Comparative Study of Nutmeg and Cheese State Gamblers" (paper presented to the Twelfth National Conference on Problem Gambling, in Las Vegas, Nevada), published in *Gaming Research and Review Journal* 5, no. 1 (1998): 1–15.

14. Maryland Department of Health and Mental Hygiene, Alcohol and Drug Abuse Administration, *Task Force on Gambling Addiction in Maryland* (Baltimore: Author, 1990).

15. Henry Lesieur, "Costs and Treatment of Pathological Gambling."

16. The eight studies were as follows: Executive Office of the Governor, *Casinos in Florida* (Tallahasse: Office of Planning and Budgeting, 1994); William N. Thompson et al., "The Social Costs of Gambling in Wisconsin," *Wisconsin Policy Research Institute Report* 9, no. 6 (1996): 1–44; Ryan et al., "Gambling in Louisiana"; William N. Thompson and Frank L. Quinn, *An Economic Analysis of Machine Gambling in South Carolina*, a report prepared in conjunction with Friends of South Carolina, presented to the Education Foundation of the South Carolina Policy Council, Columbia, South Carolina, May 18, 1999.

17. Grinols and Mustard, "Measuring Industry Externalities: The Curious Case of Casinos and Crime," Terny College of Business, University of Georgia, 2001 [online], http://www.terny.uga.edu/~dmustard/casinos pdf.

18. Dean Gerstein et al., *Gambling Impact and Behavior Study;* South Dakota Legislative Research Council, *Economic and Fiscal Impacts of the South Dakota Gaming Industry.*

19. Shaffer et al., *Estimating the Prevalence of Disordered Gambling Behavior.*

20. Grinols, "Distance Effects in Consumption."

4

GRAND ILLUSIONS

Robert Goodman

The United States has embarked on an unprecedented experiment with legalized gambling. At times in the past, everything from lotteries to roulette was tolerated and even exploited for public revenues. But recognizing the moral and material hazards involved, public authorities generally acted cautiously, subjecting such ventures to tight controls. Today, gambling enterprises of various kinds, including casinos and riverboats, are not only permitted but actively promoted by many state and city political leaders as a magic bullet for ailing local economies. Indeed, only a belief in magic can explain the willingness of so many people to accept the proposition that legalized gambling can provide jobs and tax revenues at virtually no cost to society. We are only beginning to recognize the real costs.

The rapid spread of legalized gambling has been hard to miss in recent years, insistently announcing itself through clamorous advertise-

Reprinted from *Wilson Quarterly* 19, no. 4 (1995): 24–32.

ments for lotteries and casino outings. Yet the numbers are still startling. As recently as 1988, casino gambling was legal in only two states: Nevada and New Jersey. By 1994, casinos were either authorized or operating in twenty-three states, and legalization was being proposed in many others. Casinos sprang up on more than seventy Indian reservations, thanks in large part to powers granted the tribes under the federal Indian Gaming Regulatory Act of 1988. The state of Mississippi alone was home by last year [1994] to one million square feet of riverboat casinos. In the four years since legalization, Mississippi acquired more gambling space than Atlantic City, New Jersey, did in sixteen years. Within three years after the introduction of casino riverboats in Illinois, per capita spending on gambling in that state doubled.

Between 1988 and 1994, casino revenues in the United States nearly doubled—from $8 billion to about $15 billion annually. Overall, Americans wagered $482 billion in casinos and other legal betting venues in 1994, a jump of 22 percent over the previous year. Gambling has expanded at all levels—and has even brought a rise in attendance at church bingo games. The new gambling outlets were impressive for their variety: electronic slot machines in rural South Dakota bars; imitation Wild West casinos in old Colorado mining towns; riverboats along the Mississippi River, from the distressed industrial cities of Iowa to the Gulf of Mexico; and gambling establishments on Indian reservations from coast to coast. New Orleans is now building what promoters tout as the world's largest casino, while the mayors of Chicago, Philadelphia, and other big cities enthusiastically embrace gambling proposals.

Casino companies often enjoy economic advantages that are available to few other businesses. Since they are usually granted exclusive government franchises, they are able to generate short-term profits on a scale that proprietors of other businesses can only dream about. Earnings of five to eight percent of revenues are the norm for most American businesses. In the gambling industry, however, yearly profits between 30 and 50 percent are not unusual. It is not extraordinary for companies to be able to pay off their total investments in one or two years. One Illinois riverboat company reportedly tripled the return on its investment in just six months.

More and more Americans are being persuaded to try their luck. According to casino industry sources, the number of American households in which at least one member visited a casino doubled between 1990 and 1993—from 46 million to 92 million. More than three-quarters of this upsurge was the result of people visiting casinos outside Nevada and Atlantic City. In 1994, gambling industry leaders and other business observers were predicting even more spectacular growth. "By the year 2000," said Phil Satre, president of Harrah's Casinos, one of the world's largest casino companies, "Ninety-five percent of all Americans will most likely live in a state with legal casino entertainment." By then, according to Mark Manson, a vice president of Donaldson, Luffin & Jenrette, a stock brokerage firm, lotteries, casinos, and other kinds of legal gambling "could surpass all other forms of entertainment in terms of total revenue." Manson concluded that "the movement towards gaming appears unstoppable for the foreseeable future."

The amount of money in play is huge. Between the early 1980s and the early 1990s, betting on legal games, including the lotteries that were conducted by thirty-seven states and the District of Columbia, grew at almost twice the rate of personal incomes. Last year, legal gambling in the United States generated nearly $40 billion in revenues for its public- and private-sector proprietors.

What has made gambling attractive to politicians and local business leaders is the prospect of new jobs for workers and easy money to fill the coffers of local government and business. An activity that was once feared for its ability to sow moral corruption, its corrosive impact on the work ethic, and its potential to devastate family savings has suddenly been transformed into a leading candidate to revive the fortunes of towns and cities across America. In Chicago, casinos were proposed to bail out the city's overbuilt hotel sector. In Gary, Indiana, they were supposed to offset declines in a once-booming steel industry. In Detroit, they were touted as a way to replace lost jobs in automobile manufacturing. In New Bedford, Massachusetts, gambling was going to provide jobs for fishing industry workers thrown out of work by the exhaustion of Atlantic fisheries.

Advocates eagerly seek to cleanse gambling of its traditional connotations. It certainly looks on the surface more reputable than it once did. An industry created by the likes of "Bugsy" Siegel and Meyer Lansky and financed with laundered drug money and other ill-gotten gains is now operated by business school graduates, financed by conglomerates, and listed on the New York Stock Exchange. "Much of the moral argument against legalization is based upon the belief that gaming is mainly about money or greed," Harrah's president Satre told the National Press Club in 1993. 1t is not. It is about entertainment. . . . It is a true social experience. And there are no gender-based, race-based, or physical barriers to access." Politicians and others have joined in the effort to de-moralize the debate over gambling. No longer do they speak of "gambling," with all its unsavory overtones, but in euphemisms such as "gaming" and "casino entertainment."

Legalization tends to have a snowball effect. When one state allows games of chance, other states have a greater incentive to do so as well. If your citizens are going to gamble anyway, why not at least reap some of the benefits by letting them do so at home? In 1985, Montana became the first state to allow slot machines in bars, effectively creating minicasinos throughout the state. Four years later, South Dakota's legislature gave its state lottery agency authority to install "video lottery terminals"—which in reality are little more than slot machines—in bars and convenience stores. Soon afterward, Oregon, Rhode Island, West Virginia, and Louisiana legalized similar machines. By 1991, Oregon had also legalized betting on sports teams and electronic keno machines through its state lottery.

Iowa took a much bigger leap into gambling in 1991 when it became the first state to legalize casino gambling on riverboats. To ensure that the floating casinos would remain low-key tourist operations, the state government limited stakes to $5 per bet and total losses of any player to $200 per cruise. But these restrictions were soon dropped after politicians in Illinois, Mississippi, and Louisiana authorized riverboat gambling with unrestricted betting. Iowa had to keep up with the competition.

By late 1994, however, there were signs that the days of expansion without end were over. The casino boom of the early 1990s was not built on a broad base of popular support for legalization. The laws were changed in response to unprecedented, well-financed campaigns by the gambling industry, countered only by the underfunded, ad hoc efforts of opposition groups. But as casinos proliferated and their social and economic costs became more widely recognized, more and more communities rallied to defeat them.

Where statewide referendums have been held on casino gambling, voters have mostly voted no. In 1994, despite the gambling industry's promises of riches to come, not a single one of the four state casino referendums passed. (In seven other states where gambling was already legal, measures to expand it got mixed results.) In Florida, casino companies mounted their costliest promotional campaign ever, yet the voters rendered a decisive no. Where casino gambling has been legalized, it usually has been by direct action of state legislators or by legislature-approved referendums on the town, city, or county level. When the target is a single community starved for jobs and tax revenues, the industry has regularly been able to gain approval.

Yet Americans appear to be recognizing that the promises made by gambling proponents are rarely if ever realized by cash-strapped cities and towns. The municipalities' hopes are based largely on what happened in Las Vegas—a remote desert city that for decades held a virtual monopoly on gambling. The city was able to draw huge numbers of tourists who spent freely, not only at the tables and slots but in local hotels, restaurants, and stores. Something at least remotely similar has been achieved, at the reservation-based casinos. The Indian reservations have several things in common with early Las Vegas, notably remote locations and no existing economic bases to speak of. They have, in short, nothing to lose.

But there aren't likely to be any more Las Vegas-style success stories. With the proliferation of casinos around the country, the nature of the game has changed. Cities and towns entering the gambling market now face fierce competition, and they will be hard-pressed to draw patrons from outside their regions. Most of the people pumping money into their slot machines will be local residents. Instead of bringing in new dollars from outside the local economy, gambling will siphon away consumer dollars from other local businesses. At the same time, these communities will be saddled with enormous new costs as they deal with the economic and social consequences of open gambling. Not the least of these costs is an increase in the local population of chronic gamblers, who bring with them not only their personal tragedies but a host of related problems, from bad debts and family breakups to crime, often of the white-collar variety. Estimates of the annual private and public costs imposed by each problem gambler range from my own $13,200 (in 1993 dollars) up to $52,000. A mere 100 additional problem gamblers, in other words, exact a monetary toll of more than $1 million.

The sad lesson of gambling as an economic-development strategy is that it creates far more problems than it solves. It doesn't even deliver the goods it promises. In Atlantic City, for example, about one third of the city's retail establishments shut their doors during the first four years after the casinos' arrival. Many could not compete with the low-price restaurants and services offered by the casinos to lure customers. In 1993, unemployment in Atlantic City was double the state average.

One of the worst long-term consequences of legalizing gambling is the difficulty, if not impossibility, of undoing the decision. New gambling ventures create powerful new political constituencies that fight to keep gambling legal and expanding. These operations can radically alter the balance of power in state and local politics.

"Casino gambling is not a 'try it and see' experiment," observes Stephen P. Perskie, the politician who led the battle to legalize gambling in Atlantic City, and a former chair of New Jersey's Casino Control Commission. "Once the casino opens and the dice begin to roll, gambling creates an instant constituency. People depend on it for jobs. Governments depend on it for revenues." Perskie, who went on to become vice president of Players International, a casino development company, elaborates: "You've got economic realities created. You've got infrastructure investments, you've got public policy commitments. . . . The public official who will stand up and say close that casino and put those 4,000 people out of work is somebody I haven't met yet."

Once the novelty of a new casino or a new game wears off, as it inevitably does, revenues tend to fall or flatten, forcing legislators to look for new gambling ventures and gimmicks to keep the money coming in. And as enterprises suffer lower revenues from increased competition or fading consumer interest, they turn to government for regulatory relief and sometimes direct subsidies.

Even in New Jersey, where the casino industry is prohibited by law from lobbying, casino operators wield enormous political power. The state's experience offers an instructive example of the ways in which gambling regulations weaken over time. In Atlantic City, the original rules governing casinos included regulations that sought to reduce problem gambling. They prohibited twenty-four-hour gambling, restricted the amount of floor space that could be dedicated to slot machines (considered by many experts one of the most addictive forms of gambling), outlawed games such as electronic keno, poker, and sports betting, and created rules for jackpots and prizes designed to ensure that players wouldn't be taken advantage of too outrageously. But over time, especially as competition from casinos in other states increased during the early 1990s, casino companies pressed for relief from these restrictions. Gambling got its way. By 1994, all these rules had been dropped, with the single exception of limits on sportsbetting. (New Jersey's Casino Control Commission ruled that it simply had no legal power to change these rules because federal law restricts sports betting.)

New Jersey's powerful casino constituency was the force behind a number of public projects that were designed to restore Atlantic City's luster as a tourist destination—and thereby bolster the gambling business. In 1993, the state announced plans to spend about $100 million to expand Atlantic City's airport, rebuild the city's convention center, and beautify the approach roads to the casinos and their surrounding Boardwalk areas.

The plans had little to do with reversing the massive deterioration of the other Atlantic City beyond the Boardwalk. In fact, they were aimed at concealing the city's mean streets from casino visitors. As an article in the *New Jersey Casino Journal*, a voice for local casino owners, explained, "The need to negotiate passage through a depressed and deteriorated urban war zone is not especially conducive to a memorable entertainment experience."

The public debt that many cash-poor communities must assume to build or improve boat docks, parking facilities, highways, water and sewer systems, and other infrastructure creates problems of its own. The hope is that a continuous stream of revenue from taxes on casino income will help pay off this debt. But the community is also in a trap. To close down or curtail these operations if they falter or prove disruptive would be almost impossible—indeed, the community has every incentive to promote even more gambling.

Some of the biggest costs of gambling expansion are the hardest to quantify. They are what economists refer to as "opportunity costs." The more energy government officials and business leaders expend on gambling as an economic development strategy, the less they can devote to the cultivation of other kinds of business enterprises that may be less flashy and more difficult to establish. Over the long term, such businesses would almost certainly be more beneficial to towns and cities than those built on the exploitation of the gambling itch.

If gambling ventures continue to proliferate and expand, the political power of the gambling industry will grow as well, making it increasingly difficult to control gambling. A taste of what may come was provided in the spring of 1994, when the Clinton administration proposed a 4 percent federal tax on gross gambling revenues to fund its new welfare reform programs. The industry's response was swift and forceful. Thirty-one governors promptly wrote to the president complaining of the potential damage to their gambling-dependent state budgets. Governor Bob Miller of Nevada flew to Washington and presented President Clinton with a scenario of silent casinos and layoffs by the thousands in the gambling industry. Owners of horse and dog racetracks lobbied Congress with similar visions of economic devastation. The administration quickly withdrew its tax proposal.

The seed planted in the Nevada desert some fifty years ago is now bearing very dangerous fruit indeed. America's unprecedented gambling boom has created grand illusions worthy of the gaudiest and most grandiose Las Vegas casino. Only in one place could the notion flourish that a magical way could be found to create new jobs, generate fresh revenues for public coffers, and revive cities at virtually no cost: a fantasy land.

5
COMMUNITY SATISFACTION WITH CASINO GAMBLING

An Assessment after the Fact

B. Grant Stitt, Mark Nichols, and David Giacopassi

The presence of casino gambling in a community is controversial, and the decision to legalize it is often accompanied with rancorous debate. Nevertheless, many communities have initiated casino gambling in the hope and belief that the benefits from casinos will exceed the costs. In the early 1990s, casino gambling in the United States experienced tremendous growth fueled by the expectation that casinos would provide economic stimulus to areas that were economically stagnant. Casino gambling grew from two jurisdictions (Nevada and New Jersey) in 1978 to twenty-six states that now have Native American or other legal casinos operating within their borders. However, the growth of casino gambling, along with the presence of slot machines outside of casinos,

This project was supported by Grant No. 98-IJ-CS-0037, awarded by the National Institute of Justice, Office of Justice Programs, U.S. Department of Justice. Points of view in this document are those of the authors and do not necessarily represent the official position or policies of the U.S. Department of Justice.

has given rise to questions surrounding the wisdom of state-sanctioned gambling as public policy. This concern is evidenced by the 1999 call from the National Gambling Impact Study Commission for a pause in the spread of gambling in the United States until more is known about its costs and benefits.[1] In Australia, "harm minimization"—policies and procedures thought to minimize the costs associated with problem gambling—is being implemented.[2] The presence of slot machines outside of casinos is also being questioned in Canada and Holland.

A Gallup Poll conducted in 1993 found that Americans have a love/hate relationship with casinos. On the one hand, only 41 percent of a national sample of adults were in favor of casino gambling coming to their communities. On the other hand, 63 percent indicated they were in favor of "resort casinos." This disparity seems to indicate that the majority of Americans do not morally object to casino gambling but do view casinos as potentially harmful if they were established within their community.

Despite all the stories in the popular media concerning casino gambling, few systematic studies have been conducted to determine citizens' views of the costs and benefits associated with casino gambling in newly established casino communities. This essay will first review the literature and then report the results of a survey of citizens residing in eight new casino jurisdictions to determine their attitudes toward casinos and their perceptions of the impact of casinos on their communities.

REVIEW OF THE LITERATURE

To determine citizen attitudes toward casinos, Pizam and Pokela telephoned 400 households in an area in Massachusetts which was considering legalizing casino gambling. Nearly one-half (48 percent) of respondents opposed or strongly opposed legalization of a casino in their area, with 40 percent favoring or strongly favoring legalization. Respondents saw the greatest potential benefit of casino gambling being economic revitalization, but feared that their community environment would be negatively affected and there would be an increase in traffic congestion and crime.[3]

Caneday and Zeiger surveyed community residents and business owners in Deadwood, South Dakota, to determine the impact of casino tourism on the community. They found that residents whose jobs depended on tourism perceived the casinos to have a greater impact on the community, both positively and negatively, than did residents whose employment was not tourism-related. Both residents and business owners perceived economic benefits from the casino-related tourism but believed that the effects went beyond a narrow economic impact and changed many aspects of life in the small town.[4]

A study of four communities with limited-stake casino gambling— Deadwood, South Dakota, and Black Hawk, Central City, and Cripple Creek, Colorado—showed that residents perceived both positive and negative changes associated with casinos; for example, seeing a significant increase in jobs but also believing that casinos brought traffic congestion and crime.[5] In a further analysis of the same data, Long compared the findings from the South Dakota towns to data from a noncasino control community in Colorado. He found that, in both states, fewer than 10 percent of the casino community residents would recommend legalization of casinos for other communities, while 59 percent of the Colorado residents and 34 percent of the South Dakota residents would not recommend further legalization. The remaining residents stated that their recommendations depended on such factors as the conditions within the respective communities.[6] Clearly, in these small towns, casinos continued to be controversial, with divided opinion among the residents concerning the desirability of casinos within their communities.

In Ontario, Canada, a telephone survey was conducted of 2,682 residents before the opening of a casino and repeated with 2,581 residents one year later.[7] Before the casino opened, 54 percent approved of the casino; after one year, 66 percent approved. Approval rates increased for both males and females. In another Canadian study, Room et al. examined the impact of the Niagra casino on quality of life. Surveying residents both before and after the casino opened, they concluded: "Comparing expectations in 1996 with these perceptions of what actually happened, the general picture is that reality turned out to be less dramatic, both for good and bad, than expected."[8]

In an attempt to determine how residents perceived the impact of casino gambling on their communities, the National Gambling Impact Study Commission (NGISC) asked the National Opinion Research

Center (NORC) to randomly select ten communities with a population of at least 10,000 residents that were within fifty miles of a major casino. Although many of those interviewed could be considered community leaders, this status was not a condition for being interviewed. Results indicated that one community strongly favored of the legalized casino gambling, six communities were slightly favorable, two showed mixed attitudes, and one community was decidedly opposed to the legalized gambling. From the interviews, it appeared that the economic impact was judged favorably but that respondents in a majority of the communities also believed there was an increase in bankruptcies and an increase in residents who were problem gamblers.[9]

An earlier phase of the present study examined the perceptions of 128 community leaders in eight new gambling jurisdictions regarding casino gambling's impact on their communities: A clear majority (59 percent) of community leaders interviewed were in favor of the casino in the community, believing that the casino enhanced the quality of life in the community (65 percent), improved the economy (77 percent), and had little or no effect on crime (69 percent). However, responses varied by community and by leadership position within the community. Leaders in three communities were overwhelmingly positive (80 percent or more favored or strongly favored casinos in their communities), whereas in two communities, approximately 25 percent of the leaders interviewed opposed or strongly opposed the casinos.[10]

One of the major determinants of community leader attitudes was the degree of economic impact the casino had on the community. In communities where the casino had a major economic impact, leaders tended to be more favorable in their evaluation of casinos generally. In communities where the impact of the casino was less significant, leaders tended to be moderate in their assessments and more likely to find some problems accompanying a casino's presence. More critical evaluations of a casino's impact appeared to be associated with community leaders who had first-hand knowledge of someone suffering from problem gambling.

The research findings reported here will present data from the same eight casino jurisdictions to determine how average citizens perceive the effects of casinos on their communities.

METHODS

The present analysis is part of a larger study to determine the effects of casino gambling on crime and the quality of life in new casino jurisdictions. Since possible effects on crime were critical to the study, the police departments were required to make available crime data for their communities dating back at least four years prior to the opening of casinos in their community. All the communities selected for the study initiated casino gambling in the 1990s and have had casino gambling for a minimum of four years. This time frame allows comparisons to be made before and after the casinos were in operation. A number of communities with casinos could not be included in the study because of incomplete, nonexistent, or inaccessible data.

The communities included in the study are Sioux City, Iowa; St. Joseph, St. Louis City, and St. Louis County, Missouri; Alton, Peoria, and East Peoria, Illinois; and Biloxi, Mississippi. Of these communities, Alton has had gambling the longest, since September 1991, whereas St. Joseph has had it for the shortest time, since June 1994. All the cities lost population between 1980 and 1990. Of the eight jurisdictions, only Peoria does not have a casino at this time. Peoria had a riverboat casino in 1991, but for regulatory reasons, it was moved to East Peoria in 1993, directly across the Illinois River and easily accessible from Peoria. However, Peoria shares in the tax revenue from the riverboat with East Peoria, and many citizens of Peoria are employed by, or are customers of, the casino. Peoria, therefore, presents a unique case for study. Each of the other cities has one riverboat casino, except for Biloxi, which at the time had nine casinos located on a bay or on the Gulf Coast on stationary barges. These barge casinos tend to be larger than the riverboat casinos, and their number and concentration have resulted in the casinos and the tourists they draw playing a much larger role in Biloxi than in the other communities studied. At the other extreme is St. Louis, a relatively large city with a single riverboat casino within the city limits, but with several other casino riverboats nearby (in East St. Louis, St. Charles, Maryland Heights, and Alton). In comparison with the other communities in the study, St. Louis has experienced relatively little impact on tourism and on the overall economy of the city and county from its riverboat casino.

The data for the present study were obtained from the community survey portion of the larger study, in which 2,678 anonymous computer-assisted telephone interviews (CATI) were conducted among persons of legal gambling age who resided in the community both before and after the introduction of casino gambling. The number of completed interviews for each community varied, with the numbers for East Peoria and Peoria and for St. Louis City and County being smaller because they were treated as combined jurisdictions. We believe that these samples are large enough to ensure the reliability of results.

Responses to the following four questions relative to citizen satisfaction with casino gambling in their communities are examined in this analysis.

- In balance, casinos are good for a community (agree, disagree, don't know).
- Since the introduction of casino gambling, is your community a better place to live, a worse place to live, or about the same?
- The community made the right choice when it legalized casino gambling (strongly disagree, somewhat disagree, somewhat agree, strongly agree).
- What kind of effects, if any, did you expect casino gambling to have on your community (negative effect, no effect at all, positive effect)?

RESULTS

Responses to Question 1 appear in Table 1 which indicates that respondents were almost equally divided in their assessment of whether casinos were good for communities, with 49.3 percent disagreeing and 50.7 percent, agreeing that casinos were good for a community.

However, when comparisons are made between jurisdictions, significant differences are found. Residents of Biloxi feel strongly that casinos are good for the community, with 74.1 percent agreeing and only 25.9 percent disagreeing. At the other extreme are the residents of East Peoria and Sioux City, with 65.6 percent and 62.5 percent respectively believing that casinos are not good for a community and 34.4 percent and 37.5 per-

Table 1. Views on Whether Casinos Are Good for a Community, by Jurisdiction

					CITY				
	Biloxi	Alton	St. Joseph	Sioux City	St. Louis City	East Peoria	Peoria	St. Louis County	All
Disagree	25.9%	43.7%	45.6%	62.5%	55.5%	65.6%	53.6%	57.6%	49.3%
Agree	74.1%	56.3%	54.4%	37.5%	44.5%	34.4%	46.4%	42.4%	50.7%
Total[1]	(374)	(364)	(384)	(379)	(319)	(93)	(293)	(288)	(2494)
	100.0%	100.0%	100.0%	100.0%	100.0%	100.0%	100.0%	100.0%	100.0%

[1] Only responses for those who chose to answer the question are included in the table. The total number of respondents was 2,768. Of those, 254, or 9.2 percent, said they did not know and 20, or 0.7 percent, refused to answer.

$\Pi^2 = 139.89$　　$p < .001$

cent believing that they are good. The other five communities are less strongly supportive or opposed. Overall, five of the eight communities' respondents feel casinos are not good for a community if a simple majority is the criterion used.

Table 2 presents comparisons for the question, "Since the introduction of casino gambling, is your community a better place to live, a worse place to live, or about the same?" Here, 17.5 percent, of the respondents felt the community was a worse place to live, while 13.3 percent, felt it was better. A substantial majority, 69.2 percent, believed it was about the same.

As was the case for the question regarding whether casinos are good for communities, the responses indicating whether it is a better or worse place to live reveal significant differences between communities. In some, the overwhelming majority of respondents indicated strong agreement that their community is about the same since the advent of casino gambling, such as St. Louis City (86.8 percent), St. Louis County (83.5 percent) and St. Joseph (82.5 percent). However, 54.8 percent of Biloxi respondents indicated that their community is a worse place to live since casinos arrived. Alton and East Peoria both have a considerable minority of respondents, 30.7 percent and 20.2 percent respectively, who feel the same. Interestingly, it is also Biloxi where the greatest number of respon-

Table 2. Views Regarding Effects of Casinos on the Community, by Jurisdiction

					CITY				
	Biloxi	Alton	St. Joseph	Sioux City	St. Louis City	East Peoria	Peoria	St. Louis County	All
A Worse Place to Live?	54.8 %	30.7 %	7.4 %	7.4 %	3.9 %	20.2 %	9.1 %	4.1%	17.5 %
About the Same?	25.6 %	60.1 %	82.5 %	74.9 %	86.8 %	68.7 %	75.4 %	83.5 %	69.2 %
A Better Place to Live?	19.5 %	9.3 %	9.3 %	17.6 %	9.3 %	11.1 %	12.4 %	12.4 %	13.3 %
Total[1]	(394)	(398)	(417)	(403)	(355)	(99)	(309)	(339)	(2714)
	100.0 %	100.0 %	100.0 %	100.0 %	100.0 %	100.0 %	100.0 %	100.0 %	100.0 %

[1] Only those responses for those who choose to answer the question are included in the table. The total number of respondents was 2768. Of those 47 or 1.7% said they did not know and 7, or 0.3%, refused to answer.

$\Pi^2 = 669.48$ $p < .001$

dents, 19.5 percent, believe the community is a better place to live. Sioux City has 17.6 percent of its respondents who think the community is a better place to live. These figures not withstanding, six of the eight communities have about 75 percent or more of their respondents perceiving no change.

Responses to the question on whether the community made the right choice when it legalized casino gambling appear in Table 3, which shows that 24.9 percent strongly agreed, 31.0 percent somewhat agreed, 16.0 percent somewhat disagreed, and 28.2 percent strongly disagreed. Clearly, there is little agreement on this issue. When the "agrees" and "disagrees" are combined, 55.9 percent agree that the community made the right choice in legalizing casino gambling and 44.2 percent disagree. Once again, the comparisons show significant differences between communities.

Examining differences between the communities, the strongest sup-

Table 3. Agreement/Disagreement with the Statement: The Community Made the Right Choice When It Legalized Casino Gambling, by Jurisdiction

	Biloxi	Alton	St. Joseph	Sioux City	St. Louis City	East Peoria	Peoria	St. Louis County	All
					CITY				
Strongly Disagree	18.4%	26.0%	25.7%	33.8%	31.6%	35.8%	31.1%	30.1%	28.2%
Somewhat Disagree	6.6%	16.8%	13.2%	22.3%	15.4%	25.3%	16.6%	19.3%	16.0%
Somewhat Agree	25.1%	31.2%	34.6%	31.0%	32.2%	20.0%	35.8%	30.7%	31.0%
Strongly Agree	49.9%	26.0%	26.5%	13.0%	20.9%	18.9%	16.6%	19.9%	24.9%
Total[1]	(391) 100.0%	(388) 100.0%	(408) 100.0%	(400) 100.0%	(345) 100.0%	(95) 100.0%	(302) 100.0%	(332) 100.0%	(2661) 100.0%

[1] Only responses for those who chose to answer the question are included in the table. The total number of respondents was 2,768. Of those, 97, or 3.5 percent, said they did not know and 10, or 0.4 percent, refused to answer.

$\Pi^2 = 213.66$ $p < .001$

port for the community making the right decision to legalize casinos is evidenced in Biloxi, where 49.9 percent strongly agree and 25.1 percent somewhat agree, yielding 75 percent in the "agree" category. This is followed by St. Joseph where a combined 61.1 percent agreed. To a lesser extent Alton, St. Louis City, and Peoria tended to agree with 57.2 percent, 53.1 percent, and 52.4 percent, respectively. St. Louis County was evenly divided with 50.6 percent in the "agree" categories and 49.4 percent in the "disagree" categories. However, more respondents in St. Louis County strongly disagreed (30.1 percent) than strongly agreed (19.9 percent). Two communities disagreed that the community made the right decision; in East Peoria 61.1 percent disagreed and in Sioux City 56.1 percent disagreed. Clearly, few communities have attained a consensus regarding the appropriateness of casino legalization.

Table 4. Agreement/Disagreement with the Statement: The Community Made the Right Choice When It Legalized Casino Gambling, by Expected Effects

What kind of effects, if any, did you expect casino gambling to have on your community?	The community made the right choice when it legalized casino gambling				
	Strongly Disagree	Somewhat Disagree	Somewhat Agree	Strongly Agree	Total
Negative Effect (33.7 %)	57.2%	19.5%	15.8%	7.4%	(877) 100.0%
No Effect at All (22.0 %)	18.1%	21.0%	40.5%	20.4%	(558) 100.0%
Positive Effect (44.3 %)	11.3%	10.7%	37.2%	40.7%	(1166) 100.0%
All (100.0 %)	28.3%	15.9%	30.7%	25.1%	(2601) 100.0%

$\Pi^2 = 759.23$ $p < .001$

Table 4 examines the question of whether people's expectations were met regarding the effects that casinos might have on their communities. Here community-by-community comparisons are replaced by a cross-tabular analysis comparing expected effects with whether or not the community made the right decision to legalize gambling. Overall, 44.3 percent of the respondents expected a positive effect, 33.7 percent expected a negative effect, and 22.0 percent expected no effect at all. Clearly those who expected a negative effect believed that the community made the wrong choice, since 76.7 percent of those expecting a negative effect answered in the "disagree" categories. Conversely, of those expecting a positive effect, 77.9 percent believe the community made the right choice. In the middle category, of those who expected no effect, 60.9 percent believe the community made the right choice, as opposed to 39.1 percent who think the community made the wrong choice. To determine the extent to which beliefs and attitudes might have changed, we can look at the results for those who expected a negative effect, but believe the community made the right choice, versus those who expected a positive effect and believe the community made the wrong choice. The results are virtually identical, in that 22.2 percent of those who expected negative effects believe the community made the right choice, while 22.0 percent who expected positive effects believe the community made the wrong choice. These results clearly reflect the division of opinion regarding the effects that casinos have had on these new casino jurisdictions.

DISCUSSION

The responses from residents in eight new casino jurisdictions indicate that community satisfaction with casino gambling is far from unanimous. This disagreement was first evidenced in that 49.3 percent of those responding disagreed with the statement that "in balance, casinos are good for a community." This left a 50.7 percent majority who agreed. This nearly equal division of opinion results largely from to the fact that Biloxi respondents so substantially believed that casinos are good for a community. However, in five of the eight other communities, more respondents disagreed with this statement than agreed. The question of whether the community had become a better or worse place to live yielded a significant majority of respondents who felt the community was virtually unchanged (69.2 percent). Responses to whether the community had made the right choice in legalizing casino gambling revealed that 55.8 percent agreed to some extent, while 44.2 percent disagreed. While this response indicates greater support for casinos than the first question, it seems to further validate the idea that neither satisfaction nor dissatisfaction is not strongly felt. Finally, most people's preconceptions regarding likely negative and positive effects were borne out in their own view, and virtually equal percentages of respondents seem to have had their expectations invalidated, indicating that both positive and negative effects have occurred, but in some cases not in the expected directions. From the totality of results across communities, it is apparent that community satisfaction with casinos is indeed mixed.

The analysis clearly indicates significant differences among communities in level of satisfaction with casino gambling. A surprising finding is that residents of Biloxi overwhelmingly agree that casinos are good for a community and that the community made the right choice in legalizing them (74.1 percent and 75 percent, respectively). However, 54.8 percent believe that their community is a worse place to live since casinos have been introduced. None of the other communities had such strong, or such divided, opinions about casino gambling, a finding which suggests that Biloxi is experiencing effects attributed to casinos that other communities are not, presumably in both positive and negative directions. What is known is that Biloxi has the highest concentration of casinos, with nine at the time of this study, and that Biloxi has been transformed into a major resort and tourist destination as a consequence of casino gambling's presence. As a result, the level of economic prosperity in Biloxi is probably at an all-time high, with many new jobs, new residents, and new recreational opportunities. In fact, as reported elsewhere, 81.5 percent of the Biloxi respondents indicated that the standard of living had increased since casinos were introduced into their community.[11] At the same time, we can speculate that traffic congestion and drains on community services are also at an all-time high. Without question, the crimes of robbery, simple assault, forgery, fraud, credit card fraud, embezzlement, prostitution, drug violations, public disorder, and DUIs have significantly increased, even taking into account the number of tourists (the population most at risk).[12] The increase in crime was recognized by a majority of Biloxi respondents, with 54.1 percent indicating that crime had increased since the advent of casinos.[13] Additionally, 38.6 percent of the respondents believed that fear of crime had increased since casinos arrived. Both percentages represent the greatest magnitude of perceived increases in these measures of all of the jurisdictions. Thus, Biloxi seems to have experienced both the greatest positive and the greatest negative effects resulting from casino gambling.

Biloxi stands out as a community strongly affected by casino presence and, in most instances, favorably inclined toward the casinos. There are, however, other communities where respondents indicated dissatisfaction with casinos. As mentioned earlier, 61.1 percent of East Peoria respondents and 56.1 percent of Sioux City respondents believed the community did not make the right decision in legalizing casino gambling. Also, 65.6 percent of East Peoria respondents and 62.5 percent of Sioux City respondents disagreed with the statement that, on balance, casinos are good for a community. As reported elsewhere, Sioux City "stands out as being the most polarized in its citizens' perceptions of casino effects on quality of life." This disparity may be due to the significant opposition to casinos that existed on moral grounds. As also reported previously, 32 percent of the Sioux City and 29.4 percent of the East Peoria respondents felt there was some decrease in the quality of family life as a result of casino gambling.[14] Perhaps significantly, residents from the small town of East Peoria were third highest of all community respondents to perceive an increase in crime and fear of crime.

CONCLUSIONS

Clearly, community satisfaction with casino gambling is mixed. The structures and dynamics of each community seem to interact in very complex ways to determine what effects casinos will have. The one thing that is apparent, both from this analysis and others reported elsewhere, is that satisfaction is a multidimensional factor. Other analyses have found strong support for the economic boosts that casinos bring to communities. This result was most notable when members of the research team queried community leaders with regard to impacts of casinos on their communities. A next step might be to further analyze specific social and economic variables affected by casino presence in a variety of community settings. The impact of casinos on communities and the evaluation of this impact by members of the community, are extremely complex issues that will require large-scale and sophisticated analyses to resolve.

NOTES

1. National Gambling Impact Study Commission, *Final Report* (Washington D.C.: Government Printing Office, 1999), pp. 1–7.

2. Australian Productivity Commission, *Australia's Gambling Industries: Inquiry Report* (Canberra: Commonwealth Government, 1999).

3. Abraham Pizam and Julianne Pokela, "The Perceived Impacts of Casino Gambling on a Community," *Annals of Tourism Research* 12 (1985): 147–65.

4. Lowell Caneday and Jeffrey Zeiger, "The Social, Economic, and Environmental Costs of Tourism to a Gaming Community as Perceived by Its Residents," *Journal of Travel Research* 30 (1991): 45–49.

5. Richard P. Perdue , Patrick Long, and Yoong-Song Kang "Resident Sup-

port for Gambling as a Tourism Development Strategy," *Journal of Tourism Research* 33 (1995): 3–11.

6. Patrick Long, "Early Impacts of Limited Stakes Casino Gambling on Rural Community Life," *Tourism Management* 17, no. 5 (1996): 341–53.

7. Richard Govoni et al., "First-Year Impacts of Casino Gambling in a Community," *Journal of Gambling Studies* 14, no. 4 (1998): 347–58.

8. Robin Room, Nigel Turner, and Anca Ialomiteanu, "Community Effects of the Opening of the Niagara Casino," *Addiction* 94, no. 10 (1999): 1449–66.

9. National Opinion Research Center, *Overview of National Survey and Community Database Research on Gambling Behavior* (Chicago: University of Chicago Press, 1999), pp. 62–63.

10. David M. Giacopassi, Mark Nichols, and Grant Stitt, "Attitudes of Community Leaders in New Casino Jurisdictions Regarding Casino Gambling's Effects on Crime and Quality of Life," *Journal of Gambling Studies* 15, no. 2 (1999): 123–47.

11. Mark Nichols, Grant Stitt, and David Giacopassi, "Community Assessment of Effects of Casinos on Quality of Life," *Social Indicator's Research* 57, no. 3 (2002): 229–62.

12. Grant Stitt, David Giacopassi, and Mark Nichols, "The Effect of Casino Gambling on Crime in New Casino Jurisdictions," *Journal of Crime and Justice* 23, no. 1 (2000): 1–23.

13. Nichols, Stitt, and Giacopassi, "Community Assessment of Effects of Casinos."

14. Ibid.

Section 3

LAW, CRIME, AND COMMERCIAL REGULATION

♥♠♣
6
GAMBLING AND THE LAW®

The New Millennium

I. Nelson Rose©

Twice before in American history, legal gambling has spread across the nation, only to crash down in scandal and complete prohibition. At the beginning of 2002, at least twenty-five states and three territories of the United States had legalized casino gaming. Twelve or more state lotteries are in the quasi-casino business with video lottery terminals (VLTs) and keno. Every state except Utah, Tennessee, and Hawaii had some form of commercial gambling; and Hawaii is considering allowing a casino near Honolulu to help tourism.

If the future depended solely on advances in technology, the future of gambling could be summed up in two words: "video poker." It is the closest thing we have to the perfect gambling device: fast, fun, and easy to learn, with the potential for large jackpots allowing even novice players to gamble without being intimidated, and with at least the illusion that skillful participation will change the results. But we are not about to see legal video poker machines in every corner grocery store, nor legal sportsbetting on home computers. The technology already exists, but other important factors will determine which forms of gambling are allowed under the law.

The proliferation of legal gambling is shaped by such factors as historical legal baggage, feelings of morality and tradition, demographics, social and psychological factors, and pure irrationality. Gambling spreads in a haphazard manner, with long-term recurring patterns played out against a background of local politics and unpredictable technology.

THE THIRD WAVE OF LEGAL GAMBLING

In my 1986 book, *Gambling and the Law*,[1] the proliferation of gambling is described as a third wave. In the New Millennium, this description appears too conservative. It is not a wave but a virtual explosion.

Every year Americans spend about $10 billion at the nation's approximately 36,000 movie screens. This sum includes all ticket sales (a record $7.7 billion in 2000), plus popcorn and confections[2]. The total for all forms of recorded music is less than $14 billion.[3] By comparison, lotteries operating in thirty-seven states, the District of Columbia and three U.S. possessions,[4] sell more than $46 billion in lottery tickets.[5] Add to this pari-mutuel betting on horses, dogs, and jai alai; total "action" in casinos and on slot machines; wagers on sports; bets made in licensed card rooms; and expenditures before prize payments in charity gaming and Indian bingo, and the total amount wagered legally in the United States was estimated to be well over half a trillion dollars: $638.6 billion.[6] Looking just at revenue, Americans spent more money on gambling—$50.9 billion, than they did on all live events, such as concerts and plays, all movies in theaters, all spectator sports, and all forms of recorded music—combined. It may say something about us as a nation, or it may just be that Baby Boomers' children are growing up, but in 1994, for the first time, adults in America spent more money on their gambling games than they did on toys for their children.[8]

It is not just the money but the general availability of gambling venues that is the real story. Legal gambling has become such an accepted part of American life that it is often not even noticed, even when its impact is extraordinary. The May 20, 1996, issue of *Forbes* magazine featured a cover story on "Getting Rich Outside Corporate America." The editors did not feel it newsworthy to point out that two of the four individuals pictured on the cover made their money from gambling: a professional poker player and the chairman of a tribe with a casino. The most dramatic reversal of the law's traditional antipathy toward gambling came in the Supreme Court's 1986 decision that a full-time gambler could declare himself to be in the trade or business of gambling for tax purposes.[9]

Even Indian gaming has become so commonplace and respectable that it has passed the ultimate test: gaining access to legitimate financing. The Mohegan Sun was the first tribal casino to receive financing from Wall Street, placing $175 million in high-yield bonds with institutional investors.

What does the spread of gambling mean for the future? It is important to remember that the prior two gambling waves ended with nationwide prohibitions on virtually all forms of gaming. Is the current boom headed toward the same bust?

CYCLES OF LEGALIZATION

Like a prophecy fulfilled, we are apparently doomed to repeat our history, having failed to learn the lessons of the past. Twice before players could make legal bets in almost every state, until such legal gambling was outlawed.

Americans are not sure of what role law should have in society. Should the law be used only against acts that everyone agrees should be illegal, like murder? Or should law be used as a tool to enforce morality, as it was during Prohibition? We have the most trouble with the morally suspect industries—alcohol, drugs, abortion, and gambling. Although the Prohibition era is the best example, there have always been limits and prohibitions in American law that large numbers of the population violated on a fairly regular basis, often without even knowing they had broken the law.

The antigambling prohibitions epitomize the traditional approach taken by American laws. These laws are designed not only to protect people from themselves but also, as part of a greater moral framework, to reflect an imagined ideal society. Surveys and election results have shown that voters want most of the antigambling laws to stay on the books, even if they do not want those laws actively enforced.[10]

Perhaps our cycles from complete prohibition to complete permissiveness and back again can be explained by the tendency of Americans to go to the limits, and beyond. Congress passed the Indian Gaming Regulatory Act with the image of tribal bingo halls in mind. Entrepreneurs took the poorly written law and used it to create some of the largest casinos in the world.

Gambling has followed a recurring, consistent pattern throughout the country's history. When gambling is illegal, there is pressure for legalization, first of one game and then, gradually, of all forms. Although it may be illegal, many people are gambling—at social games or underground commercial lotteries, race books or casinos. The laws are difficult to enforce and the general population does not want arrests made, anyway, if it means taking police resources away from more serious crimes. The result is widespread evasion of the law, leading to disrespect and corruption. The response by the public is a demand for reform, for something to be done to prevent involvement by officials in these areas of moral ambiguity. The perceived solution is often a demand for legalization—if it is not a crime, there will be no reason to bribe law enforcement or public officials.

Sometimes the breakthrough comes from the legalization of a seemingly benign form, such as charity bingo. Once one form of gambling has been legalized, the antigambling arguments based on morality begin to fade away. Legalization of gambling seems to correspond with a general trend toward permissiveness in society. The Victorian morality that says *nothing is permitted* is replaced by the belief that *everything is permitted, so long as you do not hurt another person.* And gambling is the least harmful of the victimless crimes.

Many people see hypocrisy in the remaining prohibitions. Even the legalization of a game by a neighboring state can start the decline of the moral barriers against gambling. It is difficult for a state official to argue that a lottery would be immoral when his constituents are going across the state line by the millions to buy tickets.

Proponents can direct discussion toward cost/benefit analyses of various other games that might be legalized. Once all of the states in a region have the same game, the first to legalize a new game has an advantage and can siphon off the disposable income of its neighbors. A domino effect is created. Meanwhile, the police and prosecutors are finding it increasingly difficult to enforce those antigambling laws that are still on the books, and venality is growing. Even the police begin to see hypocrisy in trying to prohibit a wager when an almost identical game is being actively promoted by the state.

Most of the states are presently at this point in the cycle. The tidal wave of legalized gambling is still rising throughout the nation. In the past, the wave continued to grow until many forms of gambling became legal, widespread, and commercialized. In the past, everyone seemed to be playing and the amounts of money involved were staggering. Those few prohibitions that still existed were virtually ignored by the police, and venality and corruption became widespread and open.

Historically, the next stage has been a devastating deluge of public scandals. Legal gambling is very big business with very few paper records; of the at least $600 billion that is bet each year, most is in the form of untraceable cash. It is not difficult to understand the temptation to rig the outcome of a legal game.

The combination of highly publicized scandals and a reawakened morality close the games. Constitutional amendments are passed to outlaw gambling forever. Of course, this stage of prohibition only leads, inevitably, to the next stage where demand once again builds for the legalization of some form of gambling.

HISTORICAL BAGGAGE FROM THE FIRST AND SECOND WAVES

America's first wave of legal gambling began even before there was a country: The earliest settlements were funded, in part, by lotteries in England.[11] The first race track was set up in New York in 1666.[12] Gaming was usually outlawed by statute; the Massachusetts Bay Colony banned the possession of cards, dice, or gaming tables, even in private homes.[13] But both the colonies and the newly formed states were awash in lotteries, licensed by both state and federal government.[14]

Technological and social developments radically changed the nation's attitude toward gambling between the colonial period and the Civil War. The invention of the steamboat led to the establishment of riverboat commerce. The Golden Age of the almost always crooked riverboat gamblers ended with Civil War blockades and the invention of the railroad.[15] Lotteries, run by private individuals without government oversight, were everywhere. The lotteries were hit by widespread scandals, the worst being drawings that often were not held at all. In addition, the 1820s and 1830s saw the birth of a reform movement, which became centered on Andrew Jackson's call for a clean sweep to "throw the rascals out." The mix of the two—lottery scandals and a newfound morality—led to the near-complete prohibition of lotteries. The feelings of emotional revulsion were so strong that reformers attempted to lock out lotteries for what they thought was forever by writing bans into their state constitutions. By 1862 Missouri and Kentucky were the only states that had not banned lotteries altogether.[16]

The most important pieces of legal debris from the collapse of the first wave of legal gambling are the state constitutional bans on lotteries. So much time has passed that sometimes the meaning of the term "lottery" has been lost or warped to include other forms of gambling, creating enormous problems for proponents of bingo, pari-mutuel wagering, and casinos.

Amending a state constitution is difficult, requiring a vote of the people. A century after the antilottery provisions were written in, long after the memory of the scandals that led to their creation had died away, proponents of state lotteries were able to win constitutional elections in over two dozen states. Proponents of casinos have not fared as well. Voters have almost always rejected amending their state constitutions to bring in high-stake casinos. However, many state legislatures have been able to legalize casinos when no vote was required.

The second wave began with the Civil War and the continuing expansion of the western frontier. The South turned to state-licensed lotteries as a painless way to raise revenue.[17] Licensed casinos dominated the heart of Gold Rush San Francisco. Frequently, gaming houses were explicitly made legal in part so that the government could raise revenue through licensing and in part to avoid the problem epitomized by Prohibition, having criminal statutes on the books that no one obeyed. Often the games were illegal but ignored by law enforcement because it was difficult to outlaw this typical frontier diversion.[18]

The establishment of permanent cities brought the desire for law and order, and Westerners wanted to be viewed as respectable in the eyes of the established East Coast.[19] With civilization often came statutory prohibitions on casinos. Betting on horse races was not viewed as a problem when bettors had to be physically present at the track. The invention of the telegraph, telephone, and totalizer machines in the late nineteenth century made it possible for the average working man to bet on races taking place in another part of the country. The establishment of these "pool rooms" led to the passage of antibookie statutes prohibiting the transmission of gambling information. The nineteenth century ended with a second round of lottery scandals. The Louisiana lottery was the greatest, both in the size of its operation and in the magnitude of the scandal. The lottery operators were accused, correctly, of attempting to buy the Louisiana state legislature. Operators promoted their legal lottery tickets throughout the nation. Technological advances had allowed the Louisiana lottery to operate without being in close geographic proximity to its customers. But Congress closed it down by barring lottery tickets from the U.S. mails and interstate commerce.[20] The prohibitions have been expanded as technology developed, now including radio, television, and the use of agents.[21]

The rise of Victorian morality, outrage over scandals, and the desire for respectability brought the second wave crashing down in the West. The territories of New Mexico and Arizona were told that to gain statehood they would have to close their casinos.[22] In 1909, even the Nevada legislature outlawed casinos.[23] By 1910 only Maryland, Kentucky and New York were left, and in that year New York closed its racetracks. The United States was once again virtually free of legalized gambling.[24]

THE THIRD WAVE: THE DEPRESSION TO THE PRESENT

The Depression gave birth to the third wave of legal gambling. Nevada relegalized casino gambling in 1931.[25] Twenty-one states opened racetracks with pari-mutuel betting in the 1930s, with additional states allowing pari-mutuel betting in every decade since.[26] Charities played bingo, at first illegally, until many states changed their laws in the 1940s and 1950s to permit charitable and social gambling. And then New Hampshire rediscovered the state lottery in 1964.

For the last twenty years, the fight has been over casino games, particularly slot machines. Part of the problem comes from sloppy legal work done decades ago. Operators of roulette wheels and slot machines were sometimes convicted of running illegal "lotteries." In some jurisdictions, the states' highest courts ruled that the word *lottery* was synonymous with gambling.

Today, state attorneys generally find themselves making exactly the opposite argument. Federally recognized Indian tribes are allowed to operate any form of gambling permitted by state law.[27] A federal judge in Wisconsin ruled that "lottery" means any game of prize, chance, or consideration. The state operates a lottery; therefore, the state had to negotiate to allow Indian tribes to have any games of prize, chance, or consideration, including blackjack and video poker machines.

WHAT HAPPENS WHEN PROHIBITION IS REPEALED?

It is widely believed in this third wave of legal gambling that anyone, including the government, can get rich quick. All one needs to do to grab a piece of the action is to own, operate, or tax some form of legal gambling. An endless flow of instant, unlimited wealth will follow. This delusion is a typical symptom of a classic speculative bubble. All bubbles grow out of unrealistic expectations, like the one preceding the Great Crash of 1929,[29] the South Sea Bubble, and Dutch Tulipmania.[30] Fortunes really can be made during such wild speculation.

The dream of instant, unending riches is not limited to Americans. Canada, Australia, and Europe have the legal gambling bug as badly as we do, or worse. With the opening of Ontario's Casino Niagara, Canada's gaming industry employs more than 46,000 people—twelve times the size of the nation's commercial fishing industry.[31] And nothing compares to the percentage growth of lotteries, casinos, and pari-mutuel betting in the newly freed former Soviet bloc.

Unlike tulip bulbs, commodities, or stock index futures, legal gambling can, in fact, generate revenue. However, it will not be on the scale imagined nor can it expand endlessly in the face of direct competition. Suppose that Prohibition of alcohol had just been repealed. The hypothetical owner of the first and only liquor store in a state would make a fantastic return on investment. But soon, if there were no government controls, there would be liquor stores throughout the state, as there would be few barriers to entry. Excess profits would disappear and returns on investment would descend to normal levels.

The government makes the situation worse. The fantasy that there is an infinitely elastic demand for gambling seems to hit politicians harder than entrepreneurs. Sin taxes are always the easiest to raise. Casinos, like liquor stores and tobacco retailers, are easier targets than more politically acceptable businesses. Government's thinking is that people should not be gambling anyway and that they will continue to make wagers, no matter how much the cost. So, even though a quarter of the gaming establishments in a jurisdiction might go bankrupt, the state continues to consider raising taxes on gambling.

Resorts International opened the first legal casino on the East Coast on May 26, 1978, spending $45.2 million to refurbish the old Chalfonte-Haddon Hotel in Atlantic City.[32] Its first-year gross revenue of $224.6 million made it the most profitable casino in the world.[33] The state of New Jersey, for merely allowing the casino to open, collected $18 million in taxes that first year.[34] Twelve more casinos quickly followed. The Trump Taj Mahal, the thirteenth and last Atlantic City casino to open, cost over $1.1 billion.[35] The Taj opened in April 1990; it declared bankruptcy in July 1991. Of the thirteen casinos opened in Atlantic City, eight have been involved in formal bankruptcy proceedings.[36]

The explosion of legal gambling has finally settled the question of whether availability creates demand. It does. The metropolitan area of

Biloxi-Gulfport-Pascagoula, near the Mississippi casinos, with a population in 1995 of 112,993,[37] ranks as the eighth most important feeder market for casino gaming in the nation, far above such massive cities as Houston and Seattle, which did not even make the top ten.[38] But even though availability creates demand, that demand is not endless. Even a casino in New Orleans will fail if Louisiana and Mississippi are already saturated with competing forms of gambling.

A TIDAL CHANGE IN ATTITUDES

Until the November 1996 elections, all high-stakes casino-style gambling in the United States, with the exception of Atlantic City, had been created without voter approval by state legislatures (even Nevada voters were never asked whether they wanted casinos) and Indian tribes.[39] Before 1996, high-stakes casinos had won only one statewide election, in New Jersey in 1976.

There had been a few successful elections at the local level, with cities and counties approving high-stakes casinos. But statewide, the only way to win a casino election had been to promise the voters that gambling would be isolated onto a mountaintop or surrounded by water or that stakes would be low. Colorado and South Dakota voters approved five-dollar maximum blackjack and slots, and Missouri voters accepted riverboats with $500 loss limits. But all these casino electoral victories occurred in the last decade. Even on the local level, far more campaigns to legalize gambling were, and still are, lost, than won.

One reason for such electoral defeats in the past is Americans' attitudes toward legal gambling. Most people simply do not take gambling seriously, unless they are asked to approve it in their own backyards. Then, if it is viewed as one of the "safe kinds," bingo or a state lottery, it will be allowed. If it can be isolated to a mountain town, or somehow sanitized by surrounding it with thirty feet of river water, it is somehow also viewed as acceptable. But if the general population is asked to vote for casino gambling or slot machines where their children might be tempted to play them, then they will say no.

November 1996 marked the greatest victory in American history for legal gambling, particularly for casino gaming. Unprecedented breakthroughs occurred in virtually every area of the country. For the first time in American history, the citizens of a state (actually two: Michigan and Arizona) voted, in the face of active opposition, to bring in new, high-stakes casinos. Also for the first time in American history, local citizens throughout a state (Louisiana) voted unanimously, in the face of active opposition, to retain high-stakes casinos.

News articles written immediately after the elections called the results mixed, contrasting these wins against an even greater number of losses, including casino initiatives in Arkansas, Colorado, Ohio, and Guam. Yet twenty years ago, casino gambling would have lost every election. The votes to keep casinos, and especially to bring in new ones, indicate a tidal change in the way Americans feel about legal gambling. Voters, for the first time ever, have accepted local gambling as a normal part of their lives. Voters have in the past approved state lotteries. They often vote in favor of horse racing. But, in dozens of attempts over the last 200 years, never before 1996 had the citizens of a state voted, in the face of active opposition, to bring in new, high-stakes casinos.

Organized antigambling activists have almost never been a significant factor, but powerful politicians are another matter.[40] In 1990, professors William N. Thompson, University of Nevada, Las Vegas, and John Dombrink, University of California, Irvine, published their study, *The Last Resort: Success and Failure in Campaigns for Casinos*.[41] Examining virtually every election up to the date of publication, Thompson and Dombrink found that statewide casino campaigns never succeeded, as long as a single powerful political actor was opposed. They called this phenomenon the veto factor.

But something new and unprecedented occurred in Michigan and Arizona in 1996. There, all political voices seemed to be unified in opposition to casinos. The governors of both states actively campaigned against the initiatives. Yet, for the first time ever, statewide voters approved allowing new high-stakes casinos.

The tidal change in the public's attitude toward legal gambling was confirmed two years later. Proponents of legalized gaming won virtually every race in the November 1998 elections. Tribal casinos won by a landslide in California.[42] In Missouri, voters approved "riverboat" (actually "boats in moats") casinos for the third time. In New Jersey, voters approve off-track phone betting; in 1980 they had voted down innocuous

Sunday horse racing. In Arizona, a large majority voted to extend the state lottery despite repeated crises and religious opposition.

Gaming opponents can rarely gather enough signatures to get a repeal on the ballot. They failed in 1998 in both Michigan and Mississippi. But a vocal opposition can sometimes force fearful legislators to let the voters decide. Antigambling forces did have a couple of victories. A nasty fight in Maryland ended with a win for incumbent governor Parris Glendening, a vocal opponent of racetrack slot machines, but even here, surveys showed that gambling was not an issue; voters were most concerned about education. The only antigambling victories in 1998: Voters in Arizona and Missouri outlawed cockfighting.

The November 2000 elections reconfirmed the tidal change in the way voters view legal gambling. In a self-congratulatory (and fund-raising) newsletter to its followers, the Rev. Tom Grey, Executive Director of the National Coalition Against Legalized Gambling, portrayed the results of the November 7, 2000, races as follows: "By their votes at the polls Americans proved that they are waking up to the threat facing our country and have soundly rejected legalized gambling in Arkansas, Maine, West Virginia, New Mexico and Wisconsin."[43]

Not exactly.

The Arkansas election was certainly a defeat. But the proposal was so bizarre that it was not a fair test of the voters' feelings toward legal gambling. West Virginia's election was even stranger. Only voters in rural Greenbrier County cast ballots, and there were only 7,065 "no" and 5,109 "yes" votes. They rejected the plan to put a casino, open only to registered guests of the Greenbrier Hotel, in a converted bomb shelter.[44]

Elsewhere legal gambling won big. In South Dakota, voters approved keeping their video lottery terminals and raising the maximum betting limits in casinos in Deadwood from $5 to $100. South Carolinians voted to establish a state lottery. Voters in Colorado approved joining multistate lotteries, and those in Massachusetts voted to keep their greyhound racing.

The best that the Rev. Tom Grey could say about these smashing statewide defeats of the antigambling movements was, "In those states where gambling was defeated, it was by a much higher margin than in those states where gambling initiatives passed." The margins of victory could be significant if they were part of a national trend. But history has demonstrated that the trend is exactly the opposite of what the antis want. Fifty years ago every one of these progambling proposals would have been defeated at the polls, and by margins of two- or three-to-one. The fact that any of them made the ballot, let alone won, shows that voters have come to accept legal gambling as merely another part of everyday life.

One of the most interesting results of the fall 2000 election shows how political power has shifted in the last decade. Democrat Maria Cantwell beat Washington State's most powerful politician, incumbent senator Slade Gorton, by less than one-tenth of one percent, with the help of $1 million from gaming tribes.

REASONS FOR THE SPREAD OF LEGAL GAMBLING

1. **The morality argument is dead.** It is no longer considered acceptable to oppose gambling on the ground that it is immoral. Once churches started running bingo games and governments began selling lottery tickets, gambling opponents lost their main moral spokesmen. With no one to say what is right or wrong, everything has become a cost/benefit analysis. Gambling makes money, even accounting for social costs, particularly if it is run as a monopoly.

2. **Government has said it is okay.** A large segment of American society believes government knows best.

3. **The outrageous becomes acceptable if taken in small doses.** The power of incremental change is tremendous. The first state lottery of this century, the New Hampshire Sweepstakes authorized in 1964, cost three-dollars, required players to fill out a form, and was held twice a year; it was a financial failure. But drawings went from twice a year to weekly to daily to rub-off tickets. We now have video lottery terminals, where the lottery player can put money into a machine and be paid on the spot. Thirty years ago it would have been unthinkable that states would be operating such slot machines.

4. **The domino effect.** New Hampshire was first with a state lottery this century, but 80 percent of its players came from New York,

Massachusetts, and Connecticut. The second lottery state was New York and the third its neighbor, New Jersey. When every state has lotteries, the first to introduce off-track betting or casinos has an advantage, until that form of gambling also spreads.

5. **The easy money is not so easy; states are hooked on gambling revenues.** Lottery tickets are poor consumer items—people buy them for a while and then stop. States are forced constantly to come up with more promotions and new games. States like Iowa, which thought it could sit back and make millions on five-dollar-maximum casinos on riverboats, find that the state has to constantly support the enterprises, particularly during winter, and come to the rescue of failing operations. After half its casino riverboats sailed south, the Iowa legislature raised the betting limits to match those of nearby Illinois.

6. **Gambling begets gambling.** Players always want games that are faster and easier, with at least the illusion of player participation. Many casinos are becoming nothing more than video slot machine warehouses. Eventually, we will see video poker machines and lottery terminals in every American city.

7. **Competition for the gambling dollar is fierce.** Casinos in Nevada have had to introduce megabucks and million-dollar keno games to compete against California's lottery. The racing industry has been particularly hard hit by the introduction of lotteries and tribal casinos. The surviving tracks are asking state legislatures to let them have slot machines, to avoid putting hundreds of people out of work. In May 1997 the Association of Racing Commissioners International approved a resolution urging Congress to pass legislation regulating gambling on the Internet, "to ensure . . . [that the] racing industry receives the appropriate portion of such handle."[45]

8. **Operators push to the limits.** If the law allows "pull-tabs," operators will construct devices with a slot and video screen and call the machines "video pull-tabs."

IMPACT OF TECHNOLOGY ON LEGAL GAMBLING

Although it is possible to see the general trends and cycles in gambling, it is impossible to predict how exactly it will develop because the games are dependent on so much technology. In his book, *Cleopatra's Nose*, Daniel J. Boorstin analyzed the differences between what he calls the new "Machine Kingdom" and the traditional designations of the "Animal, Vegetable, and Mineral Kingdoms."[46] The development of the Internet in general and gambling on the Net in particular illustrates Boorstin's point: invention creates a demand formerly that did not formerly exist because the technology itself did not exist.

Inventions redefine experience. Modern technology has played havoc with traditional legal categories. The New Jersey State Lottery and casinos in Atlantic City battled over which would have the right to run keno games. The law can react to unexpected technological developments, but inventions cannot be uninvented. If the demand has been created, technology will eventually find ways of getting around the legal barriers.

As Boorstin points out, "[the] most potent machines assimilate all environments."[47] Every form of gambling can now be played on a computerized video screen. Inventions expand experience—technology creates its own demand.[48] Video games and home computers created the ability to play faster games more conveniently; the video poker machine created the need for games that play like video poker machines. Inventions are increasingly intrusive. In Boorstin's words, "The advance of technology in our times attests our increasing inability to exclude novelties or their consequences from our daily lives."[49] Whether this phenomenon is a bad thing is difficult to judge. To quote Boorstin again, "Our nation has grown by its need for the unnecessary, another name for human progress."[50] Law constantly has to adjust to technological developments in gambling by designing new means of control. As Boorstin put it, "For us invention has become the mother of necessity."[51]

NOTES

1. I. Nelson Rose, *Gambling and the Law*, (Hollywood: Gambling Times, 1986).

2. Box-office sales should pass $8 billion in 2001. See Claudia Eller and James Bates, "Hollywood Box Office News Is Boffo," *Los Angeles Times*, November 11, 2001, A1.

3. "Weekday Trader: Slow Business –2: Movie Costs Cause Concern," Dow Jones News Service, 27 May 1998; "1994 Southern Economic Survey: The Urban South," *Atlanta Constitution*, April 17, 1994, sec. R, p. 11.

4. Puerto Rico, the Virgin Islands, and the Northern Mariana Islands.

5. Eugene M. Christiansen, "The United States Gross Annual Wager: 1997," *International Gaming and Wagering Business*, August 1998, p. 29.

6. Ibid., p. 3. However, this number, called the "handle," is inflated because it includes all wagers: If a player bets twenty-five-dollars and wins and then bets twenty-five-dollars and loses, a total of fifty-dollars has been wagered, even though no money has changed hands. A more accurate number for making comparisons with other industries is the gross revenue or "win," i.e., the amount players lose. Since this is money left behind by customers after the gambling transactions, it corresponds nicely with gross revenue or sales from other retail businesses.

7. Ibid., pp. 9 and 17.

8. Total sales of durable toys and goods were $39.0 billion compared with $39.9 billion in gross revenue for gambling. Eugene M. Christiansen and Will E. Cummings, "The United States Gross Annual Wager," *International Gaming and Wagering Business*, August 1, 1995, p. 29.

9. *Commissioner of Internal Review v. Groetzinger* (1986), 480 U.S. 23.

10. Thomas Mangione et al., "Citizen Views of Gambling Enforcement," Commission on the Review of the National Policy toward Gambling, *Gambling in America: Final Report* (Washington, D.C.: U.S. Printing Office,1976), *Gambling in America*, Appendix 1, pp. 240–300.

11. John Ezell, *Fortune's Merry Wheel: The Lottery in America* (Cambridge: Harvard University Press, 1960)

12. National Institute of Law Enforcement and Criminal Justice, Law Enforcement Assistance Administration, *The Development of the Law of Gambling: 1776–1976* (Washington, D.C.: United States Department of Justice, 1976), p. 41.

13. Records of the Court Assistants of the Colony of Massachusetts Bay, vol. 2, (1631), cited in National Institute of Law Enforcement and Criminal Justice,

The Development of the Law of Gambling: 1776–1976.

14. Henry Chafetz, *Play the Devil: A History of Gambling in the United States from 1492 to 1955* (New York: Bonanza Books, 1960).

15. James Philip Jones, *Gambling Yesterday and Today: A Complete History* (London: Newton Abbot, David & Charles, 1973), p. 23.

16. See George Sullivan, *By Chance a Winner: The History of Lotteries* (New York: Dodd, Mead, 1972).

17. National Institute of Law Enforcement and Criminal Justice, *The Development of the Law of Gambling*, p. 282.

18. Virgil W. Peterson, "Obstacles To Enforcement Of Gambling Law," *Annals of the American Academy of Political and Social Science: Gambling* 9 (1950): 269; Virgil W. Peterson, "Gambling: Should It Be Legalized?" *Journal of Law and Criminology* 40 (1949): 290.

19. John M. Findlay, *People of Chance: Gambling in American Society from Jamestown to Las Vegas* (Oxford: Oxford University Press, 1986).

20. Now at 18 U.S.C. §1302.

21. 18 U.S.C. §1301.

22. Nevada made casino gambling legal in 1869 through the Act of March 4, 1869, c. 71, Nev. Laws 119; legal casino gambling in the territories of New Mexico and Arizona is described in John Currie, "The Transformation of the Southwest: Through the Legal Abolition of Gambling," *Century Magazine*, April 1908, p. 905; Ariz. Laws 1909, c. 92.

23. Act of March 24, 1909, c. 210, Nev. Laws 307: "An Act prohibiting gambling, providing for the destruction of gambling property and other matters relating thereto"; Currie, "The Transformation of the Southwest." For a discussion of Nevada's changing public policy toward gambling during this era, see *West Indies v. First Nat. Bank of Nevada*, 67 Nev. c. 13, 23, 214 P.2d 144, 149.

24. David Weinstein and Lillian Deitch, *The Impact of Legalized Gambling: The Socioeconomic Consequences of Lotteries and Off-Track Betting* (New York: Praeger, 1991).

25. *Nevada Act of March 4, 1869*, c. 71, Nev. Laws 119 (made casino gambling legal); *Act of March 24, 1909*, c. 210, Nev. Laws 307 (outlawed casinos); *Act of March 19, 1931*, c. 99, Nev. Laws 165 (made casino gambling legal again).

26. John Dombrink and William N. Thompson, *The Last Resort: Success and Failure in Campaigns for Casinos* (Las Vegas: University of Nevada Press, 1990).

27. *California v. Cabazon Band of Mission Indians*, 480 U.S. 202 (1987); Indian Gaming Regulatory Act, Pub. L. 102 Stat. 2467, 100–497 (17 October 1988).

28. *Lac du Flambeau Band of Lake Superior Chippewa Indians v. Wis-*

consin, 770 F. Supp. 480 (W. D. Wisc. 1991), appeal dismissed for lack of jurisdiction 957 F.2d 515 (7th Cir. 1992).

29. John Kenneth Galbraith, *The Great Crash*, 1929 (London: H. Hamilton, 1961).

30. J. Bulgatz Ponzi Schemes, *Invaders from Mars and More Extraordinary Popular Delusions and the Madness of Crowds* (London: Harmony Books, 1992).

31. Casino J., "Top Ten Casino Feeder Markets," *National Gaming Summary*, April 3, 1995, p. 10.

32. Michael Satchell, "Atlantic City's Great Gold Rush," *Parade*, June 10, 1979, p. 8.

33. New Jersey Casino Control Commission, *Annual Report 3* (Atlantic City: Casino Control Commission, 1979); D. Janson, "Resort Wins a Permanent License to Operate a Casino in Atlantic City," *New York Times*, February 27, 1979, A1, B5.

34. New Jersey Casino Control Commission, *Annual Report 3*. In their first fifteen years in operation, the casinos of Atlantic City, which never numbered more than thirteen, claim they paid a total of $6 billion in local, state, and federal taxes.

35. Allan Sloan, "And Now, Trump's Taj Mahal: The Soap Opera" *Los Angeles Times*, November 12, 1990, D5.

36. "Atlantic City's Sands Declares Chapter 11 Bankruptcy," *Casino Journal*, February 1998, p. 30; "Playboy Tangles with Casino in Chapter 11," *Los Angeles Times*, November 16, 1985, iv; Hancock Institutional Equity Services, "Industry Review, United States Casino Gaming Industry Update: Hedge Your Bets" 4 (June 19, 1992); "Resorts International Bankruptcy," AP Newswire story 2013 (March 21, 1994).

37. *World Almanac and Book of Facts* (Mahwah, New Jersey: Funk & Wagnalls, 1995), pp. 381 and 403.

38. Casino J., *National Gaming Summary*, "Top Ten Casino Feeder Markets."

39. Other political players have been involved. In the case of Indian-owned casinos, for example, tribal governments, state governors, federal agencies, and Congress have given their approval, often because of adverse court rulings.

40. Opponents of legal gambling have become more organized and do, occasionally, make a difference in a close election. In November 1999, antigambling activists led by churches and the National Coalition Against Legalized Gambling, won a surprising victory against a proposed state lottery. Of course, the massive casino industry in neighboring Mississippi and Alabama's own race-

tracks may also have played a role in blocking the creation of a new competitor.

41. John Dombrink and William Thompson, *The Last Resort,* p. 11.

42. Citing my 1986 book, *Gambling and the Law*, the California Supreme Court ruled that Proposition 5 violated the California Constitution. *Hotel Employees and Restaurant Employees Int'l Union v. Davis* (1999), 21 Cal.4th 585, 981 P.2d 990, 88 Cal.Rptr.2d 56. The state's tribes easily gathered enough signatures to put the issue back on the ballot, this time as an amendment to the state constitution. Voters approved Proposition 1A in March 2000 by an overwhelming margin, giving tribes a monopoly on casinos in California.

43. Tom Grey, letter dated November 2000 to "Dear Friend," accompanying NCALG Newsletter 8, no. 3 (November 2000).

44. See *West Virginia Limited Gaming Facility Act*, W.Va. Code §§29–25-1 et seq.

45. *Bulletin of the Association of Racing Commissioners International Inc.* 63, no. 15 (May 9, 1997): 1.

46. Daniel J. Boorstin, *Cleopatra's Nose: Essays on the Unexpected* (New York: Random House, 1994).

47. Ibid.,

48. Did anyone want to play a video poker machine before it was invented?

49. Boorstin, *Cleopatra's Nose.*

50. Ibid.

51. Ibid.

7
IS IT A CRIME TO BET ON THE NET?

Michael E. Hammond

For decades, Americans have weighed the entertainment value of gambling against the social ills that seem to accompany the practice.[1] Only recently, however, has this debate been thrust into the computer world, for only in recent times have casinos and bookmakers turned to the Internet. This business strategy has been a financial boon. Conservative estimates approximate that online casinos and bookmakers will bring in over $3 billion in annual revenue by 2003.[2] This revenue comes from Internet sites like *Intertops*, *Sports Interaction*, and *Virtual Vegas*. The simple fact is that Americans are flocking to cyberspace as fast as they can to put five, ten, or fifty dollars down on their favorite team or to play cards or slot machines.[3]

Internet gambling can be performed in almost all the traditional manners. The most popular types of betting are online casinos, which feature nearly every game available in regular casinos, as well as sports wagering. In May of 1999, there were over 250 online casino Internet sites and 139 online sportsbooks.[4] Through the Internet, almost everyone has the ability to wager on any major professional or amateur athletic event in the world. This ease of access, combined with the ethical stigma placed upon gambling, will inevitably lead to myriad new federal and state regulations seeking to restrict access to these types of Web sites, as well as the application of existing laws to Internet gambling establishments.

IS INTERNET GAMBLING ALREADY ILLEGAL?

Although there has been considerable debate concerning currently proposed legislation that addresses Internet gambling, this type of activity is, arguably, already regulated by various federal and state laws. The debate concerning the validity and applicability of these laws has just begun.

State Laws

Until recently, the regulation of gambling had been relegated to state legislatures. Predictably, states have varied in their degree of regulation. Utah, generally considered a conservative state, does not permit its citizens to participate in any form of gambling. Nevada, in contrast, openly declares in its statutory law that gambling is vital to the state's economy. The essence of Kentucky's gambling statutes can be found in the statement: "The principal concept of the entire gambling chapter is to punish those who make a business or profession of gambling rather than the player who makes the business possible."[5] This purpose is accomplished by establishing a system in which a person can be only punished for the promotion of gambling (bookmaking) or for permitting gambling. Here a *player* is defined as "a person who engages in any form of gambling solely as a contestant or bettor." Such a person cannot be guilty of bookmaking, according to the statute. Thus, the individual gambler would not be prosecutable under Kentucky state law for placing bets on the Internet.

Federal Laws

Congress decided to institute its own regulations on gambling because of the inconsistencies in state legislation and enforcement. To prevent a wide variation among neighboring states, Congress resolved to exercise its power to control interstate commerce.[6] The majority of these federal statutes were passed before the introduction of online wagering, however.

The Wire Wager Act of 1961

The statute that most directly restricts the use of the Internet to place bets is the Wire Wager Act, which directly prohibits the use of a wire transmission facility to foster a gambling pursuit.[7] It reads, in part:

> Whoever being engaged in the business of betting or wagering knowingly uses a wire communication facility for the transmission in interstate or foreign commerce of bets or wagers or information assisting in the placing of bets or wagers on any sporting event or contest, or for the transmission of a wire communication which entitles the recipient to receive money or credit as a result of bets or wagers, or for information assisting in the placing of bets or wagers, shall be fined under this title or imprisoned not more than two years, or both.[8]

Two different views of this statute can be taken. Some regulatory advocates feel that it broadly covers any interstate use of the Internet that is related to placing or receiving bets. Supporters of this assertion emphasize the phrase "*use* [o]f a wire facility." For example, if this law does indeed apply to online wagering, a bookmaker would violate the act simply by e-mailing a point spread across state lines if the purpose was to "assist . . . in the placing of bets."

Challengers to the applicability of the act point to two issues. First, the words "wire communication facility" apply only to transmissions that use wires. Currently, wireless Internet access is already being provided by cellular phone companies and with handheld computers. The proliferation of such services is inevitable. The Wire Wager Act may not apply to companies that allow wagering or provide information to assist in a wager through a wireless service. Second, the Act may apply only to wagering upon sporting events (not card games or other games based upon chance). The first portion of the Act refers to "bets or wagers on any sporting event or contest." However, only a few phrases later, the act becomes more expansive by referring generally to "bets or wagers."[9] The legislative history of the act suggests that its purpose was to regulate sports betting and activities, such as numbers games, that were related to organized crime.[10] Nevertheless, the challenge is a valid one.[11]

Another relevant shortcoming of the Wire Wager Act is its significance only to those "being engaged in the business of betting or wagering."[12] This phrase limits the act to professional bookmakers who set up online facilities. Online gamblers, Internet service providers, and those arranging for wagering without making a profit (office pools, for example) would be excluded. Despite these limitations, the Wire Wager Act contains language that is broad enough to allow the law to serve as the primary basis in the attempt to hold operators of online gambling operations criminally liable.

The Travel Act of 1961

The second federal statute relevant to the regulation of Internet gambling is the Travel Act, which penalizes any person who "travels in interstate or foreign commerce or uses the mail or any facility in interstate or foreign commerce, with intent to . . . further any unlawful activity."[13] An *unlawful activity* is defined as including "any business enterprise involving gambling." Peter Brown comments, "Although the purpose of the Act was to prohibit illegal syndicated gambling, the scope of the Act may reach online gamblers who use interstate facilities, such as telephone lines, to access the Internet in furtherance of illegal activities."[14]

The plain language of the statute indicates that it could apply to both online casino operators and individual bettors. However, the intention of the statute was not to reach online gamblers but, as indicated by the definition of an unlawful activity, to focus upon those who are involved in a "business enterprise involving gambling."[15]

The Interstate Transportation of Wagering Paraphernalia Act of 1961

The Interstate Transportation of Wagering Paraphernalia Act also applies to Internet gambling. This Act prohibits individuals or entities from "knowingly carrying or sending in interstate or foreign commerce any 'paraphernalia' or 'other device' to be 'used . . . or designed for use' in illegal gambling."[16] Clearly, the primary interpretation required for the implementation of this law is the definition of *other device*. A broad interpretation could include the Web site software necessary to place wagers online, which would be shipped by companies to potential customers.

Another phrase in the Act could extend liability to Internet service providers. The law punishes anyone who "knowingly carries or sends" devices used for illegal gambling. For example, an Internet service provider could be found criminally liable if it learns that its facilities are being used to expedite online wagering and it does nothing to prevent such acts. However, such a broad interpretation would require that the Web site itself be considered a "device."

Like the other federal statutes analyzed earlier, the Interstate Transportation of Wagering Paraphernalia Act would not apply to individual gamblers, only to those who "send" the paraphernalia or device.

The Professional and Amateur Sports Protection Act of 1992

This federal statute makes it illegal for any person to

> [sponsor], operate, advertise or promote, pursuant to the law or compact of a governmental entity, a . . . betting, gambling, or wagering scheme based, directly or indirectly . . . on one or more competitive games in which amateur or professional athletes participate . . . or on one or more performances of such athletes in such games.[17]

At first glance, this statute seems very inclusive. However, there are some exceptions. Nevada, Oregon, and Delaware are not subject to the restrictions "with respect to state authorized sports betting in existence prior to enactment of the statute."[18] This federal statute would make it illegal for anyone to operate a gambling business (whether online or not) in which the results of amateur or professional sports form the basis for winning bets.

There are limitations with this statute. First, it applies only to bookmakers who take bets on sporting events, making it inapplicable to all of the cybercasinos that do not provide sportsbetting. Second, it does not apply to the individual bettor, only to those who operate the gambling scheme. Finally, as mentioned earlier, the statute contains exceptions for specific states.

The Federal Aiding and Abetting Statute of 1948

Although this statute does not specifically mention gambling, it applies to online gambling, nevertheless. It provides that "[w]hoever commits an offense against the United States or aids, abets . . . or procures its commission, is punishable as a principal."[19] In order to be punished under this act, the perpetrator must assist in the commission of the offense with the intent to assist and have "guilty knowledge" of the offense. Further, the illegal act must actually be performed by the principal lawbreaker.

Plainly, this statute would apply to anyone who assists someone in operating an illegal online gambling business. "Thus," as Brown notes, "those involved in the operation and maintenance of cybercasinos, those who assist users in accessing gambling Web sites, and possibly those who provide access to cybercasinos would all face potential penalties under the aiding and abetting statute."[20] The typical Internet service provider would not face criminal liability, however, under normal circumstances because their actions do not normally satisfy either of the "guilty knowledge" or participation requirements.

All of these federal statutes appear to pertain, to some degree, to online gambling. Nevertheless, the actual prosecution of these types of companies or their officers is uncommon. One reason for this scarcity in prosecutions is the inability of enforcement officials to coerce the defendants to appear in the United States to stand trial, although in December 2001, Duane Pede and Jeff D'Ambrosia did plead guilty in a Wisconsin federal court to gambling and tax charges based on the Wire Wager Act.

INTERNATIONAL JURISDICTION

The enforcement of extraterritorial jurisdiction provides the single largest obstacle in the regulation of Internet gambling. The process of obtaining jurisdiction is difficult when a prosecutor is facing acts that are performed in another state. This process becomes radically more complex when the actions that make up the cause of action are committed in a different country. Jurisdictional determination is not unique to actions committed online. These debates have existed since the first multinational corporation began doing business, and because of this history, there is a basis for determining the appropriate standards in determining jurisdiction.

There are two prerequisites for the exercise of jurisdiction by a United States court over a foreign defendant. The court must have both *subject matter* jurisdiction over the controversy and *personal* jurisdiction over the defendant.

Subject Matter Jurisdiction

The test for determining whether subject matter jurisdiction is present in a particular case has two prongs. The purpose of these prongs is to determine whether the particular act has had an impact upon the United States or its citizens, or whether the substantive law that is at issue was intended by Congress to be decided by U.S. courts.

With certain issues, Congress has clearly expressed an intent for U.S. courts to exercise jurisdiction; for example the Iran and Libya Sanctions Act of 1996 and the Antiterrorism and Effective Death Penalty Act of 1996. However, none of the areas involve online gambling, and therefore, the two-pronged test established by the judiciary must be utilized.

The two-part inquiry used by the courts is generally known as the effects test. In *United States* v. *Aluminum Co. of America* (Alcoa),[21] the United States Second Circuit Court of Appeals addressed whether the Sherman Antitrust Act could be applied to acts committed while abroad. The Court ruled that foreign entities could be held liable under the antitrust laws in circumstances where intentional foreign conduct affects United States commerce or where the conduct results in a demonstrated actual or presumed effect in the United States. The U.S. Supreme Court implicitly endorsed the effects test in *American Tobacco* v. *United States*.[22]

Subsequent to the *Alcoa* and *American Tobacco* cases, the U.S. Supreme Court created an additional test known as the true conflicts test.

In *Hartford Fire Insurance v. California*,[23] the court held that the assertion of extraterritorial subject matter jurisdiction is valid if the effects test is met and there is no genuine contradiction between United States law and the law or policy of another nation.

Online gambling sites would most likely satisfy the two-pronged effects test. Internet sites make their service available to U.S. customers by knowingly accepting memberships to individuals from the U.S., making payments to the U.S. through checks or credit card transactions, or simply by making the site available in the states. Any of these connections could be seen as an intentional foreign act affecting U.S. commerce or, at the very least, as leading to a demonstrated effect in the United States.

Satisfying the true conflicts test is more challenging because some countries are beginning to recognize legalized online casinos and bookmakers. In Australia's Northern Territory resides Lasseters Online, the world's first government-licensed, fully regulated online casino. U.S. Justice Department officials claim that the operation of this casino is a violation of U.S. law if Americans use the site. However, according to the true conflicts theory, a court would have to determine (through a balancing test) that United States interests outweigh the incentive for maintaining harmonious foreign relations before American jurisdiction could be exercised. The exercise of such jurisdiction over a foreign defendant operating an online gambling operation has not yet been tested.

Personal Jurisdiction

The Due Process Clause of the Fifth Amendment to the U.S. Constitution protects not only United States citizens, but also foreign defendants, from unfair assertions of jurisdiction over them. The Due Process Clause's requirements were formalized in *International Shoe Co. v. Washington*,[24] and a two-pronged test was developed. The first prong focused upon the nature and quality of the defendant's contacts with the U.S. forum, and the second analyzed the sufficiency of these contacts.

The Court first noted that involuntary contacts were insufficient to satisfy the minimum contacts standard.[25] Next, the type of voluntary contacts that would satisfy the minimum contacts standard was clarified in

World-Wide Volkswagen Corp. v. Woodson,[26] in which the court stated that contacts with a foreign jurisdiction would meet the minimum contacts standard if (1) the defendant "purposely avail[ed]" himself of the protections provided by the forum state's laws and (2) it was reasonably foreseeable to the defendant that her actions would force her to be subject to the forum state's jurisdiction. Finally, the Court provided further clarification concerning the degree of relation required between the defendant's actions and the contacts with the forum state in *Helicopteros Nacionales de Columbia v. Hall.*[27]

In *Helicopteros*, the Court set up two categories for personal jurisdiction analysis. The category labeled general jurisdiction is used when the defendant's contacts with the forum state are so "continuous and systematic" that personal jurisdiction may by granted even if there is no connection between the contacts and the act which has led to the claim. The category labeled specific jurisdiction is utilized when the defendant's actions which are the basis for the claim "aris[e] out of or [are] related to the defendant's contacts with the forum." If a court can legitimately claim that general or specific jurisdiction exists, then the minimum contacts between the defendant and the forum state exist and personal jurisdiction can be exercised.

The contacts between an online gambling company and a state within the United States could, certainly, vary. If the site developed a large number of customers from one particular state, then the general jurisdiction parameters might be met. Even if the general jurisdiction standards were not met, however, specific jurisdiction requirements would surely be satisfied. This is because the suit would arise from the contacts that the defendant made with the forum state. In other words, specific jurisdiction conditions would be met because the defendant's contact with the state (the customers activity with the company) is the basis for the criminal claim against them.

One further level is added to this puzzle by the U.S. Supreme Court's decision in *Asahi Metal Industry Co. v. Superior Court.*[28] In this case, the Court found that even when the minimum contacts with a forum are present, the exercise of personal jurisdiction is unreasonable when these contacts "arose out of the defendant's mere placement of its goods into 'the stream of commerce.'" Thus, if a court were to rule that the defendant online gambling company simply placed its services into the stream of commerce without advertising or further soliciting its services to the residents of the forum state in question, then the assertion of personal jurisdiction would be unreasonable.

In recent cases, courts have focused upon the type of transmission used by the Internet company. In Bruce P. Keller's words, courts "have developed a continuum, whereby personal jurisdiction can be asserted over a Web site operation depending on the degree of interactivity the site allows or encourages with users in the forum state."[29] Courts generally do not find personal jurisdiction if the Web site is purely passive (simply provides information).[30] However, courts have usually found jurisdiction in cases where the site interacts with users or conducts online business.[31]

As the portrayal just provided suggests, the exercise of jurisdiction over foreign online gambling companies is anything but certain. Only recently has the first case with a defendant online gambling operation gone to the trial stage. In February, the U.S. attorney for the Southern District of New York obtained a conviction against Jay Cohen, the co-owner of the World Sports Exchange sports book. This conviction was upheld by the U.S. Court of Appeals for the Second Circuit, indicating that U.S. Courts will exercise jurisdiction over these type of defendants.

FIRST AMENDMENT CHALLENGES

First Amendment challenges to the restrictions placed upon gambling have largely been unsuccessful. State and federal governments have been free to regulate gambling in any manner they wished without the worry that their actions would be ruled unconstitutional violations of free speech by the Supreme Court. However, a recent Supreme Court decision indicates that the Court could be willing to treat online gambling differently from more traditional forms.

In *Reno* v. *ACLU*, the Court rejected the government's primary justification for the Communications Decency Act, the protection of minors.[32] Even though the Court admitted that not all indecent materials could be kept away from minors with the current technology, it nevertheless struck down the law because of a refusal to "reduce the adult population . . . to . . . only what is fit for children." If the protection of minors was proffered as a justification for current or future online gambling restrictions, the Court could rule that this rationale was invalid in that context also.

This theory seems less relevant to online gambling than to pornography, however. Because of the necessary use of a credit card or a wire transfer, Internet gambling has a built-in method for limiting access to adults. Thus, most challengers to current or future statutes probably would not even attempt to use this theory. Instead, the basis for any restrictions would be the preservation of state laws that outlaw gambling.

Another potential First Amendment issue is vagueness. The Court noted that the term "indecent" was problematic because its vagueness could lead to discriminatory enforcement of the law and have an "obvious chilling effect" upon free speech. In *Reno*, the Court was afraid that individuals would be unsure whether particular material was indecent and, to avoid a potential prison sentence, would choose not to post such materials.

This same argument could be made with online gambling restrictions. Both the Wire Wager Act and the proposed Internet Gambling Prohibition Act penalize individuals for "the transmission of information assisting in the placement of bets or wages."[33] This language could be interpreted by the Court as an attempt to regulate the content of the Internet. For example, individuals living in Oregon (where gambling is legal) might fear prosecution for mentioning the odds of a game in an e-mail message or chat room. Instead of taking the risk that someone in Utah (where gambling is illegal) would see the information, the individual will refrain from posting the information.

COMMERCE CLAUSE

Federalism

The U.S. government was designed as a federalist system, which requires that the federal and state governments limit each other's power. The power allocated to states is best described as a police power, including the power over the welfare of the citizens of that state. The federal government's power is based on a Constitutional provision that grants it the authority to regulate foreign or interstate commerce.

In general, gambling is an issue involving the health and welfare of state citizens. Hence, the power to regulate gambling generally is granted to state governments. However, the effects of gambling have the ability to cross state borders; therefore if gambling in one state can affect the commerce of another state, then the federal government is permitted to regulate this activity pursuant to the Commerce Clause. There are two competing viewpoints with regard to the scope of powers granted to the federal government pursuant to this Clause.

The federal government's power via the Commerce Clause has recently been scrutinized by the U.S. Supreme Court. In United *States* v. *Lopez*, the Court sought to restrict the federal government's seemingly limitless Commerce Clause powers, stating that an activity must "substantially affect interstate commerce" for the government's regulation in that area to be constitutional.[34] This limitation on the government's Commerce Clause powers could result in Internet gambling regulations being deemed unconstitutional.

The legality of gambling in some states suggests that Internet gambling regulations may not have a substantial effect upon interstate commerce. It would seem difficult for the federal government to argue that Internet gambling has any more effect on interstate commerce than existing legalized gambling does. In other words, since the federal government cannot constitutionally regulate legal gambling in states like Nevada, which affects neighboring states, there is no reason why they should be able to regulate the same forms of gambling over the Internet.

Federal legislation regulating interstate lottery advertisements provides a useful parallel to the Commerce Clause problems inherent in Internet gambling. In *Valley Broadcasting Co.* v. *United States*, the U.S. Court of Appeals struck down a federal ban on casino broadcast advertisements that could be viewed in states in which gambling was illegal.[35] The government attorney argued that only a total ban could prevent ads that originated in states in which gambling is legal from spilling over into states in which gambling is illegal. However, the court dismissed this argument because ads that were not subject to the federal ban (originating from state lotteries or Native American casinos) were already being viewed in these areas.

Gambling advertisements are particularly relevant to Internet gambling. The fact that gambling advertisements can legally enter a nongambling state through such media outlets as television and radio suggests to gambling proponents that states should also be able to decide whether they want to permit Internet gambling.

This argument is countered by the proponents of federal regulation, who point to the U.S. Supreme Court's decision in *United States* v. *Edge Broadcasting*.[36] In this case, the issue before the Court was a federal statute that prohibited lottery advertisements transmitted via television and radio to states in which this activity was not authorized. The Court's decision was based on two crucial theories.

First, they emphasized the comprehensiveness of Congress's power under the Commerce Clause by upholding a 1903 decision known as the Lottery Case, in which the Court had validated a Congressional act that made it illegal for the Louisiana lottery to sell tickets in interstate or foreign commerce.[37] In approving the Lottery Case, the Court in *Edge* confirmed the federal government's ability to regulate gambling that occurs outside the United States in a jurisdiction that has legalized gambling.

Second, by embracing the Lottery decision, the *Edge* court accepted the theory that the Commerce Clause should evolve with technological advances. This case pointed out that the powers obtained by Congress pursuant to the Commerce Clause "are not confined to the instrumentalities of commerce . . . known or in use when the Constitution was adopted, but . . . keep pace with the progress of the country, and adapt themselves to the new developments of time and circumstances."[38] This approach clearly indicates that Internet transactions, including those that cross state and national borders, should be within the scope of the Commerce Clause.

In view of the competing perspectives relative to the powers within the scope of the Commerce Clause with regard to Internet gambling, it is apparent that this issue is set to evolve in the upcoming months and years.

State Concerns

The use of state law to prosecute the proprietors of online casinos and sportsbooks may also be impeded by the Commerce Clause. As Bruce P. Keller explains, "Dormant Commerce Clause jurisprudence forbids individual states—even absent congressional action—from regulating within their borders commerce that is essentially national in character in such a way as to burden interstate commerce."[39] In a recent decision from the federal district court in New York, the court found that the Internet was, like an interstate highway or railroad, national in character.[40] The court found that applying a state indecency law to Web pages would "highlight the likelihood that a single actor might be subject to haphazard, uncoordinated, and even outright inconsistent regulation by states that the actor never intended to reach and possibly was unaware were being accessed."[41] The court noted its preference to avoid the application of a state law to conduct that occurs, for the most part, outside the state, even though this application is consistent with the theory of the Dormant Commerce Clause.

Although the New York decision was based on the unique attributes of an indecency action, Internet cases and their application to the Dormant Commerce Clause have also been analyzed in other contexts and could theoretically apply to state Internet gambling regulations. If a state passes a law attempting only to regulate the online gambling that occurs within its borders and provides a remedy that does not restrain gambling sites from states that have not declared the practice illegal, then the regulation could survive.

POTENTIAL FUTURE

As stated above, there are a group of problems that exist with any attempt to regulate online gambling at the state or federal level. These challenges can only be resolved through prosecutions and judicial interpretation. Despite the opinions of skeptics, the U.S. Senate has proposed a variety of bills that are relevant to online gambling regulation. Meanwhile, those with First Amendment and Commerce Clause concerns have stated a preference for state-based regulations. The only certainty is that this issue will continue to be debated. None of the proposed legislation has yet passed into law.

Internet Gambling Prohibition Act

This bill has been commonly referred to as the Kyl Bill because of its initial proposal from Senator Jon Kyl (R-AZ). His basic purpose was to create an updated version of the Wire Wager Act so that Internet gambling would be unmistakably addressed. Initially, the IGPA added "section 1085 to the U.S. Code making it unlawful for a person to place, receive, or otherwise make a bet, or for parties engaged in the business of betting or wagering to do so via the Internet or a non-closed circuit interactive computer service in any state."[42] This language was significant because it targeted individual bettors. The comprehensiveness of this bill was questioned immediately. As one observer noted, "e-mail your picks to the office football pool, and under Kyl's bill you would face a $2,500 fine and six months in jail. Phone in your picks and you would remain free."[43]

Brownback/Leahy Bill

The National Collegiate Athletics Association (NCAA) has advocated a bill that would make it illegal to place bets on any amateur or collegiate athletic contest. The bill, sponsored by Senators Sam Brownback (R-Kansas) and Patrick Leahy (D-Vermont), would supplement the Professional and Amateur Sports Protection Act by eliminating exceptions (relating to wagers on amateur sports) for states already allowing gambling in this form and punishing the individual gambler. This bill, if passed, would lead to the enforcement and Commerce Clause issues described earlier.

State Enforcement

In order to avoid federalism concerns, some analysts have proposed a state enforcement mechanism. There are two main objections to this type of system. The first reason, that state regulation would violate the Dormant Commerce Clause, has already been discussed. Second, it is argued that enforcement in states making online gambling illegal would be impossible. However, this problem is present even when the practice is illegal nationwide. International bookmakers already avoid U.S. laws. By allowing states to make their own laws in this area, online gambling site operators could be regulated (reducing fraud) and tax revenue could be increased.[44]

Internet gambling clearly raises a variety of legal issues. Inevitably, the moral associations with gambling in this form will lead to federal regulations. Enforcing these regulations effectively, however, is burdensome. Because the operators of online gambling sites can easily locate themselves outside the extradition power of the United States, enforcement must eventually focus on the individual bettor or Internet service provider.

NOTES

1. See generally *Valley Broad v. United States* (1993), 107 F.3d 1328, 1331-1332 (9th Cir. 1997), *cert. denied,* 118 S. Ct. 1050.

2. MSNBC News. "Internet Roulette" [online], http://www.msnbc.com/news/ROULETTE_Front.asp.

3. See http://www.msnbc.com/news/ROULETTE_Front.asp (showing that 67 percent of online gambling customers are located in North America).

4. [Online] http://www.msnbc.com/news/ROULETTE_Front.asp.

5. See K.R.S. § 528.010 (Banks-Baldwin 1994).

6. See for example, *United States v. Edge Broadcasting* (1993), 509 U.S. 418, 421 (stating that "Congress has, since the early 19th century, sought to assist the States in their respective efforts").

7. See Bruce P. Keller, "The Game's the Same: Why Gambling in Cyberspace Violates Federal Law," *Yale Law Journal* 108 (1999): 1569.

8. 18 U.S.C. § 1084(a) (1994).

9. Ibid..

10. See, for example, H.R. REP. NO. 87-967, at 2-4 (1961); S. REP. NO. 87-588, at 2-5 (1961).

11. See Adam Snyder, "Guilty Verdict in Net Betting Trial," MSNBC News [online], http://www.msnbc.com/news/369978.asp. [2001].

12. 18 U.S.C. § 1084(a) (1994).

13. 18 U.S.C. § 1952(a) (1998).

14. Peter Brown, *Regulation of Cybercasinos and Internet Gambling,* 1999, 547 PLI/Pat 9, p. 23.

15. 18 U.S.C. § 1952(b) (1998).

16. 18 U.S.C. § 1953(a).

17. 28 U.S.C. § 3702 (1998).

18. Brown, *Regulation of Cybercasinos*, p. 24.

19. 18 U.S.C. § 2 (1998).

20. Brown, *Regulation of Cybercasinos*, p. 25.

21. 148 F.2d 416 (2d Cir. 1945).

22. 328 U.S. 781 (1946).

23. 509 U.S. 764 (1993).

24. 326 U.S. 310 (1945).

25. See *Hanson v. Denckla*, 357 U.S. 253.

26. 444 U.S. 286 (1980).

27. 466 U.S. 408 (1984).

28. 480 U.S. 102 (1987).

29. Keller, *The Game's the Same*, p. 25.

30. See *Bensusan Restaurant Corp. v. King*, 937 F. Supp. 295, 297 (S.D.N.Y. 1996), *aff'd*, 126 F.3d 25 (2d Cir. 1997); see also *Cybersell, Inc. v. Cybersell, Inc.*, 130 F.3d 414, 419 (9th Cir. 1997).

31. See *Compuserve, Inc. v. Patterson*, 89 F.3d 1257, 1268 (6th Cir. 1996); *Mieczkowski v. Masco Corp.*, 997 F. Supp. 782, 787 (E.D. Tex. 1998).

32. See *Reno v. ACLU*, 117 S.Ct. 2329 (1997).

33. See 18 U.S.C. § 1084(a) (1994); See also *Internet Gambling Prohibition Act of 1997*, S. 474, 105th Cong.

34. 514 U.S. 549 (1995).

35. 107 F.3d 1328 (9th Cir. 1997)

36. 509 U.S. 418 (1993).

37. *Champion v. Ames*, 188 U.S. 321 (1903).

38. Ibid. (quoting *Pensacola Tel.*, 96 U.S.).

39. Keller, *The Game's the Same*, pp. 253–54.

40. See *American Libraries Ass'n v. Pataki*, 961 F.Supp. 160 (S.D.N.Y. 1997).

41. Ibid.

42. Steve Kish, *Betting on the Net: An Analysis of the Government's Role in Addressing Internet Gambling*, 51 FCLJ 449 (1999), p. 51.

43. Tom W. Bell, quoted in "Internet Gambling Ban Faces Losing Odds," *Times-Union* (Albany, New York), January 6, 1998, A7.

44. Kish, *Betting on the Net*, p. 51.

♥ ♣ ♠ ♦
CASINO GAMBLING AND CRIME

Jay Albanese

CRIME VOLUME VERSUS CRIME RATES

The purpose of measuring crime is to assess risk. Nearly twenty years ago, then-New York State Attorney General issued a report in which he opposed casino gambling, part of his justification being a dramatic increase in crime in Atlantic City since the introduction of casinos there. Having worked in Atlantic City before the introduction of casino gambling, I saw with my own eyes how the city's population surged during the summer months with beach-goers and vacationers, and how it was almost a ghost town during the winter months. The addition of nine large casino-hotels in a period of five years obviously expanded the number of visitors year round. It is apparent that crime would increase in

---

Testimony to the National Gambling Impact Study Commission, Biloxi, Mississippi, September 10, 1998.

Atlantic City as the average daily population also rose. This was documented in my 1985 study of crime in Atlantic City,[1] which found that the increase in Index crimes in Atlantic City was offset by the increase in the average daily population of the city, meaning that the risk of being the victim of a serious property or violent crime actually *dropped* in Atlantic City after the introduction of casinos. The risk of crime is measured by the crime *rate*, the most useful measure of crime; changes in the volume of crime do not provide an indication of risk, and that is what most concerns individual citizens and policy makers.

WHAT THE EVIDENCE SAYS AND WHY

Since my study was conducted, a large amount of subsequent research has shown (with some exceptions) that the introduction of casino gambling does not have a significant impact on crime rates.[2] This finding generally has been consistent across jurisdictions for several reasons:

- First, the individual risk of being a crime victim does not increase because the average daily law-abiding population in casino jurisdictions is much larger than any increase in the crimes committed.
- Second, in most casino jurisdictions, casino gambling is a very small part of the local economy. No other city is dominated by casinos like Atlantic City and Las Vegas. As a result, the impact is limited in ways similar to other forms of economic development in the recreational sector, such as amusement parks and nightclubs.
- Third, casinos are distinguished from most other forms of economic development in that they contribute to their own regulation. In most casino jurisdictions, casinos help to fund security, law enforcement, and problem-gambling initiatives that may contribute to lower crime rates.

WHITE-COLLAR CRIME

Existing studies of the casino-crime connection have focused on street crimes. These crimes are committed most often by people aged sixteen to twenty-four. Casino patrons are typically much older than that. It has been argued that casino gambling may contribute to white-collar crimes by casino patrons who are problem gamblers. These people might steal from their employers, pass bad checks, or engage in other crimes to support their gambling habits. There are anecdotes of particular incidents where those who gamble have committed white-collar crimes, but there has been no systematic study of the problem to examine the extent to which it is widespread or consists of isolated occurrences.

I am currently researching the link between gambling and white-collar crime by analyzing arrests for the crimes of embezzlement, forgery, and fraud in some of the largest casino jurisdictions, both before and after the advent of casinos, and also in comparison with arrest trends in comparable noncasino jurisdictions. Preliminary results indicate that trends in embezzlement, forgery, and fraud vary considerably among casino jurisdictions.[3] For example, they have increased in Gulfport, Mississippi, since the introduction of casinos. However, arrests for these crimes also have risen in Mobile, Alabama, and many other jurisdictions that do not have casino gambling. Vicksburg, Mississippi, has seen arrests increase for fraud and embezzlement but decrease for forgery since the introduction of casino gambling. Jackson, Mississippi, has experienced the exact same trend without having casino gambling. In order to sort this out, it is necessary to determine the extent to which these arrests are gambling-related, which is a difficult task. Except in the most obvious cases, it is difficult to claim that gambling "caused" a person to commit a white-collar crime or that the person would not have committed the crime anyway without the presence of a local casino.

Importantly, this study of white-collar crime in casino and noncasino jurisdictions provides the first systematic look at the crimes committed by the persons who typically patronize casinos rather than the teenagers and very young adults who commit most street crime.

ORGANIZED CRIME

My fourth point is the issue of organized crime involvement. Research conducted in 1995 highlights some significant issues[4]:

- First, organized crime infiltration of the casino industry is a shadow of what it once was, due primarily to the entrance of large, publicly held corporations into the casino industry. The immense size of these companies, and their attention to stock prices, public image, and the regulation of the Securities and Exchange Commission make it easy for them to resist attempts at organized crime infiltration.
- Second, the primary opportunity for organized crime involvement comes from ancillary businesses that do business with casinos, such as cleaning, construction, furniture, entertainment, liquor, and garbage services. These vendors must be screened carefully and continuously for links to organized crime.
- Third, instances of successful organized infiltration are now few, although they do occur. In recent years, criminal charges have been lodged in several cases of organized profit skimming and cheating in Mississippi, Louisiana, and Connecticut. In virtually every case, there was co-optation of someone on the inside, pointing to the need for careful background screening and monitoring of casino employees.

THE NEED FOR PLANNING, FURTHER STUDY, AND VIGILANCE

The National Gambling Impact Study Commission has an important role to play in informing decisions on whether to legalize forms of gambling in more jurisdictions. It appears that many jurisdictions do not properly study or learn from the experiences of the past, and as a result, some jurisdictions may be condemned to relive it.

The case of Windsor, Ontario, is an example of a well-planned effort to introduce a single casino into a city. It may provide a model for other jurisdictions to emulate. Ontario brought together experts in travel, transportation, tourism, crime, and other areas to help predict who the visitors would be and where they would come from and to plan the impact on everything from employment and local businesses to police, parking, and traffic flow.[5] All economic development has benefits and incurs costs, whether it be casinos, manufacturing, convention centers, or amusement parks. Too few cities have carried out this assessment objectively to assess the suitability of different forms of economic development, given their geographic location, economy, and local public opinion. The result is a politicized atmosphere of dueling experts and ideology rather than a reliance on objective evidence and rational decision making. The National Commission would perform a useful service by providing a framework for jurisdictions considering casino gaming to follow in assessing all aspects of its impact on the community so that more informed decisions are made and fewer mistakes are repeated.

Further study of the impacts of gambling, both legal and illegal, is sorely needed. Lotteries and Internet gambling have the potential to reach far more people than casinos ever will. The gambling-crime link has been studied only in a comparatively small number of jurisdictions, most of those studies cover limited time periods, and few examine factors that more time and funds are needed to explore. For example, interviews with white collar and organized crime offenders in different jurisdictions are needed to assess their connection to gambling and the similarities and differences in their opportunities and motivations of these offenders. Only in this way can we become better informed about what to expect in the future.

Finally, all forms of gambling must be regulated closely wherever they are introduced because of the speed at which cash is accumulated. Unlike other cash businesses, where a business must wait for a product or service to be used or exhausted (e.g., a drink, food, entertainment) before the customer can be solicited again, games of chance move quickly. Multiple bets and payouts occur in seconds, permitting many transactions in a short period and resulting in large cash accumulations. This will always be a significant temptation for organized crime elements. Effective models of monitoring and enforcement levels now exist, and the Commission would do a great service by recognizing and describing those models of regulation and enforcement that are effectively keeping the risks of crime low.

NOTES

1. Jay S. Albanese, "The Effect of Casino Gambling on Crime," *Federal Probation* 64 (1985): 39–44.

2. For example, Peter Reuter, *The Impact of Casinos on Crime and Other Social Problems* (1997); WEFA Group, *A Study Concerning the Effects of Legalized Gambling on the Citizens of the State of Connecticut* (Prepared for the state of Connecticut, Department of Revenue Services, Division of Special Revenue, June 1997); Semoon Chang, "The Impact of Casinos on Crime: The Case of Biloxi, Mississippi," *Journal of Criminal Justice* 24 (1996).

3. The final report of this study has been published as Jay S. Albanese, *Casino Gambling and White-Collar Crime: An Examination of the Empirical Evidence* (Washington, D.C.: American Gaming Association, 1999).

4. Jay Albanese, "Casino Gambling and Organized Crime: More Than Reshuffling the Deck," in *Contemporary Issues in Organized Crime*, ed. Jay Albanese (Monsey, N.Y.: Willow Tree Press, 1995), pp. 1–17; Jay S. Albanese, *Organized Crime in America*, 3d ed. (Cincinnati: Anderson, 1996).

5. Jay S. Albanese, "The Impact of Casino Gambling on Crime and Law Enforcement," in *Gambling: Public Policies and the Social Sciences*, ed. William R. Eadington and Judy A. Cornelius (Reno: University of Nevada Press, 1997).

♥ ♠ ♣
9

A FAIR DEAL FOR THE PLAYER?

Regulation and Competition as Guarantors of Consumer Protection in Commercial Gambling

David Miers

A s a consumer of a commercial gambling product, do you trust your bookmaker to give you a price that fairly reflects the probability of the horse you have backed winning the race? And when you have won, that the bookie will honor the debt now owed to you? Do you trust the bingo or lottery operator both to channel all the players' money to the win pool and to pay out on all winning tickets? And where the state derives a specific and intended benefit from the lottery, do you trust the state government properly to balance its interest in the generation of that benefit against the promotion of particularly seductive games that encourage damaging overconsumption? Do you trust the casino not to bias the roulette wheel or the gaming machine operator not to deceive you about the odds against you hitting winning lines? Does the provider of any gambling service provide you with accurate and accessible information about the probabilities against you winning your bet or about other aspects of the price and quality of that service? These questions, suitably adapted, might be asked about the provision of any consumer service.[1]

Consumer protection may be justified as a means by which consumers can exercise informed choices in a competitive market, choices that contribute to the development of fairly priced goods and services that offer value for money.[2] For the gambler, the key items are the price of the bet and the information on which that price is determined. The price may be thought of as the margin of loss experienced by the player on each bet, or, conversely, as the margin of gain to the supplier. "In other industries," the *Gambling Review Report* published in Great Britain in 2001 observes, "we might ask whether the price is fair; in the case of gambling we have to consider whether the margin of loss (more generally known as the gross gaming margin) is fair."[3] Fairness will be compromised, the *Review* continues, where there is fraud or dishonesty, inadequate information or inadequate competition.

The purpose of this essay is to evaluate the role of regulation and competition as the primary means by which the state, in permitting or promoting certain forms of commercial gambling, may seek to embed an element of fairness for the consumer in the supply. In the following section, the evaluation will proceed to identify how the regulatory controls almost universally imposed on its operators will inevitably secure a degree of consumer protection. This will be so whether the objective in permitting commercial gambling is the production of benefit to the economy (economic regulation) or the reduction in the social costs of individual gambling activity (social regulation). But regulation also inhibits competition, and according to the *Gambling Review*, "[C]ompetition between suppliers of gambling activities offers the most effective way of providing a fair deal for the [player]."[4]

The choice between regulation and competition (or, more usually, a mix of the two) is particularly highlighted where the public interest lies in the generation of benefits to a local or national economy. Here, two questions arise: first, are those benefits best secured by the creation of a regulated monopoly supplier or by the operation of a degree of competition between regulated suppliers? and, second, what are the implications for the gambler's fair treatment of the choice between monopoly and competition? The role of competition as a means of delivering price and quality control for the player will be discussed later in this essay.

The discussion will be illustrated chiefly by reference to the British experience, which offers examples both of economic and social regulation, together with the as yet unimplemented introduction of the *Gambling Review Report*'s recommendations.[5] Attention will also be given to the role of regulation and competition in the protection of child and problem gamblers. The issues addressed in this essay are, however, by no means peculiar to Great Britain, but are of universal relevance, as can be readily seen in the substantial reviews recently published in Australia, New Zealand, and the United States.[6]

REGULATION AND CONSUMER PROTECTION

The Role of Regulation

Although their details vary, most regulatory regimes governing commercial gambling display four principal features.[7] The first comprises measures designed to provide a workable method for screening out undesirable elements from the gaming enterprise and ensure the continued integrity of the operation.[8] The paradigm of such prior clearance schemes lies in quality controls imposed on prospective suppliers of casino gaming, but a system of supplier control applies, to a greater or lesser extent, to all regimes. The other three features comprise (1) standards to be met by the supplier in the delivery of the gambling medium, (2) measures controlling the conditions under which participation by the player occurs, and (3) compliance procedures. How then, do these four measures work to protect the player?

First, the probity checks implicit in the prior clearance provisions are intended to eliminate those operators who might be tempted to be dishonest in their dealings with players or to manipulate information and prices to the players' detriment. According to the British Department for Culture, Media, and Sport (DCMS):

> Two of the key principles underlying regulation are to keep criminals and crime out of the industry and to ensure that the [player] has a fair and transparent deal. The key to achieving these objectives is a rigorous licensing system for the individuals who manage gambling activities.[9]

Licensing systems frequently ask the question, is the operator a "fit and proper person"? This is also one of the key statutory tests in the United Kingdom's system for regulating the provision of financial services.[10] In addition to honesty, competence, financial probity, and solvency, prior clearance provisions may require operators to demonstrate an understanding of their social responsibility toward gamblers; in particular "their knowledge of problem gambling and the help that can be offered to people who get into difficulty."[11]

Second, the performance standards imposed on those who meet the entry criteria may require operators to provide training or simple diagnostic skills in problem gambling for their employees. This is done, for example, in Nevada and the Netherlands. Apart from this more recent development, performance standards imposed on the conduct of the regulated market are typically intended to ensure financial integrity in the handling of the players' money and the collection and transmission of gambling revenues. These standards may also specify rates of return or the provision of information to the player, discussed later.

Third, participation controls may be used to limit both the general availability of gambling opportunities, for example by controlling the sites (both physical and electronic) on which they are accessed,[12] or their availability to specific groups, typically children. Such controls vary according to the prevailing regulatory objective. In the United States and Australia, for example, any adult may walk into a casino and play; in Great Britain, in contrast, the would-be player has to become a member of the club in which the facilities are offered and then wait for twenty-four hours before the first spin of the wheel. The reason: a key feature of social regulation, at least as it has been conceived in Great Britain, is to protect individuals against impulse gaming. Where the objective is social regulation, player participation may also be discouraged by the imposition of controls on advertising and marketing, as well as on the availability of such standard consumer facilities as credit, price discounting, or other incentives to purchase.

More, it may be thought appropriate to regulate the games themselves, perhaps by specifying what games may be played or by requiring operators to submit new game designs for approval. In these ways, games that contain features encouraging repeated participation may, for certain purposes, be forbidden. In the case of Great Britain's National Lottery, for example, the operator is required to obtain the National Lottery Commission's approval for new lottery products. The regulator has in the past refused to approve video lottery terminals.[13] Though ubiquitous in North America, these terminals are in effect gaming machines and pose particularly acute issues of fairness to the player.[14] By contrast, the *Gambling Review Report* has, in the case of smaller scale good-cause lotteries, cautiously recommended that interactive lottery games should be approved.[15] A significant factor in these decisions is that the minimum age for the purchase of a lottery ticket is sixteen; in other venues with a higher age threshold, the weight to be attached to that factor alone will be less.

Or the regulator may insist, as a condition of approval, that the game design incorporate some inhibitor to fast play (a key component in the development of repeat and problem gambling); in the case of a gaming machine, for example, that it is programmed to introduce particular time-lapses between games, or, where it has a smart-card facility, programmed to automatically eject the card after the player has spent, say, US$5, thus requiring a positive action for continued play. A game's attractiveness may be controlled, likewise, by specifying what constitutes a permissible wager (for example, in casino games) or the applicable prize limits. Generally speaking, the greater the prize, the greater the attraction, irrespective of the probability of a win. This incentive is especially important in the case of lotteries and also raises serious questions concerning the use that players make of the information that is given to them. At the core, however, "what is offered should be fair and transparent; any equipment that is required should be tested; staff should be properly trained; and [players] should be fully informed about the returns."[16]

Information Disclosure

In terms of the promotion of consumer sovereignty, a number of the controls outlined in the previous section are significant in that their purpose is not to *enhance* but to *eliminate* choice for the player. But many controls are intended to *inform* choice. Mandatory information disclosure rules are a primary feature of modern consumer protection regimes. Apart from the promotion of the "informed consumer" as a central tenet of consumer policy, disclosure rules reflect those political philosophies which argue that the function of the state is, with the exception of those who are particularly vulnerable to exploitation, only to ensure that purchasing decisions are freely made in a market in which choices are informed. In the present context, therefore, it is the state's function to protect children from gambling opportunities; beyond that, "the combination of informed [gamblers] and competition among businesses best serves the cause of consumer protection."[17] On this view, gamblers who fail to inform themselves of the conditions and consequences of their betting preferences will command little sympathy if they later complain.

While we might accept as axiomatic the view that "the [player] should be fully informed about the odds that he is facing and the proportion of stakes retained by the operator,"[18] two major obstacles stand in the way of the educational development of the informed gambler. The first concerns the accessibility of information about the probabilities against winning, especially in games determined purely by chance. Such information is technical and complex, and when reduced to what might be regarded as more readily understandable propositions, potentially misleading. Take for example, the price of a bet. In general terms, as indicated earlier, this may be conceived of as the margin of loss to the player, but this generality disguises the components that contribute to that loss. While important in any commercial gambling context, the consumer's understanding of these components may, merely by virtue of their popularity, be considered particularly significant in the case of lotteries, and even more acutely so where they are promoted by the state. The Productivity Commission commented:

> The most popular lottery games do not disclose the real price of the gamble. However, this is an inevitable aspect of the way these complex gambling forms are organized—accumulating jackpots, varying prize pools and the possibility of multiple winners make it hard to know the true price.[19]

As the Commission observes, the price of a lottery ticket is not the amount that the purchaser pays for it but that amount less the expected value of the return. That is dependent on three factors, only one of which can be known to the player at the time of purchase: the odds against winning. Of the other two, the value of the prize, which will depend on the number of purchasers together with any prize money carried forward from a previous game ("rollovers"), can be known and may be publicized for the purpose only of heightening the excitement of the draw since tickets cannot be bought at this time. The third factor, how many players have selected the winning numbers and thus will share the jackpot, will not be known until the draw is concluded. In short, players "cannot calculate either the expected value of the prize, or the true price of the lottery with any certainty."[20]

A second example may be drawn from statements about the rate of return to the player, in particular concerning gaming machines. The *Gambling Review Report* contains the following table, showing the approximate percentage of money returned as winnings in the British gambling market, after tax.[21]

Gambling Medium	Rate of Return (%) (after tax)
Table gambling	97
Licensed cash bingo	68
On-course betting—horses	89
On-course betting—dogs (bookmaker)	80
On-course betting—dogs (tote)	77
Off-course betting	78
Spread betting—financial	83
Spread betting—sports	88
Gambling machines—single sites	78–82
Gambling machines—other	85–95
National Lottery	46.8
Societies' lotteries	27
Football pools	33

It would, however, be very ill-informed players who thought that each time they played a game on a gaming machine, they would enjoy at least a 78 percent chance of winning, when in truth the odds against their winning on any occasion are, on a typical machine, very poor. The problem is that bald statements, such as those approved by the Gaming Board for Great Britain that "This Machine has an Average Payout of 80 percent or Greater," are meaningless without reference to the probabilities against hitting a winning line. In its analysis of information disclosure in respect of Australian poker (gaming) machines, the Productivity Commission noted that in the game Black Rhino, five rhinos in a line will pay out 5,000 times the amount bet, but the probability of such a line-up is about ten million to one. The Commission concluded that: "payout tables without the corresponding odds provide very little useful information to players."[22] The question is, therefore, what information to give and how to give it. The Commission suggested that a notice indicating how many button pushes it would take the player to have just a 50 percent chance of hitting five black rhinos (6.7 million), how long it would take (391 days of continuous 24-hours play), and how much it would cost on the ten-cent machine (AU$330,000), would alert the player to the commitment needed for the advertised payoff. This suggestion also illustrates the inherent dilemma. To make meaningful statements about probabilities requires the publication of more information than the bald propositions quoted earlier, but the greater its volume and complexity, the less accessible the information becomes.

The second major obstacle concerns the player's receptivity to the information that is available. Even when presented with accessible and accurate information, many gamblers are poor judges of the probabilities of winning in the chosen medium. For example, those who prefer combination bets on horseraces or other sporting events can be shown to overestimate quite seriously the probability of a specific sequence of events coinciding. Such faulty estimations may be driven by or simply ignored on account of the magnitude of the prize. Following its comments, quoted earlier, on the obstacles to the consumer's ability to determine the price of complex lottery products, the Productivity Commission continued: "Even so, people reveal a strong preference for such lotteries to conventional lotteries, in which a winning ticket with a known prize and known number of contestants is drawn randomly."[23] Gamblers also display many fundamental misconceptions about random events. A common misconception, known as "the gambler's fallacy," is the belief that the more frequently one result occurs, the more likely the opposite result becomes. And, as is readily evidenced in a wide range of popular media, a great deal of superstition and ritual surrounds the playing of chance-based games, much of which purports to improve the player's chances, implying an illusion of control over what will always remain a random outcome.[24]

In short, considerable evidence shows that in assessing the utility of different payoffs, gamblers do not necessarily choose the bet that objectively offers the best return. Misbuying is, however, commonplace in the purchase of other financial products, a fact that raises the question, to what extent should the law protect players from their own folly? In the analogous area of investor protection, the chief objective is to ensure that "reasonable people are not made fools of."[25] To this end, the law imposes substantial regulatory obligations on those who would sell financial products to private investors, most notably the obligation to disclose information. But the regulators also contemplate a significant role for competition among these products. If the state is content to permit competition in respect of financial products on which consumers rely for their old age (pensions) or to guard against sudden loss (insurance), why should it not also permit competition on what are, arguably, far less significant financial decisions?

COMPETITION AND CONSUMER PROTECTION

The Impact of Regulation on Gambling Markets

As noted earlier, regulation has two broad impacts on the commercial gambling market. First, it creates barriers to market entry and simultaneously raises the profit margin of those who own sites.[26] Second, it inhibits competition and thus runs counter to the prevailing conceptions in most modern economies about the best way of delivering services to the consumer. As the *Gambling Review Report* commented:

> Gambling as a whole competes with other forms of household expenditure. Within gambling, one form competes with another and, within one form, suppliers compete with each other. Competition between suppliers helps the [player] by holding down costs and profit margins. This may result in better odds, or where returns are fixed by law, as in the case of some forms of gaming, in better facilities.[27]

It is generally accepted that competition is likely to be effective where products or services are purchased frequently, their quality and performance are readily identifiable, and their characteristics are fairly stable." As noted in *Cranston's Consumers and the Law*, "By contrast, competition is weak in markets which involve substantial information gaps."[28] I have already considered some benefits and limitations of regulatory efforts to address information deficits in gambling markets. I turn now to consider further how competition might benefit the consumers of gambling products and services, in particular in betting markets.

The Role of Competition

An exemplar of a competitive market is SP (starting price) horserace betting. Horserace betting can be organized either on *pari-mutuel* lines, that is, essentially as a lottery in which those who backed the winning horse draw their prizes from the pool of bets (which, like a lottery, may amount to very little if there are many prize winners) or at odds struck between the individual gambler and a bookmaker. These odds may be determined at any time before the race but are typically set at the time the race begins. The SP for any horse is the function of a bookmaker's estimate of the likelihood of the horse winning, mediated by the need to ensure that whatever the outcome, the bookmaker is not in deficit. That estimate is itself dependent not only on any race-winning qualities that the horse or its jockey may display (as affected by any handicapping) but also on the similar qualities of the other horses and riders, the environmental conditions under which the race is to be run, and, crucially, the weight of money backing any horse. If it becomes apparent that a number of gamblers believe that a horse with a price of nine to one has a better than 10 percent chance of winning, other bookmakers will "shorten" the odds, say, to four to one (a 20 percent chance of winning). As with any market, the activities of its members determine the price at which the commodity being traded may be bought and sold. In Great Britain as in other countries, it is primarily the on-course bookmakers who determine starting prices. For the gambler who is also at the course, it is nearly a perfect market. Simply by moving around the betting ring, he or she can compare the odds being offered on each horse by each bookmaker and, so informed, choose one set of odds in preference to another. However, most bets are struck with off-course bookmakers, and for these bettors a number of factors may distort the market to their detriment. It is not possible here to explore these factors in detail, but their primary features can be identified.

The setting and the reporting of starting prices may distort the market. An on-course market that is "thin" (i.e., only a few bookmakers trading in only a small number of bets), is vulnerable to asymptomatic betting: One large bet may significantly alter the on-course odds. As the Gambling Review Report notes, "[O]ff-course bookmakers can . . . easily reduce the odds on a race favorite and thereby greatly reduce the potential gains of those who have backed the winner at the starting price."[29] "Laying-off," or "hedging," a bet is a standard feature of betting (and other financial) markets; the question is whether this practice unfairly distorts the SP market. In any case, the reporting of on-course SPs to off-course bookmakers needs to be transparent and fair, reflecting the prices available from a representative sample (in terms of both its quantity and its robustness) of the on-course market. Fair reporting is likewise threatened where there is common ownership of tracks, betting facilities, and the means by which race and betting information is transmitted to the off-course market. The *Gambling Review Report* found no evidence of malpractice here but expressed its concern that the competition authorities should be alert to the implications of linked ownership.[30]

The results of sporting events (whether horseraces or sports) are susceptible to corrupt practice (e.g., match or race fixing, and bribery of players, jockeys, or umpires). This potential for corruption in such sports as college basketball has grounded the objection to making sportsbetting legal throughout the United States, whose illegal market is, even on the most conservative estimate, substantial.[31] Dishonestly conducted games are properly addressed by the relevant disciplinary bodies; in terms of fairness to the gambler, they represent information deficits. The gambler is placing his or her bet in a market in which other consumers have access to private information; in financial markets this practice, known as insider trading, is illegal. If competition is to provide the means by which all gamblers will have access to fair prices, the market must be regulated to ensure that they all have access to the information on which those prices are based.

There is one final matter to be addressed: the enforcement of gambling contracts. The law here is both inconsistent and anachronistic. It is inconsistent in that some gambling contracts (pool betting and lotteries, to which spread betting has more recently been added) are enforceable in Great Britain, while others, typically those with bookmakers, are not. In the case of gaming, while a casino can sue upon the check that a patron has presented for his or her gaming losses, the underlying debt remains unenforceable. This legal disability, the product of the very different social context of the Gaming Act 1845, was later exported from Britain to North America and Australia.

The law is anachronistic because gambling now constitutes a regular and lawful feature of 70 percent of British citizens' social life,[32] and is actively promoted by the leisure industry as a normal aspect of social life, like visiting a pub or a leisure center. If this is so, why should purchases from this particular service sector not be treated in law like any other? In a competitive market, assuming that it is operating efficiently, suppliers and consumers ought to be able to rely on the law to enforce the decisions that regulators have made. For example, section 13 of the Supply of Goods and Services Act 1982 provides that where a service is supplied and the supplier is acting in the course of business, "there is an implied term that the supplier will carry out the service with reasonable care and skill." This provision is particularly apt in the case of the betting industry, where bookmakers currently have no duty in law to deliver to the individual gambler any particular level of service, for example, in betting options. So far from consumer protection, it is probable that many bookmakers have perceived gamblers as fair game, mugs who bet at their peril and are there to be fleeced.

The *Gambling Review Report* was critical of a number of practices that operate to the player's detriment and recommended that its proposed Gambling Commission have power to monitor the terms and conditions that bookmakers offer. More important, it also recommended that gambling debts be enforceable at law, both by the player and by the operator.[33] As with those who purchase other leisure services, gamblers will seldom pause to consider the legal consequences of their purchase, but that is not the point. A central debate within consumer protection policy concerns the *balance* that should be struck between the responsibilities that are to be imposed on the suppliers of consumer goods and services and the responsibilities of the consumers to inform themselves and to take avoiding action where it would be prudent. The tenor of much that has been written in the recent past on gambling as a broad-based consumer product emphasizes the importance of "responsible gambling."[34] This responsibility cuts both ways. For operators, it means the assumption of socially responsible policies toward their consumers; for gamblers, it means assuming individual responsibility for their gambling decisions.

Gambling for Good Causes

Many of the gambling products currently available throughout North America, Australasia, and Europe are promoted by the state for the purpose of generating public benefit. Where economic regulation is the objective, it will, as noted earlier, be important to ensure that consumers are not overexploited, if for no other reason than that they might choose to purchase other (possibly illegal) gambling products. The regulatory agency responsible for Great Britain's National Lottery, for example, is under a statutory duty to maximize the revenue to good causes. But that duty is subordinate to two other duties, to ensure that the lottery is run "with all due propriety" and that "the interests of all participants are protected."[35]

Two issues concerning fairness to the player arise in connection with state-sponsored gambling, in particular lotteries. The first is that governments committed to the expansion of gambling opportunities in the name of good causes may be perceived as having too close an interest in their citizens' losses. In the pursuit of greater revenue, or, in response to a decline in lottery sales, state-operated lotteries may therefore, in the words of William Eadington, "acquire many of the attributes that they would have been expected to acquire if they had been part of the private commercial gambling sector."[36] By way of example, consider controls on advertising. Where social regulation is the objective, the extent of permissible advertising tends to be in inverse proportion to the attractiveness of the gambling medium to repeated participation. In Great Britain, for example, in addition to the universally applicable standards that advertisements be legal, decent, honest, and truthful, there have traditionally been very strict controls on the advertising of casinos (but less so on the football pools). By contrast, where economic regulation is the objective, advertising plays a key role in encouraging initial and repeat purchases. At one time some state lotteries in the United States quite deliberately targeted the unemployed on the day that their unemployment benefits were payable, drawing their attention to the huge prizes that could be won, a practice that was extensively criticized.[37] The odds against winning tend to be less prominently displayed. I have already shown that simple statements concerning probabilities are potentially misleading. For example, the British National Lottery's first major advertising slogan, "It could be YOU!" (with a large, soft-focus finger pointing at the reader), while true, was clearly intended to downplay the odds against winning. Even setting aside the Productivity Commission's view that gambling, like the consumption of alcohol, is a public health issue, it might well be advisable to follow the slogan with a warning: "But it is almost certainly going to be SOMEONE ELSE!"

Concern about the influence of advertising in the promotion of state lotteries may be intensified where the promotion is in the hands of a monopoly operator. From the government's perspective, the allocation of monopoly rights may well be the best guarantee of maximizing public revenues, but as the *Gambling Review Report* commented regarding another state monopoly (on pool betting for horseracing): "[A]s far as the consumer is concerned the presumption is that monopoly arrangements are against the public interest as they allow excessive profits and reduce the incentive to control costs."[38] It may be that the monopoly license is allocated by means of competitive tendering, in which such matters as consumer protection will have figured, but once allocated, there is no competition within the National Lottery market. Among other matters, this means that there will only be one source of information about the expected value of a lottery ticket, even allowing for the fact that that source will be subject to probity checks imposed by the regulator.[39]

By definition only a very small proportion of purchasers will win or share jackpot prizes; in this sense, state lotteries resemble credence goods (goods whose quality or value the consumer cannot test through experience). The best example is investment products. Purchasers of pensions, for example, will not know whether they have made a good choice until many years after the purchase is made. In addition to their reliance on the predictions made by the supplier, consumers are likely to rely heavily on the supplier's credibility within the financial services market. For this reason, scandals concerning pensions and other investment products are particularly damaging. Similarly, the management of a state lottery must retain its credibility, for example, in the integrity of the draw or in its commitment to ensure the preferred anonymity of jackpot winners.

CONCLUSIONS

The commercial provision of gambling opportunities has traditionally been viewed not just as another set of consumer choices, like the purchase of CD players or cinema tickets, but as a leisure product which, like its customary stablemates, tobacco and alcohol, presents potentially detrimental effects not associated with other choices. These effects may harm individuals or generate wider social costs. For these reasons, where states have permitted gambling, they have typically done so within strict regulatory standards. While we may distinguish gambling from other consumer choices, there is compelling force in the argument that players ought to be afforded the same rights to fair prices and quality of service as apply to all other consumers. Such protection may be regarded as particularly important where technological advances simultaneously make it easier to access gambling opportunities and threaten the integrity of such consumer safeguards as do exist. The *Gambling Review Report* has conveniently summarized the particular characteristics of online gambling that "may make regulation even more desirable":[40] it is available twenty-four hours a day; there is greater continuity of gambling activities; stakes can be lower; it is easier to use; entry conditions are negligible; and social barriers are easier to overcome. These considerations lie behind the view that it is better to regulate the domestic provision of Internet gambling, offering the opportunity to its off-shore operators to "benefit from the kudos that regulation would bring,"[41] rather than to try, as has been suggested in the United States, to prohibit it.[42]

By way of conclusion, I return to the analogy of financial services. Section 5 of the Financial Services and Markets Act 2000 provides that in securing the statutory objective of an "appropriate degree of protection for consumers," the regulator must consider:

1. the differing degrees of risk involved in different kinds of investment or other transaction,
2. the differing degrees of experience and expertise that different consumers may have in relation to different kinds of regulated activity,
3. the needs that consumers may have for advice and accurate information, and

4. the general principle that consumers should take responsibility for their decisions.

From what has been said in this essay, the parallels with gambling products do not need to be further spelled out. Suitably adapted, these principles offer a powerful framework within which decisions concerning how the balance between regulation and competition best ensure fairness for the gambler may be made.

NOTES

1. Colin Scott and Julia Black, eds., *Cranston's Consumers and the Law* (London: Butterworths, 2000), p. 1

2. Department of Trade and Industry (DTI), *Modern Markets: Confident Consumers* (London: Stationery Office, 1999).

3. Department for Culture, Media, and Sport (DCMS), *Gambling Review Report* (London: Stationery Office, 2001).

4. DCMS.

5. For a discussion of the *Review*'s main recommendations and their implications for the commercial gambling market in Great Britain, see David Miers "OFGAM? OFBET? The Regulation of Commercial Gambling as a Leisure Industry," *Entertainment Law* 1 (2002): 19–50. The British government has accepted almost all of its recommendations and has committed itself to their early implementation (DCMS, "A Safe Bet for Success: Modernizing Britain's Gambling Laws" London: Stationery Office, 2002).

6. Productivity Commission, "Report of the Inquiry into Australia's Gambling Industries" [online], http://www.pc.gov.au [1999]; Department of Internal Affairs, *Gaming Reform in New Zealand: Towards a New Legislative Framework* (Wellington, 2001); *National Gambling Impact Study Commission: Final Report* [online], http://www.ngisc.gov [1999].

7. David Miers, "Objectives and Systems in the Regulation of Commercial Gambling," in *Gambling Cultures: Studies in History and Interpretation*, ed. Jan McMillen, (London: Routledge, 1996), pp. 288–311.

8. Stephen Breyer, *Regulation and its Reform* (Cambridge: Harvard University Press, 1982); Anthony Ogus, *Regulation* (Oxford: Clarendon Press, 1994).

9. DCMS.

10. *Financial Services and Markets Act 2000*, sec. 41 and Schedule 6 (London: Stationery Office, 2000).

11. DCMS.

12. It is not possible to prevent off-shore operators from providing gambling media via the Internet, but it is possible to offer jurisdiction-based operators the opportunity to be licensed and thus provide players the guarantee that they are betting with an honest operation.

13. Director General of the National Lottery (OFLOT), *Annual Report* (London: HMSO, 1994–1995).

14. Cory Aronovitz, "To Start, Press the Flashing Button: The Legalization of Video Gambling Devices," in *Gambling, Public Policy and the Social Sciences*, ed. William Eadington and Judy Cornelius (Reno: Institute for the Study of Gambling and Commercial Gaming, University of Nevada, 1997), pp. 621–52.

15. DCMS.

16. Ibid.

17. Scott and Black, eds., *Cranston's Consumers and the Law*, p. 319.

18. DCMS.

19. Productivity Commission, p. 16.11.

20. Ibid., p. 15.11

21. DCMS, Figure 16.i.

22. Productivity Commission, p. 16.17.

23. Ibid., p. 16.11.

24. Ellen Langer. "The Illusion of Control," *Journal of Personality and Social Psychology* 32 (1975): 311–28; Mark Griffiths, " The Role of Cognitive Bias and Skill in Fruit Machine Gambling," *British Journal of Psychology* 85 (1994): 351–69; Alex Blaszczynski, *Overcoming Compulsive Gambling* (London: Robinson Publishing, 1998); Paul Rogers "The Cognitive Psychology of Lottery Gambling: A Theoreical Overview," *Journal of Gambling Studies* 14 (1998): 111–34.

25. Scott and Black, eds., *Cranston's Consumers and the Law*, p. 213.

26. These surpluses are known as economic rents. The question which then arises is how these rents might be allocated, for example, to the public good. William Eadington, "Ethical and Policy Considerations in the Spread of Commercial Gambling," in *Gambling Cultures: Studies in History and Interpretation*, ed. Jan McMillen (London: Routledge, 1996), pp. 243–62.

27. DCMS.

28. Scott and Black, eds., *Cranston's Consumers and the Law*, p. 22.

29. DCMS.

30. Ibid.

31. Sportsbetting is illegal in all but two states (Nevada and Oregon); esti-

mates of the value of the illegal market range from $80 billion to $380 billion. NGISC, pp. 3-9.

32. Kerry Sproston, Bill Erens, and Jim Orford, *Gambling Behavior in Britain: Results from the British Gambling Prevalence Survey* (London: National Center for Social Research, 2000).

33. DCMS.

34. Greg Coman, Barry Evans, and Rob Wooton, *Responsible Gambling: A Future Winner* (Proceedings of the eighth National Association for Gambling Studies Conference, Melbourne, 1997).

35. David Miers, "The Implementation and Impact of Great Britain's National Lottery," *Journal of Gambling Studies* 12 (1996): 343–73.

36. William Eadington, "Issues and Trends in World Gaming," in *Gambling in Canada: Golden Goose or Trojan Horse?* ed. Colin Campbell and John Lowman (Burnaby, B.C.: Simon Fraser University Press, 1989). See also Jeff Dense, "State Lotteries and Public Policy: An Appraisal," in *Gambling, Public Policy and the Social Sciences*, ed. Eadington and Cornelius, pp. 575–606; and Susan Summers, David Honeyman, and James Wattenbarger, "Resource Suppression and Redistribution Effects of an Earmarked State Lottery," in *Gambling, Public Policy and the Social Sciences*, ed. Eadington, and Cornelius, pp. 537–60.

37. Charles Clotfelter and Peter Cook *Selling Hope: State Lotteries in America* (Cambridge: Harvard University Press, 1989); J. Mikesell, "Lotteries in the State Fiscal System," *Journal of Gambling Studies* 6 (1990): 313–30.

38. DCMS.

39. In the United States, state lotteries appeal disproportionately to the poor. Mikesell, "Lotteries in the State Fiscal System"; and Clotfelter, *Selling Hope*. This poses a further problem, in that the evidence suggests that disclosure rules are unlikely to equalize the disadvantages under which they make their purchasing decisions.

40. DCMS.

41. Ibid.; see also Productivity Commission, chap. 17.

42. NGISC.

Section 4

THE "ADDICTION" DEBATE

♥ ♠
♣
10

A CRITICAL VIEW OF PATHOLOGICAL GAMBLING AND ADDICTION

Comorbidity Makes for Syndromes and Other Strange Bedfellows

Howard J. Shaffer

Misery acquaints a man with strange bedfellows.
　　　　　　　　　　—William Shakespeare, *The Tempest*

Recently, there has been increasing focus on pathological gambling, how it develops, and the population segments that might be disproportionately vulnerable to developing this disorder.[1] Throughout the literature on gambling-related problems, scientists, clinicians, and public policy makers alike commonly consider excessive, intemperate or compulsive gambling as an addictive behavior.

Preparation of this essay was supported in part by a grant from the National Center for Responsible Gaming and a grant from the Center for Substance Abuse Treatment (#1U98TI00846). Portions of this essay derive from H. J. Shaffer, "Strange Bedfellows: A Critical View of Pathological Gambling and Addiction," *Addiction* 94, no. 10 (1999): 1445–48.

　　The author extends thanks to Debi LaPlante, Kathleen Scanlan, Chrissy Thurmond, and Joni Vander Bilt for their thoughtful comments on earlier versions of this article. Special thanks to David Korn, who patiently contributed and encouraged me to refine many of the ideas included in this chapter.

When pathological gambling was first included in the diagnostic system of the American Psychiatric Association, the associated diagnostic criteria were derived from the existing criteria for substance use disorders.[2] This development implicitly suggests that the mechanisms responsible for substance use disorders and pathological gambling may be similar. However, since its first appearance in the psychiatric nomenclature, *The Diagnostic and Statistical Manual of Mental Disorders* (DSM) has included pathological gambling among the impulse disorders; substance use disorders were placed in a separate category; interestingly, both types of disorder share symptoms that are associated with impulse dysregulation.[3]

Advances in the diagnostic nomenclature have not prevented controversy and debate. For example, Widiger and Clark recently observed that while DSM-IV (the fourth edition of DSM) "does appear to be a compelling effort at a best approximation to date of such a nomenclature, . . . even its authors have acknowledged that its diagnoses and criterion sets are highly debatable. . . . There might not in fact be one sentence within DSM-IV for which well-meaning clinicians, theorists, and researchers could not find some basis for fault."[4] One of the primary concerns about DSM-IV centers on how it has advanced the reliability of psychiatric diagnosis at the cost of diagnostic validity.[5] That is, different clinicians—or the same clinician on different occasions—can use DSM-IV criteria to evaluate the presence of mental disorders with consistency; but the underlying nature of these disorders remains uncertain.[6] Beginning with DSM-III, an increasing number of observers have been raising important questions about the nature of disorders that are reliably diagnosed.[7] More recently, Constance Holden raised the general question of whether behavioral addictions exist; she then reviewed the mounting evidence supporting this notion and the challenges that remain.[8] These considerations provide the background for the primary focus of this essay: Should pathological gambling be considered an addiction?

The difficulty of this question has more to do, perhaps, with the nature of addiction than with the essence of pathological gambling. To render an informed opinion on this matter, we must be able to define addiction. Social observers have applied the notion of addiction to many and varied human activities,[9] from substance abuse to shopping,[10] eating carrots,[11] and drinking water to intoxication.[12] The contemporary use of "addiction" is almost exclusively applied to substance using behavior patterns that evidence adverse consequences, often including the emergence of neu-roadaptation (i.e., tolerance and withdrawal). Earlier applications of the term *addiction* were less onerous. When scientists began to consider the matter of behavioral addictions, the construct of addiction became more plastic and complex. Raising important questions about the nature of addiction, investigators observed, for example, that in the absence of psy-choactive substance use, excessive behavior patterns, such as pathological gambling, could stimulate the development of neuroadaptation.[13]

On Addiction

Addiction is a lay term often used by scientists. *Dependence* is a more sci-entific term, occasionally used by lay people. While there are many working definitions of addiction, the essence of the construct has remained elusive to nosologists. Consequently, addiction remains an imprecise lay concept not yet welcome in diagnostic manuals like DSM-IV or ICD-10. Recognizing the problems associated with the meaning of addiction, G. E. Vaillant suggested that, instead of seeking a strict opera-tional definition, we should think of alcoholism as we think of mountains and seasons: you know these things when you see them.[14] Clinicians working with gambling disorders often apply similar subjective strategies to its identification.

Contemporary addiction workers have come to think of addictive behavior as having three primary components: (1) some element of craving or compulsion, (2) loss of control, and (3) continuance of the behavior in question in spite of associated adverse consequences. While these dimensions provide a useful map for understanding the elements of addiction, we must remember that the map is not the territory[15] and the diagnosis is not the disease.[16] Although DSM-III and DSM-IV provided a multidimensional map for diagnosing mental disorders, these works improved the reliability of diagnosis at the considerable expense of validity.[17] In response, Alan Leshner, the director of the National Institute for Drug Abuse, asked, "When is addiction addiction?"[18] This question cuts to the heart of the matter: when clinicians and scientists identify a behavior pattern as an addiction, even if they can identify it reliably according to DSM criteria, how do they know that it is indeed an addiction? We can add to this question, when is pathological gambling pathological gambling? Further, does this pattern of behavior justify consideration as an addiction?

For scientists, the concept of addiction represents a troublesome tautology that has contributed to keeping an addiction classification from entering the diagnostic nomenclature. Consequently, the notion of addiction remains a lay concept and a very popular one, indeed. The tautology operates like this: when observers notice adverse consequences, stimulated by repetitive behavior patterns, apparently occurring against the actor's better judgment, they often infer the presence of addiction. A 1991 study concludes:

> The problem is that there is no independent way to confirm that the 'addict' cannot help himself and therefore the label is often used as a tautological explanation of the addiction. The habit is called an addiction because it is not under control but there is no way to distinguish a habit that is uncontrollable from one that is simply not controlled.[19]

Even if we consider substance use disorders and pathological gambling as the leading candidates for addiction status, diagnostic manuals will remain inadequate on the matter of addiction if social consequences and self-report direct the criteria for classification. As organized currently, diagnostic manuals like DSM-IV increase the likelihood that clinicians can repeatedly classify disorders like pathological gambling correctly. However, these systems fail to address the construct validity of what is being classified because the "addictive" disorders are assumed to exist by inference from the consequences of behaviors in question.

Diagnostic systems that rest upon a mix of self-report and corroborating perspectives do not resolve the problem. Individuals struggling with intemperate behavior suffer the burden of the fundamental attribution error.[20] This cognitive error leads actors to the perception that an external object stimulated their excessive behavior (e.g., addictive drugs or addictive gambling); conversely, observers tend to think the cause of intemperance is a relatively stable underlying trait (e.g., weak character or addictive personality). Both perspectives are biased.

Addiction, Gambling, and Gold Standards

For addiction to emerge as a viable scientific construct, whether psychoactive drug use or pathological gambling is the concern, investigators need to establish a "gold standard" against which the presence or absence of the disorder can be judged. Social consensus among scientists is insufficient to establish such a standard, though it can yield a criterion to establish concurrent validity in the absence of a bona fide gold standard. To achieve gold status, the benchmark must be independent of the disorder being judged. As with many psychiatric disorders, pathological gambling does not have an independent gold standard. Absent a gold standard, pathological gambling suffers from the "myth of mental illness" stigma. As Thomas Szasz puts it, "The psychiatric community seems determined to ground its medical legitimacy on principles that confuse diagnoses with diseases."[21] If pathological gambling represents an uncontrollable impulse and not an uncontrolled habit, then there must be independent validation of the irrepressible impulse or the impaired regulatory mechanisms to confirm the diagnosis.[22] Pathological gambling cannot be limited to intemperate bettors who lose more than they win because these gamblers also represent a group who gamble sufficiently often for statistical probability to take its inevitable toll. If pathological gambling represents a primary disorder orthogonal both to its consequences and the laws of probability, then clinicians and scientists should be able to identify the disorder without knowing the winning or losing status of the gambler.

An independent gold standard likely will come from neurogenetic or biobehavioral attributes. Early neuroscience research is encouraging. Dopaminergic and serotinergic functions have been found to be altered among pathological gamblers.[23] Biogenetic vulnerabilities also have been identified among pathological gamblers,[24] and there is evidence to suggest the presence of genetic markers for novelty-seeking behavior among normal people that can predispose these people to take chances.[25] Finally, new evidence suggests that there are common reward circuits in the central nervous system responsible for the experiences associated with such experiences as the anticipation of substance use effects, the acquisition of money, and the appreciation of beauty.[26]

The Strange Bedfellows: Psychiatric Comorbidity and Syndromes

In a recent review, Howard J. Shaffer and David Korn noted that the various versions of the DSM that have included pathological gambling as a distinct disorder have also drawn attention to the possibility that other disorders may coexist with pathological gambling.[27] For example, DSM-IV notes that pathological gamblers

> may be prone to developing general medical conditions that are associated with stress. . . . Increased rates of Mood Disorders, Attention-Deficit Hyperactivity Disorder, Substance Abuse or Dependence, and Antisocial, Narcissistic, and Borderline Personality Disorders have been reported in individuals with Pathological Gambling.[28]

The coexistence of multiple diagnostic entities represents a circumstance known as comorbidity.

Comorbidity presents a challenge to diagnostic classification schemas in general and the DSM system in particular. For example, as R. C. Carson notes, "The frequency of comorbidity in using the DSM indicates that these categorical distinctions are not derived from relatively mutually exclusive, basic invariants. Rather, one is more 'impressed by the extraordinary and obstinate heterogeneity of the . . . diagnostic groupings in terms of putative genotypal correlates.'"[29] Consequently, the current map of mental conditions that are often comorbid may derive more from how clinicians and scientists have constructed the DSM than from the nature of the disorders they evaluate. Similarly, it is difficult to determine whether clinicians and the diagnostic systems that guide their work reflect two primary diagnostic errors: (1) failing to distinguish unique disorders that coexist, thus yielding the diagnosis of a unitary problem, or alternatively, (2) identifying separate, coexisting disorders that do not exist independent of one another. In the first instance, comorbid conditions exist but the diagnosticians and current nosology do not have the capacity to distinguish the uniqueness of these problems; in the second circumstance, the appearance of comorbid conditions is an artifact of the diagnostic schema itself.

Research on treatment seekers further complicates the picture. Clinicians often report that patients who seek treatment for pathological gambling, like casino employees with gambling problems,[30] have a variety of social problems that are caused by gambling. However, treatment seekers are very different from people who have gambling problems but do not seek treatment, typically having a greater variety and intensity of psychological problems than their counterparts.[31] Among those who seek treatment, are the comorbid problems the cause or consequence of pathological gambling?

Because comorbidity reflects the coexistence of gambling with other disorders, this confluence makes it difficult to determine whether (1) gambling behavior causes a "gambling disorder" or (2) other disorders cause intemperate gambling and the problems that often accompany excessive gambling, or (3) both sets of problems reflect another underlying disorder. To illustrate, where X represents a comorbid condition and PG represents a level 3 gambling disorder, seven primary relationships can describe the association between disordered gambling and psychiatric comorbidity.[32]

1. X contributes to, is a risk factor for, or causes PG.
2. X protects against or "treats" the occurrence of or progression to PG.
3. PG contributes to, is a risk factor for, or causes X.
4. PG protects against or "treats" the occurrence of or progression to X.[33]
5. X and PG co-occur or coexist but are coincidental and completely independent.
6. X and PG share common determinants (biological, psychological, behavioral or social).
7. X and PG combined are actually components of some larger entity, disorder, or syndrome.

Despite this map of the complex relationships that can exist between gambling and comorbid disorders,

[r]esearch on psychiatric comorbidity in pathological gambling is still very much in its infancy. Consequently, there is little conclusive evidence to guide our understanding of comorbid disorders and the relationships among these conditions with gambling disorders. Therefore,

there remains a great need for longitudinal studies that can illuminate the development, temporal sequencing and relationships among these co-occurring disorders. While an overlap of symptoms belonging to a variety of diagnostic disorders is common, a more systematic analysis . . . reveals a much more tentative picture.[34]

The following section will examine these complicating factors in more depth.

Is Pathological Gambling a Primary and Unique Disorder?

The research methods associated with promulgating basic estimates of gambling prevalence have not changed much during the past twenty years. Despite exceptions, the National Research Council noted the overall weakness of research methods in the area of gambling studies.[35] Shaffer et al. observed that regardless of the quality of these studies, weak and strong methods seem to produce comparable estimates of disordered gambling prevalence.[37] Nevertheless, two critically important conceptual and methodological issues face the study of gambling and related psychiatric disorders. First, is pathological gambling a primary and unique disorder or a multidimensional syndrome? Second, are existing estimates of disordered gambling prevalence accurate in the absence of a gold standard? These concerns comingle and their confluence affects how we understand gambling disorders. For example, while clinicians may be heeding diagnostic exclusion criteria for purposes of treatment planning, researchers for the most part have simply ignored the implications of exclusion criteria during the conduct of prevalence research.[37]

One of the research consequences of ignoring exclusion recommendations is that prevalence estimates of pathological gambling may be overestimated. In addition, between the publication of DSM-III and DSM-IV, the American Psychiatric Association shifted the exclusion criteria from antisocial personality disorder to mania. This change reflects an ongoing struggle to develop a clear definition of pathological gambling in the absence of a gold standard. Much remains unknown about the nature of the overlap and interaction among, for example, antisocial personality, manic episodes, and pathological gambling. Future research that measures the prevalence of related psychiatric disorders along with pathological gambling will provide important insight into these questions. Ultimately, the field of gambling studies is in need of research that can provide additional construct validity.

If pathological gambling represents a primary disorder, then it can emerge in the absence of other comorbidity and cause sequelae independent of any other condition. However, if it is a secondary disorder subordinate to other dysfunctional behavior, then it will exist only as a consequence of another condition (e.g., manic episode, antisocial personality, alcohol abuse, obsessive-compulsive disorder, or, perhaps, even adolescence). If this is the case, pathological gambling is not a unique disorder but rather a cluster of symptoms associated with one or several other disorders. Although worldwide prevalence estimates of disordered gambling have identified pathological gambling as a relatively stable and robust phenomenon, investigators have not established with ample certainty that this phenomenon represents a *unique* construct. Further, observers have noted that the mere existence of a diagnostic entry into the taxonomy of psychiatric illnesses is not a proxy for the validity of the disorder. As S. J. Blat and I. N. Levy note, "Agreement among a committee of experts and a demonstration of reliability among judges is insufficient evidence of the validity of a diagnostic taxonomy. Operational criteria can lead to the reliability of relatively trivial distinctions that add little to the field."[38] More research on the temporal sequencing of symptoms and disorders,[39] as well as research on discriminant and concurrent validity, is necessary to begin to unravel the complexities and causal implications of the comorbid psychiatric conditions often associated with intemperate gambling. The repercussions of this type of research are significant for the development not only of treatment strategies and plans but also of social policy initiatives designed to ameliorate or regulate gambling-related problems.

Symptoms or Underlying Syndrome

The symptoms associated with pathological gambling reflect a complex syndrome—not a one-dimensional, single disorder. The comorbidity and co-occurrence of pathological gambling with other diagnostic entities may be an artifact of DSM-IV, misdirecting observers away from the likelihood that the condition is better understood as a syndrome. As mentioned earlier, the current diagnostic system often distinguishes disorders that may not exist independent of one another. For example, gambling, substance use disorders, and dysthymia share a variety of characteristics. Instead of reflecting different disorders, the presence of overlapping symptoms may represent a common underlying causal factor or factors. The heterogeneous nature of symptoms associated with gambling problems can present significant difficulties for diagnosticians. When a variety of symptoms may be associated with a disorder but not all the symptoms are always present, a syndrome is in evidence. Acquired Immune Deficiency Syndrome (AIDS) reflects this complex pattern: although an impaired immune system is responsible for an array of possible symptoms, a viral infection is the disease entity responsible for the set of assorted symptoms.

People with gambling disorders also present with many different and varying symptoms; these symptoms are not always present and can vary across individuals. Constructing pathological gambling as a syndrome emphasizes that it has both common and unique components. A syndrome's common component (e.g., depression, anxiety, impulsivity) is shared with other disorders (e.g., substance use disorders) whereas its unique component (e.g., betting increasing amounts of money or chasing) is specific to pathological gambling. The shared components, which accounts for the comorbidity evidence, reflect broad individual differences that can vary along multiple dimensions (e.g., intensity and duration); the unique component distinguishes pathological gambling from other disorders and is specific only to it.[40]

Because gambling disorders have both unique and shared signs and symptoms, pathological gambling is best understood as a syndrome. From this perspective, the most effective treatments for gambling problems will reflect a multimodal "cocktail" approach combined with patient-treatment matching. These multidimensional treatments will include various combinations of psychopharmacology, psychotherapy, financial, educational and self-help interventions: these various treatment elements are both additive and interactive, a circumstance necessary to deal with the multidimensional nature of gambling disorders.

Because syndromes are multidimensional, these disorders typically do not respond favorably to a single treatment modality. Whether we view disordered gambling as primary or secondary, unique or syndromal, intemperate gambling inflicts human suffering. If pathological gambling is a primary disorder, it often will require professional assistance; if it is a disorder secondary to another problem, it still requires specialized modalities focusing on gambling issues in addition to the problems related to the primary disorder. Future research will help clarify these theoretical, research, and clinical issues.

CONCLUSIONS

There is no simple answer to the question of what is an addiction. Therefore, we must approach this issue by considering whether a particular pattern of behavior like pathological gambling qualifies as a unique and distinct addiction with a substantial dose of scientific skepticism and uncertainty. I suggest that we need to refine our definition of addiction. For pathological gambling to find a legitimate home in the psychiatric nomenclature as a primary disorder, people will need to view it as the consequence of overwhelming and uncontrollable impulses, compromised biobehavioral regulatory mechanisms, or a combination of both. Anything short of this redefinition will leave people thinking that pathological gambling is simply the result of uncontrolled "habits." Further, gambling disorders must exist in the absence of other conditions that also can cause similar psychosocial problems if pathological gambling is to be regarded as a real disorder.

Currently, however, even the DSM-IV reflects ambivalence about the psychiatric status and construct validity of pathological gambling. In a cautionary note, the DSM-IV states that

> inclusion here, for clinical and research purposes, of a diagnostic category such as Pathological Gambling or Pedophilia does not imply that the condition meets legal or other nonmedical criteria for what constitutes mental disease, mental disorder, or mental disability. The clinical and scientific considerations involved in categorization of these conditions as mental disorders may not be wholly relevant to legal judgments, for example, that take into account such issues as individual responsibility, disability determination, and competency.[41]

By merely mentioning pathological gambling in this cautionary note,[42] the editors of DSM-IV have purposely or inadvertently removed the full standing of this problem as a psychiatric disorder—rightly or wrongly—with all of its exculpatory power.

In spite of these critical scientific views regarding the nature of addiction and pathological gambling, many gamblers increasingly believe that they are suffering from an uncontrollable impulse to gamble. These people are beginning to seek treatment in greater numbers. New public education and awareness programs have lowered the threshold for identifying problems among excessive gamblers. This trend, coupled with emerging treatment opportunities for gambling-related problems, is bringing more people into treatment and teaching them that they have an addiction. With few rigorously conducted outcome studies available, the efficacy of treatments for disordered gambling remains to be determined. Nevertheless, human suffering deserves our attention and response. Therefore, the clinical issue—as opposed to the scientific and conceptual debate—is not now, nor has it ever been, whether pathological gambling is an addiction or the result of a biobehavioral vulnerability. From a clinical perspective, this issue involves establishing a working formulation that clinicians and patients can share, and which will permit clinicians to select treatment methods that offer patients a favorable prognosis given knowledge of the problem and patient.[43]

For science, the value of improving our understanding of pathological gambling and addiction rests in the development of better theory. Improved theory can guide better research. From a community perspective, as our understanding of addiction and pathological gambling improves, then a vehicle for more effective public policy emerges. From the treatment side, there is little or no value to understanding any individual as addicted or mentally disordered unless that understanding permits clinicians to choose a treatment plan that will maximize the well-being of the patient. The value of the concept of pathological gambling or the classification of any addictive behavior, then, is dependent on the extent to which an individual sufferer benefits from its application. While the art and science of diagnosis is dependent upon comparisons among groups, clinicians should apply their choice of treatments prescriptively. Prescriptive or differential treatment requires consideration of three interactive domains: (1) the physician (medical management strategy); (2) the patient (compliance rules and expectations of care and concern); and (3) society (social mores and attributions of responsibility). Together these domains define the "sickness" that is to be treated.[44] The relationship between pathological gambling and addiction ultimately rests upon socio-cultural acceptability. As Amy Blum states, "It is best to think of any affliction—a disease, a disability—as a text and of 'society' as its author."[45]

NOTES

1. Brian Castellani, *Pathological Gambling: the Making of a Medical Problem* (New York: State University of New York Press, 2000); Renee M. Cunningham-Williams et al., "Problem Gambling and Comorbid Psychiatric and Substance Use Disorders among Drug Users Recruited from Drug Treatment and Community Settings," *Journal of Gambling Studies* 16, no. 4 (2000): 347–76; Jeffrey L. Derevensky and Rina Gupta, "Prevalence Estimates of Adolescent Gambling: A Comparison of the SOGS-RA, DSM-IV-J, and the GA 20 Questions," *Journal of Gambling Studies* 16 (2000): 227–51; Carlo C. DiClemente, Marilyn Story, and Kenneth Murray, "On a Roll: The Process of Initiation and Cessation of Problem Gambling among Adolescents," *Journal of Gambling Studies* 16 (2000); David Korn and Howard J. Shaffer, "Gambling and the Health of the Public: Adopting a Public Health Perspective," *Journal of Gambling Studies* 15, no. 4 (1999): 289–365; James Langenbucher et al., "Clinical Features of Pathological Gambling in an Addictions Treatment Cohort," *Psychology of Addictive Behaviors* 15, no. 1 (2001): 77–79; W. G. McCown and Linda L. Chamberlain, *Best Possible Odds: Contemporary Treatment Strategies for Gambling Disorders* (New York: John Wiley & Sons, 2000); Wendy S. Slutske et al., "Common Genetic Vulnerability for Pathological Gambling and Alcohol Dependence in Men," *Archives of General Psychiatry* 57, no. 7 (2000): 666–73.

2. American Psychiatric Association, *Diagnostic and Statistical Manual of Mental Disorders*, 3rd ed. (DSM-III) (Washington, D.C.: American Psychiatric Association, 1980).

3. American Psychiatric Association, *Diagnostic and Statistical Manual of Mental Disorders*, 3rd ed.; 3rd ed., rev.; 4th ed.; 4th ed., text rev. (Washington, D.C.: American Psychiatric Association, 1980, 1987, 1994, 2000).

4. Thomas A. Widiger and Lee Anne Clark, "Toward DSM-V and the Classification of Psychopathology," *Psychological Bulletin* 126, no. 6 (2000): 946–63.

5. James Barron, ed., *Making Diagnosis Meaningful: Enhancing Evaluation and Treatment of Psychological Disorders* (Washington, D.C.: American Psychological Association, 1988).

6. Jerome C. Wakefield, "The Concept of Mental Disorder: On the Boundary between Biological Facts and Social Values," *American Psychologist* 47 (1992): 373–88.

7. Sidney J. Blat and Kenneth N. Levy, "A Psychodynamic Approach to the Diagnosis of Psychopathology," in *Making Diagnosis Meaningful*, ed. James Barron; Robert C. Carson, "Dilemmas in the Pathway of the DSM-IV," *Journal of Abnormal Psychology* 100 (1991): 302–307; George E. Vaillant, "A Debate on DSM-III: The Disadvantages of DSM-III Outweigh Its Advantages," *American Journal of Psychiatry* 141, no. 4 (1984): 542–45.

8. Constance Holden "Behavioral Addictions: Do They exist?" *Science* 294 (2001): 980–82.

9. Jim Orford, *Excessive Appetites: A Psychological View of Addictions* (New York: John Wiley & Sons, 1985).

10. Gary A. Christenson et al., "Compulsive Buying: Descriptive Characteristics and Psychiatric Comorbidity," *Journal of Clinical Psychiatry* 55, no. 1 (1994): 5–11.

11. Lydek Cerny and K. Cerny, "Can Carrots Be Addictive? An Extraordinary Form of Drug Dependence" *British Journal of Addiction* 87 (1992): 1195–97.

12. L. K. Pickering and G. R. Hogan, "Voluntary Water Intoxication in a Normal Child." *Journal of Pediatrics* 78 (1971): 316–18; L. G. Rowntree, "Water Intoxication," *Archives of Internal Medicine* 32, no. 2 (1923): 157–74.

13. I. Wray and Mark Dickerson, "Cessation of High Frequency Gambling and 'Withdrawal' Symptoms," *British Journal of Addiction* 76 (1981): 401–405.

14. George Vaillant, "On Defining Alcoholism," *British Journal of Addiction* 77 (1982): 143–44.

15. Howard J. Shaffer and M. Robbins, "Manufacturing Multiple Meanings of Addiction: Time-Limited Realities," *Contemporary Family Therapy* 13 (1991): 387–404.

16. Thomas Szasz, "Diagnoses Are Not Diseases," *Lancet* 338 (1991): 1574–76.

17. James Barron, ed., *Making Diagnosis Meaningful*.

18. Alan Leshner "Addiction Is a Brain Disease and It Matters" (paper presented at the New Directions in Gambling Addiction Research, George Washington University, February 1999).

19. Akers, 1991, quoted in John Booth Davies, "Reasons and Causes: Understanding Substance Users' Explanations for Their Behavior," *Human Psychopharmacology* 11 (1996): S39–S48.

20. Lee Ross, "The Intuitive Psychologist and His Shortcomings: Distortions in the Attribution Process," in *Advances in Experimental Social Psychology*, vol. 10, ed. Leonard Berkowitz, (New York: Academic Press, 1977), pp. 173–220.

21. Thomas Szasz, "Diagnoses Are Not Diseases," p. 1574.

22. Pathological gambling is now classified in DSM-IV as an impulse disorder, meaning that it represents an irrepressible impulse—the hallmark of an impulse disorder. Unlike most characterizations of addiction as primarily ego syntonic, clinicians consider impulse disorders like obsessive-compulsive disorder as primarily ego dystonic.

23. Cecillia Bergh, Per Sodersten, and Conny Nordin, "Altered Dopamine Function in Pathological Gambling," *Psychological Medicine* 27 (1997): 473–75; Concetta M. DeCaria, Tomer Begaz, and Eric Hollander, "Serotonergic and Noradrenergic Function in Pathological Gambling," *CNS Spectrums* 3, no. 6 (1998): 38–47.

24. David E. Comings, "The Molecular Genetics of Pathological Gambling," *CNS Spectrums* 3, no. 6 (1998): 20–37.

25. Jonathan Benjamin et al., "Population and Familial Association between the D4 Dopamine Receptor Gene and Measures of Novelty Seeking," *Nature Genetics* 12 (1996): 81–83; Richard P. Ebstein et al., "Dopamine D4 Receptor (D4DR) Exon III Polymorphism Associated with the Human Personality Trait of Novelty Seeking," *Nature Genetics* 12 (1996): 78–80.

26. Itzhak Aharon et al., "Beautiful Faces Have Variable Reward Value: fMRI and Behavioral Evidence," *Neuron* 32 (2001): 537–51; H. C. Breiter et al., "Functional Imaging of Neural Responses to Expectancy and Experience of Monetary Gains and Losses," *Neuron* 30 (2001): 619–39.

27. Howard J. Shaffer and David A. Korn, "Gambling and Related Mental Disorders: A Public Health Analysis," *Annual Review of Public Health*, vol. 23 (Palo Alto: Annual Reviews, Inc., 2002) pp. 171–212.

28. American Psychiatric Association, DSM-IV, p. 616

29. Robert C. Carson, "Dilemmas in the Pathway of the DSM-IV," pp. 302–303.

30. Howard J. Shaffer, Joni Vander Bilt, and Matthew N. Hall, "Gambling, Drinking, Smoking, and other Health Risk Activities among Casino Employees," *American Journal of Industrial Medicine* 36, no. 3 (1999): 365–78.

31. David N. Crockford and Nady el-Guebaly, "Psychiatric Comorbidity in Pathological Gambling: A Critical Review," *Canadian Journal of Psychiatry— (Revue Canadienne de Psychiatrie)* 43, no. 1 (1998): 43–50; Ronald C. Kessler, "Lifetime Co-occurrence of DSM-III-R Alcohol Abuse and Dependence with

Other Psychiatric Disorders in the National Comorbidity Survey," *Archives of General Psychiatry* 54 (1997): 313–21; H. J. Shaffer et al., "Gambling, Drinking, Smoking, and Other Health Risk Activities among Casino Employees."

32. Shaffer and Korn "Gambling and Related Mental Disorders."

33. When pathological gambling "treats" the occurrence of a coexisting disorder or the progression of these problems, gambling serves as a "self-medication"; see, for example, John Khantzian, "The self-Medication Hypothesis of Addictive Disorders: Focus on Heroin and Cocaine Dependence," *American Journal of Psychiatry* 142, no. 11 (1985): 1259–64.

34. Crockford and el-Guebaly, "Psychiatric Comorbidity in Pathological Gambling," p. 48.

35. National Research Council, *Pathological Gambling: A Critical Review* (Washington D.C.: National Academy Press, 1999).

36. Howard J. Shaffer et al., *Estimating the Prevalence of Disordered Gambling Behavior in the United States and Canada: A Meta-analysis* (Boston: Presidents and Fellows of Harvard College, 1997).

37. J. H. Boyd et al., "Exclusion Criteria of DSM-III: A study of Co-occurrence of Hierarchy-Free Syndromes," *Archives of General Psychiatry* 41 (1984): 983–89.

38. Blat and Levy, "A Psychodynamic Approach to the Diagnosis of Psychopathology," p. 81.

39. Howard J. Shaffer and Gabriel B. Eber, "Temporal Progression of Cocaine Dependence Symptoms in the National Comorbidity Survey," *Addiction* (in press).

40. Widiger and Clark, "Toward DSM-V and the Classification of Psychopathology."

41. American Psychiatric Association, DSM-IV, p. xxvii

42. Readers may also consider the social impact of having only one conceptual counterpart, pedophilia, included in this cautionary note.

43. Samuel Perry, Arnold M. Cooper, and Robert Michels, "The Psychodynamic Formulation: Its Purpose, Structure, and Clinical Application," *American Journal of Psychiatry* 144 (1987): 543–50; H. J. Shaffer, "Assessment of Addictive Disorders: The Use of Clinical Reflection and Hypotheses Testing," *Psychiatric Clinics of North America* 9, no. 3 (1986): 385–98.

44. Arthur Kleinman, *The Illness Narratives: Suffering, Healing, and the Human Condition* (New York: Basic Books, 1988).

45. Amy Blum. "The Collective Representation of Affliction: Some Reflections on Disability and Disease as Social Facts," *Theoretical Medicine* 6 (1985): 221–32.

11
PATHOLOGICAL GAMBLING

What's in a Name?
Or, How the United States Got It Wrong

Mark Dickerson

The signature of President Clinton in August 1996 established the National Gambling Impact Study Commission (NGISC) which was to complete "an assessment of pathological and problem gambling, including its impact on individuals, families, businesses, social institutions, and the economy."[1] In completing these duties, the National Research Council of the National Academy of Sciences was to assist the Commission. Here then was a unique opportunity for the research domain of gambling to be critically reviewed by independent distinguished scholars. But what did they do? They modified the brief, stating that "the report focuses on a medical model of gambling problems," and is not concerned with impacts that may arise "untainted by illness." No further clarification or definitions were provided to explain the procedure for distinguishing the "taint of illness" from other impacts arising from gambling. How could such distinguished scholars be so misguided? How could the destructive schisms of alcohol abuse be so readily revisited?

The purpose of this essay is to address these questions in the context of an argument demonstrating how the language in which we frame human behavior and its consequences can either limit or facilitate progress. The end point of the arguments presented here is the recommendation that the "use by" date on the concept of pathological gambling is long past, that the diagnostic label should be dropped from our discourse, and that we use alternative language and models that will more effectively support both

- the evolution of social policy to deal with the harm to individuals and families that can and does arise from gambling, and
- psychological research into the processes that contribute to the occurrence of harmful impacts.

First and foremost, there is no dispute about the existence of the harmful impacts that can arise from a person's involvement in gambling. Since the 1950s this fact has been documented in the literature beyond dispute. Instead the debate is about an apparently far more trivial concern: namely, how to define and conceptualize these harmful impacts and the significant social implications of the models and language preferred. To this end, I will undertake a contrast between Australia and the United States and make the provocative assertion that Australia takes the lead in resolving issues concerned with legalized gambling.

In New South Wales, with an adult population of around three million, there are over 100,000 EGMs (electronic gambling machines), 20 percent of all such machines worldwide.[3] The maximum stake is AU$10 per game at an average rate of play of about thirteen games per minute, and every outcome can range from a loss of AU$10 to a win of AU$100,000 on a linked machine or AU$25,000 on a "stand alone." Such gaming is available in social clubs and hotel bars so that nobody has to travel more than a block in a town or city or a few kilometers in rural districts. This is not resort destination gambling. It is gambling as a regular leisure habit as part of day-to-day living, and 11.4 percent of the population play EGMs one to three times a week.[4]

As ease of access and regularity of use are the basis of every addictive behavior, it is not surprising that the levels of harmful impacts associated with gambling are probably higher in Australia than elsewhere in the world. In Victoria, which has a similar population to New South Wales, an integrated set of problem gambling strategies has been in operation since 1995, including education, community awareness campaigns, a toll-free help line, and specialist counseling services accessible at over 100 sites throughout the state. These strategies are continually refined and supported by systematic research and are arguably the international benchmark for problem gambling.

The past decade in Australia has witnessed the publication of an increasing number of research reports on gambling and its impacts from all disciplinary perspectives. The Institute for Gambling Research at the University of Western Sydney has a research record second to none, and an increasing number of academics and postgraduates have been attracted to the area by substantial research funding and the increasing community interest in and concern with problem gambling. Australia's Productivity Commission (PC) is an independent agency that is the government's principal review and advisory body on microeconomic policy and regulation and whose independence is underpinned by an Act of Parliament.

If such a wealth of expertise and research knowledge exist, why then did Australia not feature prominently in the critical research review completed for the NGISC by the National Research Council? The reason may be that Australia has tended to reject the mental disorder model of the harmful impacts of gambling, avoiding the use of the term "pathological gambling,"[5] and preferring the term "problem gambling" instead. Consequently, almost all Australian social policy and research has risked the inclusion of impacts of gambling "untainted by illness" and therefore not to be considered by the NRC. Fortunately, as the "taint of illness" was never defined, some Australian research findings slipped past the barrier.

A consideration of key social policy and research themes shows how the choice of "pathological gambling" or "problem gambling" has had extensive implications resulting in very different responses in the United States and in Australia to the impacts of gambling. The reports of the United States and Australia provide an immediate contrast: the former is thoroughly inconsistent, while the latter is an invaluable researcher's handbook and likely to remain so for perhaps a decade.

The topic will be considered in two main sections, one dealing with the definition and measurement of the negative impacts of gambling, and the other analysing the responses of government, the community, and the gambling industry to deal with the impacts of gambling. Each section will compare and contrast how the two different ways of conceptualizing the impacts of gambling have resulted in very different outcomes.

THE DESCRIPTION AND MEASUREMENT OF THE NEGATIVE IMPACTS OF GAMBLING

Definitions of Pathological and Problem Gambling

In 1980, for the first time, the *Diagnostic and Statistical Manual of the American Psychiatric Association* (DSM-III) included criteria for pathological gambling. The most recent version, from DSM IV, follows:

A: Persistent and recurrent maladaptive gambling behavior as indicated by five (or more) of the following:

1. is preoccupied with gambling,
2. needs to gamble with increasing amounts of money in order to achieve the desired excitement,
3. has repeated unsuccessful efforts to control, cut back, or stop gambling,
4. is restless or irritable when attempting to cut down or stop gambling,
5. gambles as a way of escaping from problems or of relieving a dysphoric mood (e.g., feelings of helplessness, guilt, anxiety, depression),
6. after losing money gambling, often returns another day to get even ("chasing" one's losses),
7. lies to family members, therapists, or others to conceal the extent of involvement with gambling,
8. has committed illegal acts such as forgery, fraud, theft, or embezzlement to finance gambling,
9. has jeopardized or lost a significant relationship, job, or educational career opportunity because of gambling,
10. relies on others to provide money to relieve a desperate financial situation caused by gambling.

B: The gambling behavior is not better accounted for by a manic episode.[6]

What the DSM-IV report means by "maladaptive" remains for me obscure. Even if the core addictive theme of impairment of control over time and money expenditure is considered, this is not necessarily maladaptive. In other leisure pursuits, participation may be enhanced by loose budgetary control; similarly, gambling may be more fun and pleasurable for some players when conducted in an out-of-control manner. This would be common to other leisure pursuits for which strict budgets may also be ignored.

These diagnostic criteria are used by trained clinicians to decide whether a person is suffering from the supposed mental disorder "pathological gambling."

The NRC accepted the DSM-IV's criteria without reviewing any theoretical or conceptual criticisms of this mental disorder approach despite the wealth of literature in the area.[7]

The leading contemporary critic, Jerry Wakefield of Rutgers University, has been especially critical of similar diagnostic criteria for substance dependence/abuse.[8] For example, criterion 9 for pathological gambling, which refers to jeopardizing or losing a significant relationship because of gambling, is almost identical to the item for Substance Abuse about which Wakefield argued: "This criteria is inconsistent with DSM-IV's own definitions of mental disorder which asserts that symptoms must not be due to conflict with society." He continues, "[Y]our spouse can now give you a mental disorder simply by arguing with you about it, and can cure you by becoming more tolerant!"[9] Wakefield also notes the public embarrassment for DSM-IV recently in when American tobacco companies, debating about whether smokers suffer from a true addictive mental disorder, held up the criteria for substance dependence to public ridicule. It is quite possible that a similar scenario could happen for the diagnosis of pathological gambling.

The NRC considered none of this literature, and its discussion of the DSM-IV was both inaccurate and uncritical. For example, the report states that: the diagnostic cut-off of five symptoms was set by the expert committee. In fact, that committee recommended a cut-off of four symptoms and this recommendation was changed to five by the central, non-specialist committee (i.e. it was a political, not a medical, decision). The three "clusters or dimensions" of symptoms are described, but there is no mention that these "clusters or dimensions" have not been supported by the two factor analytic studies published to date. Moreover, the report states that "DSM-IV criteria [of pathological gambling]) appear to have worked well for clinicians for the past five years,"[10] but no evidence is presented to support this assertion.

In contrast, the Productivity Commission observed that the above "medicalized" perspective of gambling impacts had been challenged, not only by Australian researchers but also by American researchers preferring a broader epidemiological model that includes the environment in which the gambling takes place in the causal chain.[11] The report listed a number of concerns about the limitations of the medical model, one of which resonated with what Wakefield identified as the main issue concerning the DSM-IV, the tendency for the diagnostic criteria to be over-inclusive:

> [G]ambling has much greater social acceptability in Australia than in the United States and a wider spectrum of gambling behaviors are regarded as perfectly normal. . . . [T]he use of judgments about problematic behavior based on another country's norms runs the risk of mislabeling some people as ill when they are not.[12]

This is not to say that the issue of subjective control over one's gambling behavior is not important or relevant to psychological research, or to the person in distress from the harm arising from his or her gambling. It clearly is. But there is no necessary link between uncontrolled gambling and a mental disorder. The same arguments can be developed for all the idiosyncratic ways in which people participate in gambling activities. There is not maladaptive gambling, there is simply gambling.

To turn to the DSM-IV criteria themselves, which the NRC report accepted without question, two separate studies have shown that the first and main factor accounting for about a third of the variance is best identified as preoccupation.[13] The remaining criteria are a heterogenous list of items that form no identifiable clusters. According to the DSM-IV, one risks a mental disorder by becoming preoccupied with one of the most popular leisure activities. In the Australian context, the overinclusive nature of this criterion seems very probable, and this concern will be taken up in the next section where I examine the measurement of the harmful impacts of gambling.

If criteria 3, 5, and 6 of the DSM-IV are considered, then research has demonstrated how common all such features are among samples of frequent gamblers who prefer continuous forms of gambling.[14] These criteria fail to distinguish between the normal experiences of people who regularly (weekly or more often) play electronic game machines (EGMs), bet off-course on races, or gamble at casinos and those actually experiencing harmful impacts, whom the DSM system was designed to identify as having a mental disorder.

The avoidance of these faulty criteria may not come without some costs. The PC notes that the failure to use pathological gambling as the basis for the development of treatment services runs the risk of not allocating adequate resources and that the use of problem gambling may seem to "downplay the significance of the harmful impacts generated by gambling."[15] Nonetheless, the report used problem gambling thereafter because the mental disorder model was seen as too restrictive.

"Problem gambling" has been defined by Dickerson et al. as: "the situation in which a person's gambling activity gives rise to harm to the individual player, and/or to his or her family, and may extend into the community."[16] This definition has the appearance of logic, but from a research perspective the operational definition of "harm" is likely to be very complex, and as the authors pointed out, will vary according to the perspective of the judge and from context to context. The definition does, however, shift the debate away from arguments about exactly how many "problem gamblers" there are to focus on the crucial issue of preventing, reducing and dealing with all harmful impacts of gambling.

The Measurement of Pathological and Problem Gambling

Regardless of the definition chosen for "problem gambing," once it was known that gambling could cause harm to individuals and families, one major concern for all stake-holders—government, community, and the gambling industry—was to discover how many pathological or problem gamblers there are (i.e., what percentage of the population was affected).

Despite its failing in other areas, the NRC report provides an authoritative and detailed account of the requirements for the development of measures for use in prevalence studies and concludes: "Validity also relates to sensitivity and specificity: if a net is thrown out, it must have mesh small enough to catch the cases of interest, but large enough to let escape those that do not have the attribute being sought."[17]

The best known "net" is the questionnaire called the 'SOGS' (South Oaks Gambling Screen),[18] designed to detect pathological gamblers. Details of psychological testing are usually the fine print that nobody reads, but we need to look at how such a net works in order to understand some of the major problems in measuring prevalence. When the senior author of the SOGS, Henry Lesieur, designed the test/net, he fished in an artificial pond of a set of known pathological gamblers ("known" because they were in treatment and had been very carefully assessed) and a roughly equal number of people who were known not to be cases of pathological gambling (in fact 58 percent were 'normal'; volunteer hospital staff, etc.). Using a test/net under 50:50 conditions is the best way of seeing whether your net is any good at all. With no net you have a random chance of knowing whether the person you catch is a pathological gambler; you could toss a coin with equal success. If your net tells you anything at all about pathological gambling, then the odds should shift to favor a better chance of correct identification. In fact the SOGS does this very well, identifying 98 percent of the pathological gamblers and catching only 3.6 percent of the normal group along with them in what are called "false positives."

The problem is that the net has since been used almost exclusively to fish in ponds where there are about 1 to 2 percent of pathological gamblers (i.e., the general population, using previous attitude studies to estimate what the prevalence is likely to be).[19] When there are proportionally so very many more fish who are not pathological gamblers, we would expect the net to come up with many fish besides the actual cases we are after. This is exactly what happens, and calculations show that these normal fish predominate in four out of every five cases.[20] However, the net is very good at not letting slip any fish who really are pathological gamblers; the false negatives tend to zero.

Results like these essentially are what the NRC was referring to when it specified the need for sensitivity and specificity; i.e., the ability of the net/test to detect the pathological gambler and to exclude those who are only problem gamblers. Unfortunately, the NRC then included two sets of prevalence data: their own reworking of all the previous U.S., studies included in a published meta-analysis,[21] and the most recent national study, which had used a new test (with the acronym of the National Opinion Research Center Diagnostic Screen for Gambling Problems [NODS]) designed to detect pathological gambling. In neither case did it address the issues of sensitivity or specificity although the possible level of false positives is a major concern for both sets of results. Perhaps the estimate for the United States of 1.1 percent of adults being pathological gamblers, based on the NODS needs a correction similar to that provided by the SOGS in order to account for the false positives.

Fortunately, and perhaps ironically in the context of this discussion, the SOGS has been used extensively here, too, despite the preference for problem rather than pathological gambling in Australia. The PC prevalence estimates ranged up to 2.55 percent for New South Wales, the state where EGMs were most prolific. The SOGS was used in this study and in earlier ones to provide international comparisons and from the lack of any other test. However, some attempt was made to correct for the rate of false positives first by raising the cutoff point on the test to define cases in which one could be confident that the person was experiencing severe harmful impacts of gambling, and second by using the recommended cutoff to indicate an "at risk" population.

Thus on the face of it the decision to avoid the mental disorder model and prefer the problem gambling model might appear to have had little effect on how researchers went about actually measuring the harmful impacts of gambling in Australia. In fact, the content of all so-called prevalence studies in Australia included detailed questions covering all the possible harms that might arise from gambling,

- interpersonal impacts such as depression and the disruption of relationships
- financial, debts and excessive losses
- employment impacts such as loss of productivity or loss of ajob
- legal impacts such as misappropriation of money.

The survey completed by the PC itself used a twenty-two-item "harm indicator," which it used concurrently to evaluate how best to interpret the

SOGS and other data. The development of a new measure derived from the definition of problem gambling, in terms of harm to themselves and others is very recent[22] and has yet to be rigorously tested in population surveys.

Researchers in Australia during the 1990s, may have had greater freedom to detail concerns about whether the SOGS was accurate or not. Certainly when the recommended U.S. derived cutoffs were used, a prevalence rate of over 6 percent was found, suggesting a level of harm that simply did not make sense in terms of what clinicians and social scientists were able to observe in the community. When the SOGS scores were considered alongside the survey respondents' reported gambling behavior, it appeared that the test was failing to distinguish between ordinary regular gamblers who were not experiencing any harmful impacts and those who were; the SOGS was, like its underlying theory, over-inclusive, confirming pathology where there was none.

Perhaps the Australian researchers felt freer than the Americans because in the United States prevalence studies were part of the argument about whether funding was needed to deal with the harmful impacts of gambling and whether legalization of additional forms of gambling should proceed. In Australia in contrast, the majority of prevalence studies were funded after states had decided to increase the availability of legalized gambling (especially EGMs) and had already committed funds to the development of problem gambling services and other harm reduction/prevention strategies. The first prevalence studies in Australia were therefore essentially detailed descriptive base lines from which any changes in harmful impacts would be estimated.

As research progressed, it became quite evident that the harmful impacts arising from gambling could be adequately monitored only by considering prevalence studies as just one part of the picture. At least five other data sources were needed to complete it: the Australian Gambling Statistics, which annually give per capita spending by gambling product and by state; household expenditure surveys; community patterns of gambling; calls to the toll-free help line for gamblers, and finally the annual data analysis of clients attending problem gambling counseling services.[23]

RESPONSES TO GAMBLING

The differences in the prevailing political and social contexts probably had a very significant impact not only on the language in which the definitions were couched but especially on the social policy and related strategies that were developed to deal with the impacts of gambling.

The late Robert Custer, M.D. played the pivotal role in ensuring that pathological gambling was included in the DSM-III. His professional background in the treatment of alcoholism ensured close links to the traditional conceptualization of gambling as an illness. This view is clearly reflected in his adaptation of the Jellinek stages of alcoholism[24] to the development of pathological gambling. At that time the American Psychiatric Association held that it was unethical for therapists treating alcoholics to espouse any treatment goal other than abstinence; the condition was regarded as an illness from which there was no recovery. It is in this context that the first research trial of controlled drinking as an alternative treatment came under criticism and the researchers subjected to the charge of falsifying their data.[25] These charges were never substantiated despite several independent highlevel inquiries in both the United States and Canada. The quality of the research had been exemplary.

The real problem was that the paradigm of controlled drinking as an alternative successful outcome for alcoholics did not fit with the existing model of alcoholism as an illness, with its entrenched social and political forces. This resistance remains today in some quarters despite the indisputable evidence worldwide that many alcoholics do indeed achieve controlled levels of drinking later in their lives.

That this traditional approach to the addictions generally remains the dominant paradigm in the United States today can be seen simply from the relative absence of harm-minimization strategies; the concern being that they implicitly support an addictive behavior. Within this paradigm, the imperative is that the pathology be stopped, removed, and treated, and that the cause itself be eliminated.

The strategies that flow from this conceptualization are very limited. An example can be found in New Zealand, where the policy development regarding gambling-related harm has been the responsibility of a committee that is permitted to fund services for clients only when it can be shown that they satisfy the DSM diagnosis of pathological gambling. If this restriction was applied to existing client services in Australia, over a quarter of all clients would be denied access to treatment.[26]

In Australia, the research infrastructure for the addictions generally is perhaps among the best in the world and has been particularly strong in developing harm minimization strategies. The combination of this solid research with the preference for the term, "problem gambling" has resulted in the development of social policy dealing with the harmful impacts of gambling that seems infinitely preferable to the pathologizing of the impacts. It also has at the core the essential collaboration between government, the community, and the gambling industry, with the government sometimes playing a leading role despite its obvious conflict of interest as the recipient of 12 to 16 percent of tax revenue from gambling. The strategies developed have had three interlocking themes:

- direct services (including a toll-free phone line)
- education and community awareness
- proactive harm-minimization strategies

In my experience, the language of "pathology" elicits defensiveness from the industry and a strong incentive to challenge the accuracy of the estimated prevalence of this pathology. The community may be drawn into this dispute, in conflict with the industry, leaving the government to find some acceptable middle ground that does justice to community concerns and yet permits a viable commercial opportunity for the industry.

Each collaborator has shown commitment to particular themes, with the government often taking a leadership role in the planning and development of strategies and in the allocation of significant funding, the community and NGOs tending to provide services and to influence the content and direction of all strategies, and the gambling industry generally supportive and engaged, often providing skilled advice in areas such as advertising, but, in particular, involving itself in the development of proactive, venue-based strategies of harm minimization, which more recently have been categorized as "responsible gaming" strategies.

In Australia, patron care is a well-established theme with regard to alcohol, and both the hotel industry and government have supported responsible marketing. In this context, the Codes of Practice for Gaming Machines, together with an operationally independent secretariat to monitor its results and handle complaints, seems a very natural next step for the gaming industry in Victoria to have taken.

Eliminating the concept of pathological gambling should not be interpreted as an easy way out for the industry or for governments: the industry's codes of practice and its public involvement in harm-minimization demonstrate a level of commitment to patron care higher than anywhere else in the world. Eliminating pathological gambling provides a more flexible approach that opens rather than closes doors on strategies, and certainly does not mean that these are supportive of industry development. It also provides a means of determining an accurate prevalence rate. In Australia, for example, taking the SOGS and a score of five or more as the "definition" of a problem gambler gives a prevalence of 2 percent for the general adult population, 4.67 percent for all EGM players, and 22.59 percent for frequent EGM players.[27]

Thus a flexible use of the SOGS can generate evidence that places the industry in the position of having to produce strategies that use its regular player base as something other than the key group to whom they direct their marketing. Currently in Australia the industry is having to decide whether its own provision of gaming implies that it must take extra precautions to safeguard this group of players, and indeed they may be required to do so under duty of care.

CONCLUSIONS

At a conference in Las Vegas in 2000 I commented that my publications thus far would confirm my lack of ability to anticipate or forecast the future directions that research into problem gambling would take. In the late 1980s, I wrote a piece entitled: "The Future of Gambling Research: Learning the Lessons of Alcoholism." In that paper I suggested that in the gambling domain we had avoided the schisms that had been so costly in relation to abstinence versus controlled drinking and the underlying competing explanatory models. How wrong could I be?

I went on to discuss ways in which the politics or polemics of current debates may slow rather than halt research development. My starting point was 1998 when most readers of the *Journal of Gambling Studies* had received their Winter edition, (part 4 of volume 13). When I opened this edition, I was at a loss to understand why the contents were given over to a debate about whether researchers had to be for or against gambling. Titles included "The Courage to Be Counted" and " Pursuing an Agenda for Mature Analysis."

Subsequently my own work was criticized, not regarding its accuracy or validity but because it questioned and speculated on whether there was yet adequate scientific data to prove that gambling caused many of the harmful impacts attributed to it. The criticism arose from a delegate very much aware that the funding base for treatment in his own jurisdiction would be threatened if the evidence for pathological gambling were weakened.

It is interesting to note that since that time there has been a trend to rename organizations responsible for the provision of services to deal with the harmful impacts of gambling, and the mental disorder terms are being rejected in favor of "problem gambling" or "responsible gambling." Why? To enable the organizations to develop more wide-ranging harm-prevention strategies and not be restricted to the provision of client treatment services.

It is a nice irony that the very first organization to change its name— the National Council on Compulsive Gambling, which became the National Council on Problem Gambling many years ago—was itself United States based.

The political pressures that more strongly surround researchers in the United States have made the development of collaborative strategies with the gambling industry very hazardous. In Canada, the United Kingdom, and Australia, but not in the United States, there is an emerging research literature that uses regular gamblers as respondents for surveys and in studies,[28] many of which provide unique insights not only into how psychological processes erode a gambler's ability to control his or her time and money but also into the psychological causes of addictive behaviors generally.

The conduct of this research is usually dependent on collaboration and support from venue staff and the industry at the local level. In the United States such collaboration would be difficult to do without acrimonious and heated public debate. This circumstance is regrettable, as it is just this kind of careful empirical research that the NRC, correctly this time in my opinion, noted was needed for a better understanding of problem/pathological gambling.

Perhaps the NRC itself got caught up in political pressures. But how in writing a "critical review" could twenty-eight academics, as well as a quality-control group of thirteen more experts, fail to get the basics right: specifying its literature search methods and making transparent the criteria used to reduce the original 4,000 references to the final 300? Perhaps it was simply a case of too many cooks, but whatever the reasons, a golden opportunity was squandered.

NOTES

1. National Gambling Impact Study Commission (NGISC), *Final Report* (Washington, D.C.: Government Printing Office, 1999).

2. National Research Council, *Pathological Gambling: A Critical Review* (Washington, D.C.: National Academy Press, 1999), p. 38.

3. Productivity Commission, *Australia's Gambling Industries: Final Report* (Canberra: Commonwealth Government, 1999).

4. Ibid.

5. American Psychiatric Association *Diagnostic and Statistical Manual of Mental Disorders*, 4th ed. (DSM-IV) (Washington D.C.: 1994).

6. Ibid.

7. T. Schachter and P. E. Nathan, "But Is It Good for the Psychologists? Appraisal and Status of DSM-III," *American Psychologist* 32 (1977): 1017–25; Hans J. Eysenck, "A Critique of Contemporary Classification and Diagnosis," in *Contemporary Directions in Psychopathology: Toward the DSM-IV*, ed. Theodore Millon and Gerald Klerman (New York: Guilford, 1986), pp.73–98.

8. See, for example, Jerome S. Wakefield, "Diagnosing DSM-IV, part 1: DSM-IV and the Concept of Disorder," *Behavior Research and Therapy* 36 (1997): 633–49.

9. Wakefield "Diagnosing DSM-IV."

10. NGISC, *Final Report*, p. 27.

11. Robert Politzer, C. Yesalis, and C. Hudak, "The Epidemiologic Model and the Risks of Legalized Gambling: Where Are We Headed?" *Journal of Health Behavior, Education, and Promotion* 16 (1992): 20–27.

12. Productivity Commission, *Australia's Gambling Industries,* p. 6.6.

13. Sue Fisher, *Gambling and Problem Gambling among Casino Patrons* (report to the British Casino Industry Consortium, 1996), in the United Kingdom with casino players; and Rachel Volberg, *Gambling and Problem Gambling in New York: A Ten-Year Replication Study, 1986–1996* (report to the New York Council on Problem Gambling, 1996), in New York with a large sample from the general population.

14. See, for example, Mark G. Dickerson et al., *Study 2 (Repeat): An Examination of the Socio-Economic Effects of Gambling on Individuals, Families, and the Community, Including Research into the Costs of Problem Gambling in New South Wales* (report to the Casino Community Benefit Fund Trustees, New South Wales Government, 1998); Tony Schellinck and Tracy Schrans, *Nova Scotia VL Players' Survey* (report completed by Focal Research Consultants Ltd. for the Nova Scotia Department of Health, Halifax, Nova Scotia, 1998).

15. Productivity Commission, *Australia's Gambling Industries*, p. 6.7.

16. M. G. Dickerson et al., *Definition and Incidence of Problem Gambling Including the Socio-economic Distribution* (report to the Victorian Casino and Gaming Authority, Victoria, British Columbia, 1997).

17. National Research Council, *Pathological Gambling*, p. 47.

18. Henry Lesieur and Sheila B. Blume, "The South Oaks Gambling Screen (the SOGS): A New Instrument for the Identification of Pathological Gamblers," *American Journal of Psychiatry* 144 (1987):1184–88.

19. Maureen Kallick et al., *A Survey of American Gambling Attitudes and Behavior* Research Report series (Ann Arbor: University of Michigan Press, 1987).

20. Mark G. Dickerson, "A Preliminary Exploration of a Two-Stage Method in the Assessment of the Extent and Degree of Gambling Related Problems in the Australian Community," in *Gambling Behavior and Problem Gambling*, ed. William Eadington, Judy Cornelius, and Julian Taber (Reno: Reno Institute for the Study of Gambling and Commercial Gaming, University of Nevada, 1993), pp. 336–47.

21. Howard J. Shaffer, Matthew N. Hall, and Joni Vander Bilt, *Estimating the Prevalence of Disordered Gambling Behavior in the United States and Canada: a Meta-analysis* (Boston: Harvard Medical School, Division on Addictions, 1997).

22. David I. Ben-Tovim et al., *The Victorian Gambling Screen* (Melbourne, Victoria: Gambling Research Panel, 2001).

23. Mark G. Dickerson et al., *Definition and Incidence of Problem Gambling*.

24. E. M. Jellinek, "The Phases of Alcohol Addiction," *Quarterly Journal*

of Studies on Alcohol 13 (1952): 673–84.

25. Mark B. Sobell and Linda C. Sobell, "Individualised Behavior Therapy for Alcoholics," *Behavior Therapy* 4 (1973): 49–72.

26. Alan C. Jackson et al., *Client and Service Analysis Report No. 6: Analysis of Clients Presenting to Problem Gambling Services from July 1st 2000 to June 30th 2001*, (Victoria: Department of Human Services, 2001).

27. Productivity Commission, *Australia's Gambling Industries.*

28. Mark G. Dickerson and Ellen Baron, "Contemporary Issues and Future Directions for Research into Pathological Gambling," *Addiction* 95, no. 8 (2000): 1145–60.

♥♠♣

12

IS GAMBLING AN ADDICTION LIKE DRUG AND ALCOHOL ADDICTION?

Developing Realistic and Useful Conceptions of Compulsive Gambling

Stanton Peele

News Item

On May 9, 2000, the seven-state "Big Game" lottery provided a prize of $366 million. The odds of winning were 76 million to 1. In the days before the lottery sales outlets were overrun with people buying hundreds of dollars worth of tickets. The weekend before the lottery was held, 35 million tickets were sold. Annually, Americans spend $36 billion on lotteries.

A version of this paper was originally published in the *Electronic Journal of Gambling Issues: eGambling* 3 (February 2001) [online], http://www.camh.net/egambling/issues 3/feature/index.html. Copyright 2003, Centre for Addiction and Mental Health, Toronto, Ontario.

THE PURPOSE AND DEVELOPMENT OF ADDICTION THEORY

n 1975, I proposed as a general theory of addiction in *Love and Addiction*[1] that any powerful experience in which people can lose themselves can serve as the object of an addiction. The result of this immersion is deterioration of the person's engagement with the rest of his or her life, which increases the person's dependence on the addictive object or involvement. Certain people are far more prone to form such addictive involvements—those with tenuous connections to other activities and relationships and whose values do not rule out antisocial, destructive activities.

Initially, both scientists and alcohol and drug addicts thought that the expansion of the addiction concept to such nonsubstance-based activities cheapened and minimized the value of the idea of addiction. At the same time, the popularity of the idea of nondrug addictions grew through the 1980s and beyond. This trend was fueled by the growing claims by many people who gambled destructively that they were equally at a loss to control their involvement with gambling and suffered just as much pain and loss in their lives as those destructively devoted to drugs and alcohol (and quite a few of these individuals shared gambling and substance addictions).

Since then, successive editions of the *Diagnostic and Statistical Manual* of the American Psychiatric Association have recognized compulsive (called "pathological") gambling (beginning with DSM-III in 1980). But the concept has continued to require fine-tuning, and even some major revisions, in the DSM diagnostic criteria. At the same time, some analysts continue to question whether compulsive gambling qualifies for genuine "disease" status, whether withdrawal from gambling occurs, and why many people diagnosed as pathological gamblers have no sense that that they have a gambling problem.

In fact, these fundamental objections to gambling addiction are actually commonplace questions raised with alcohol and drug addiction. These objections do not disqualify gambling as an addiction. Instead, gambling sheds light on the fundamental dynamics of addiction: (1) addiction is not limited to drug and alcohol use; (2) spontaneous remission is commonplace, and, indeed, even active—"nonrecovered" addicts show considerable variability in their behavior; and (3) fundamental addictive experiences and motivations for addiction are readily apparent in gambling, and gambling even helps to clarify the motivations of drug and alcohol addicts.

In the effort to make sense about addiction, gambling researchers and theorists fall prey to the reductionist fallacy that typifies theorizing in addiction about drugs and alcohol. Blaszczynski and McConaghy, for example, referred to data showing that there is not a distinct variety of pathological gambler but rather that gambling problems occur along a continuum, as an indication that a disease model of gambling addiction does not succeed. They then cited some preliminary findings of physiological differences that might characterize pathological gamblers as potentially strong support for the disease model.[2]

This logic is exactly backwards—with drugs and with gambling. If a model does not begin to explain the behavior in question, then any number of associations with biological mechanisms and measurements will fail to provide an explanation (and, by extension, a solution) for the problem. Science is the creation of accurate and predictive models, not an exercise in laboratory virtuosity to show, for example, how drugs impact neurochemical systems. No work of this kind will ever explain the most basic elements of addiction, including that many people show the ability to be addicted to an array of dissimilar substances and activities, that different people react differently to the same addictive activities and substances even though the same neurological systems are implicated for all these individuals, and—most patently—that people addicted to an involvement at one time and place cease to be addicted at a different time and place.[3]

GAMBLING IS ADDICTIVE; IT IS NOT A DISEASE

Defining Addiction

Saying gambling is addictive but not a medical disease begs for definitions of "addiction" and "disease." The essential element of addiction to gambling is that people become completely absorbed in the activity, which they then pursue in a compulsive manner, leading to extremely negative life outcomes. These individuals often describe a loss of control, such that, they claim, they are incapable of avoiding gambling or of ceasing after having started. All of these elements of addiction are behavioral, experiential, and phenomenological.

The disease model, on the other hand, looks to an inescapable biological source for addictions, such that some neurochemical adaptation accounts for the observed compulsive behavior. In addition, a disease model posits, these neurochemical adjustments lead to measurable tolerance and withdrawal. Because the biological systems underlying the addiction are thought to be irreversible, the disease model includes the idea of progressive worsening of the addiction, with the requirement that some kind of treatment is necessary in order to cease addiction.

Obviously, an experiential model of addiction is much easier to observe. All it requires is that people sacrifice their lives to gambling and that they assert or believe they cannot resist the urge to do so. Evidence for this model is provided nightly at Gamblers Anonymous meetings, where compulsive gamblers sincerely attest that they have sacrificed everything to their addiction and that they had no control over their habit. On the other hand, all of the elements of the medical (disease) model of addiction can be questioned, and indeed, in many cases have been explicitly disproved. Where addiction theorists and gambling researchers err is that, while finding compulsive gambling to fall short of attaining the status of a medical disease, they then discount its genuine addictiveness. In doing so, they often assume that alcohol and drug addictions fulfill criteria for an addictive disease that gambling fails to meet.

Diagnostic Studies of Gamblers in Comparison with Substance Abusers

Wedgeworth found that "patients coming into treatment do not fit the addictive disease conception of gambling behavior."[4] He interviewed (both directly and through examination of autobiographies created for treatment) twelve patients admitted to a private inpatient treatment center who were diagnosed as pathological gamblers. Yet he found the hospital patients did not meet criteria of "compulsive" gambling. Rather, he found that individuals were diagnosed for practical purposes, in order to fulfill insurer criteria while allowing gamblers to repair their personal relationships. Nonetheless, in the one case most extensively described, the patient "had burned all his bridges"—separating from his wife, losing his job, and facing embezzlement charges.[5]

To discover that those receiving hospital treatment for addiction frequently do not meet the full criteria for addiction in no way distinguishes inpatient gambling patients from alcohol and drug patients. Research has found for decades that intakes in heroin treatment centers often reveal negligible (or sometimes no) signs of opiate consumption, and that private drug and alcohol centers commonly admit anyone who shows up for intake in order to fill their treatment rolls. In 1999 the founder of the American Society of Addiction Medicine, G. Douglas Talbott, was found liable for fraud, malpractice, and false imprisonment for coercing into treatment a physician who was not alcohol dependent.[6]

Orford, Morison, and Somers compared problem drinkers with problem gamblers by employing an attachment scale, which found that problem drinkers and gamblers were equally devoted to their habits. But drinkers scored significantly higher on a severity-of-dependence scale, including both psychological and physical components of withdrawal.[7] For Orford et al., these findings call for a refocusing on subjective states rather than on withdrawal symptoms as indicators of addiction. The Orford view that addiction is best understood from an experiential and behavioral perspective is close to the position I take. However, I believe that symptoms of addiction, including withdrawal and tolerance, are simply behavioral manifestations of the same attachment that Orford et al. measured.[8]

There are reasons not to accept that withdrawal and tolerance are absent in gambling addiction, or at least any more so than they are in alcohol and drug addictions. Wray and Dickerson claimed that gamblers frequently manifest withdrawal, although their definition of withdrawal as restlessness and irritability might be questioned.[9] However, classic studies of withdrawal have found that even heavy narcotics users manifest extremely variable symptoms, which are highly subject to suggestion and environmental manipulation.[10] Moreover, the recent WHO/NIH Cross-Cultural Applicability Research Project found that withdrawal and other alcohol-dependence symptoms varied tremendously from cultural site to cultural site.[11]

Thus, Orford et al.'s view that dependence symptoms exist objectively and that factors such as treatment experiences and social learning do not determine their prevalence is not well-founded.[12] Indeed, Orford and Keddie showed that a subjective scale of dependence and prior treatment and AA experiences yielded better predictive models of alcoholism treatment outcomes (particularly with regard to the achievement of controlled drinking) than did the same severity-of-dependence measure Orford et al. used for the purpose of differentiating gambling from drinking problems.[13] In addition, DSM-IV changed the criteria for substance disorders so that the manifestation of tolerance and withdrawal is not essential for a diagnosis of dependence.

Thus, while I remain highly sympathetic to Orford and his colleagues' view that an essential element of addiction is the experience of attachment, I find the distinction they draw between an attachment-based definition of addiction and manifestations of withdrawal and tolerance unjustified and unnecessary.

DISTRIBUTION, CONTINUITY, AND SELF-IDENTIFICATION OF ADDICTIVE PROBLEMS

If there is a disease of alcoholism, or of compulsive gambling, some people should manifest a distinct addiction syndrome. Yet population studies (as opposed to clinical studies of individuals in treatment) of alcoholism, drug addiction, and compulsive gambling regularly reveal that different people display different types of problems, and that the number and severity of these problems occur across a continuum rather than forming distinct addict and nonaddict profiles. Most important of all, interview studies of general populations of drinkers (or of large populations of clinical alcoholics) find tremendous movement and variability in severity of problems, such that over time (sometimes quite brief periods), people shift in terms of the severity of their problems, including substantial numbers who are no longer found to have a diagnosable problem.[14]

At times, the fluidity of drinking problems apparent in large populations defies imagination—how could people regularly escape addiction when we so frequently observe individuals with problems as severe who tearfully testify they have tried everything to quit their addictions, but have failed time and again to do so? One subcategory of this question that occurs with addictions concerns those who are objectively measured to be in remission (that is, in a lifetime prevalence measure they score as addicted, but they do not currently score as such). Yet, these same individuals reply "no" when asked if they have ever been addicted or dependent. Hodgins, Wynne, and Makarchuk surveyed over eighteen hundred Canadians and identified forty-two respondents who revealed a lifetime gambling problem but who had had no problem in the last year.[15]

Of course, this is the clinical symptom of denial. However, it seems to be a fairly functional attitude when it permits people to leave a gambling or other addictive problem behind, perhaps more readily or with less stress than otherwise. This unselfconscious remission reminds us of the college student or military recruit who gets drunk several times a week, who graduates or leaves the service, gets married, and now only consumes a glass or two of wine with his wife over dinner. Likewise, we can observe a young person who becomes increasingly desperate as he loses bet after bet at a carnival, reaches deep into his savings in order to recoup his losses, and returns several more nights to continue this futile and destructive effort. Years later, this same person loses twenty dollars at the same carnival, shrugs his shoulders and goes home to tuck his children in bed or to mow his lawn.

WHAT DOES A GAMBLING ADDICT LOOK LIKE?

Certainly, some people have extremely destructive gambling experiences and some develop chronic gambling habits and problems. The individual loses more than he or she intended, feels bad, tries to recoup his or her losses by continuing to gamble, loses more, and good money follows bad. In a direct parallel to the principal varieties of alcoholism, the person may fail to control any individual gambling experience in a gambling binge, or else may gamble steadily and heavily over a long period, forming a chronic dependence. While the risk of gambling or prospect of winning can be exhilarating, the aftermath of gambling losses, as well as being emotionally deflating, becomes increasingly problematic from a legal, job, and family standpoint. At the same time, future gambling relieves the anxiety, depression, boredom, and guilt that set in following gambling experiences and losses.

This addictive cycle is described repeatedly in the gambling literature.[16] One critical element of the pathological gambling experience is money—for Orford et al., the problem cycle begins with "negative feelings associated with gambling losses," in addition to the "person's positive experience of the gambling activity itself, shortage of money and the need to keep the extent of gambling a secret." [17] In this sense, addictive gambling resembles compulsive shopping, where people spend irrationally and accumulate debts and problems resulting from efforts to hide and/or cover these debts. The individual who is lost in this cycle is one who relies on magical solutions—as do drug and alcohol abusers—to produce desired outcomes without following systematic or functional plans to achieve his or her goals.[18]

Some effort has been devoted to uncovering personality syndromes in gambling addicts. In recent years, Blaszczynski and his colleagues have focussed on the personality trait of antisocial impulsiveness, which includes with it other emotional disorders.[19] In this research, gambling addicts are unable to curb their urges, disregard the consequences of their actions for others, use gambling as a response to dysphoria and emotional problems, and are predisposed to substance abuse and criminality. Thus, they frequently view people in manipulative terms and readily sacrifice relationships to their urges—stealing or diverting money from family and friends and carrying on campaigns of duplicity.

Many of these traits resemble those found in alcohol and drug abusers—particularly antisocial impulsivity.[20] Likewise, addicts and alcoholics frequently demonstrate manipulative and alienated relationships. Such similarities in the lives of those addicted to disparate involvements indicate common addictive patterns and motivations, with different triggering events, social milieus, and personal predilections leading individuals to one or another type of addictive object. At the same time, a given individual often alternates or substitutes from among a variety of addictions, including problem drinking and gambling. For such individuals, it is the experiential similarities in these involvements that link the activities.

CONCLUSIONS

Gambling problems are increasingly attracting attention around the world, particularly in North America. Unlike recreational drugs, which are illegal, and alcohol, which is manufactured privately, substantial gambling initiatives originate with the state (e.g., massive state lotteries), and private gambling generates huge revenues for various levels of government. As both private and government-sponsored gambling spreads, it is also marketed more aggressively. These marketing efforts rely on addictive appeals—for example, highlighting the excitement of gambling and other escapist aspects of the experience, magical resolution of problems (through fantasized winnings), and personal gratification at the expense of family and social obligations. In this way, addiction and addictive values are being forcefully marketed to masses of Americans and Canadians. If one seeks an image of state-fostered addiction as a way of keeping the populace preoccupied, if not stupefied, and under government control, gambling is that image.

NOTES

1. Stanton Peele with Archie Brodsky, *Love and Addiction* (New York: Taplinger/Signet, 1975, 1991).

2. Alex Blaszczynski and Nathaniel McConaghy, "The Medical Model of Pathological Gambling: Current Shortcomings," *Journal of Gambling Behavior* 5 (1989): 42–52.

3. Stanton Peele, *The Meaning of Addiction* (San Francisco: Jossey-Bass, 1985/1998) and "Addiction as a Cultural Concept," *Annals of the New York Academy of Sciences* 602 (1990): 205–20.

4. Raymond L. Wedgeworth, "The Reification of the 'Pathological' Gambler: An Analysis of Gambling Treatment and the Application of the Medical Model to Problem Gambling," *Perspectives in Psychiatric Care* 34, no. 2 (1998): 5.

5. Wedgeworth, "The Reification of the 'Pathological' Gambler," p. 10.

6. Stanton Peele, Charles Bufe, and Archie Brodsky, *Resisting Twelve-Step Coercion: How to Fight Forced Participation in AA, NA, or Twelve-Step Treatment* (Tucson, Ariz.: See Sharp Press, 2000).

7. Jim Orford, Victoria Morison, and Marcia Somers, "Drinking and Gambling: A Comparison with Implications for Theories of Addiction," *Drug and Alcohol Review* 15 (1996): 47–56.

8. Peele, *The Meaning of Addiction.*

9. I. Wray and Mark Dickerson, "Cessation of High Frequency Gambling and Withdrawal Symptoms," *British Journal of Addiction* 76 (1981): 401–405.

10. Arthur B. Light and Edward G. Torrance, "Opiate Addiction VI: The Effects of Abrupt Withdrawal Followed by Readministration of Morphine in Human Addicts, with Special Reference to the Composition of the Blood, the Circulation, and the Metabolism," *Archives of Internal Medicine* 44 (1929): 1–16.

11. Laura Schmidt et al., "Cross-Cultural Applicability in International Classifications and Research in Alcohol Dependence," *Journal of Studies on Alcohol* 60 (1999): 448–62.

12. Stanton Peele, "Consumption and Dependence: Inextricable Link or Cultural/Subjective Connection?" paper presented at Measuring Drinking Patterns, Alcohol Problems, and Their Connection: An International Research Conference, Skarpö, Stockholm, April 3–7, 2000.

13. Jim Orford and A. Keddie, "Abstinence or Controlled Drinking: A Test of the Dependence and Persuasion Hypotheses" *British Journal of Addiction* 81 (1986): 495–504.

14. Deborah A. Dawson, Compare "Correlates of Past-Year Status among Treated and Untreated Persons with Former Alcohol Dependence: United States, 1992," *Alcoholism: Clinical and Experimental Research* 20 (1995): 771–79, and Stanton Peele, "Ten Radical Things NIAAA Research Shows about Alcoholism," *Addictions Newsletter* (American Psychological Association, Division 50, 1998): 6, 17–19, in the case of alcohol. Howard J. Shaffer et al., *Estimating the Prevalence of Disordered Gambling Behavior in the United States and Canada: A Meta-analysis* (Boston: Harvard Medical School, 1998) provides similar data for gamblers.

15. David C. Hodgins, Harold Wynne, and Karyn Makarchuk, "Pathways to Recovery from Gambling Problems: Follow-up from a General Population Survey," *Journal of Gambling Studies* 15, no. 2 (1999): 93–104.

16. Robert L. Custer and Harry Milt, *When Luck Runs Out: Help for Compulsive Gamblers and Their Families* (New York: Fact on File Publications, 1985).

17. Orford et al., "Drinking and Gambling," p. 52.

18. Alan Marlatt, "Alcohol, the Magic Elixir?" in *Alcohol and Pleasure: A Health Perspective*, ed. Stanton Peele and Marcus Grant (Philadelphia:

Brunner/Mazel, 1999), pp. 233–48; Stanton Peele "Love, Sex, Drugs, and Other Magical Solutions to Life," *Journal of Psychoactive Drugs* 14 (1982): 125–31.

19. Alex Blaszczynski, Zachary Steel, and Nathaniel McConaghy, "Impulsivity in Pathological Gambling: The Antisocial Impulsivist," *Addiction* 92 (1997): 75–87.

20. Stanton Peele, *Diseasing of America* (San Francisco: Jossey-Bass, 1989, 1995).

SOCIAL TRENDS, PROBLEM GAMBLING, AND THE CHALLENGE TO PUBLIC POLICY

♥♠♣

13

PAYING THE PIPER

Gambling and Problem Gambling in America

Rachel A. Volberg

THE NEW GAMBLERS IN AMERICA

Gambling among the upper classes, whether on horses, cards, casino games, real estate or stocks, has long been condoned in most Western societies. Despite the efforts of reformers, similar activities have been broadly tolerated among the working and lower classes. In contrast, until the latter part of the twentieth century, gambling among the middle classes was widely discouraged. Over a decade ago, Rosecrance argued that the rapid legalization of gambling would lead to growth in the gambling participation of the middle classes. Given the size and influence of the middle class in American society, Rosecrance believed that their

Reprinted from *When the Chips Are Down: Problem Gambling in America* by Rachel Volberg with permission from The Century Foundation, Inc. Copyright © 2001, New York. Work on this paper was supported by NIAAA grant AA12982-01 from the National Institutes of Health, Bethesda, Maryland.

acceptance of legal gambling would be an important factor in the continued expansion of lotteries, casinos and pari-mutuel wagering in the United States.[1]

There is growing evidence that Rosecrance's prediction was correct. In support of this, we can look at the results of the only two national studies of gambling that have been carried out in the United States. The first survey was carried out by the Institute for Social Research at the University of Michigan in 1975 on behalf of the Commission on the Review of the National Policy Toward Gambling.[2] The second survey was carried out by the National Opinion Research Center at the University of Chicago in 1998 on behalf of the National Gambling Impact Study Commission.[3] Although the 1975 and 1998 surveys used somewhat different methodologies, they were sufficiently similar to enable some comparisons to be made.

While there was substantial social acceptance of gambling long before most Americans had access to legal gambling opportunities, gambling participation has increased as access has grown. A Gallup poll in 1950 estimated that 57 percent of the American population had ever gambled.[4] In 1975, the first national survey of gambling in the United States showed that 68 percent of adults had ever gambled; the second national survey in 1998 found that 86 percent of adults had ever gambled.[5]

In contrast to lifetime participation, past-year gambling participation rates have not changed much since 1975. The proportion of respondents in the two national surveys indicating that they had gambled in the past year barely changed between 1975 and 1998, rising from 61 percent to 63 percent. The small increase in past-year gambling participation is at least partly explained by the fact that Americans are now more likely to participate in casino and lottery gambling, which are widely advertised and highly visible, and less likely to participate in older types of gambling with less visibility, such as bingo and horserace wagering. In 1998, the percentage of people who reported playing the lottery in the past year was two times higher than in 1975 while the increase in the percentage of respondents who reported gambling in a casino in the past year was even higher. In contrast, past-year bingo participation and past-year participation in horserace wagering both decreased by two-thirds between 1975 and 1998.[6]

Tables 1 and 2 provide more detailed information from the 1998 national survey about gambling participation among different groups in the population.

Gender and Gambling

While women are substantially less likely than men to participate in illegal types of gambling, they are just as likely as men to participate in legal forms of gambling.[7] As the availability of legal gambling has grown in America, women's gambling has started to look more like the gambling done by men.

For example, the 1975 national survey found that while 68 percent of males and 55 percent of females participated in all types of gambling, the difference in illegal gambling participation was much greater with 17 percent of males and only 5 percent of females engaging in these activities.[8] As Table 1 shows, while men still gamble more than women, the difference between the genders has narrowed to only a few percentage points, with the exception of weekly gambling. As Table 2 illustrates, past-year casino and lottery players are almost as likely to be women as men. However, men are still more likely than women to gamble in cardrooms and at unlicensed gambling establishments and to participate in private wagers among themselves. The only type of gambling that women are more likely to do than men is bingo.

Similarly, the scope of women's gambling—that is, the number of gambling activities in which they participate—is lower than the scope of men's gambling. A 1989 telephone survey of Iowa adults found that while women engaged in significantly fewer gambling activities than men, they were not significantly different from men in the frequency of their gambling, the amounts they wagered, or the time they spent gambling.[9] An analysis of gambling participation in four states surveyed between 1992 and 1994 also found that women were less likely to participate in multiple gambling domains than men.[10]

Together, age and gender are the strongest demographic predictors of participation in specific types of gambling and the results of the 1998 survey suggest that interactions between age and gender affect gambling participation. In the 1998 national survey, males and females aged

Table 1: Lifetime, Past-Year, and Weekly Gambling by Gender, Age, and Ethnicity

	Ever	Past-Year	Weekly
Total	85.6	63.3	16.3
Male	88.1	67.6	20.9
Female	83.2	59.3	12.0
18–29	83.7	65.2	11.8
30–39	87.5	66.2	15.7
40–49	90.2	66.6	15.5
50–64	86.1	65.7	21.4
65+	79.8	50.0	18.9
White	87.5	65.1	15.4
Black	77.7	56.4	22.3
Other	83.1	60.4	15.4

Source: Gambling Impact and Behavior Survey, Public Use File (weighted RDD-patron sample).

eighteen to twenty-nine were just as likely as adults aged thirty to sixty-four to have gambled in the past year at a casino and on lotteries; females thirty to thirty-nine were just as likely as males aged eighteen to twenty-nine to have ever gambled at a store, bar, restaurant, truck stop, or similar location; and females aged fifty to sixty-four were more likely than any other gender and/or age group to have gambled at an Indian-owned casino.[11]

Age and Gambling

Numerous studies have found that older Americans are less likely than younger Americans to gamble and, when they do gamble, more likely to be involved in only a few activities.[12] The 1998 national survey found that while lifetime gambling participation had increased for all age groups since 1975, the increase was far more dramatic for older adults than for younger adults. In contrast to lifetime gambling, past-year gambling participation actually decreased among young adults but increased in the forty-five-to-sixty-four age group and doubled among persons aged sixty-five and over. In spite of this increase in gambling among older adults, seniors are still under-represented in the total population of past-year gamblers.

Table 2: Past-Year Gambling Participation by Gender, Age, and Ethnicity

	Male	Female	18–29	30–39	40–49	50–64	65+	White	Black	Other
Casino	27.0	24.4	25.6	26.2	26.3	31.5	17.8	26.1	24.0	24.6
Track	9.5	6.8	8.2	7.1	8.8	9.5	7.2	8.2	7.9	7.6
Lottery	55.3	47.9	49.1	55.7	56.2	55.8	38.5	52.4	47.7	49.7
Bingo	3.0	6.8	6.3	4.8	3.8	5.3	4.8	4.8	3.3	7.6
Charitable	4.6	4.3	3.9	4.4	4.1	6.5	3.3	5.3	1.1	2.8
Cardrooms	3.2	0.5	3.9	1.6	1.2	1.6	0.4	2.2	0.8	1.0
Private	14.4	5.7	18.2	10.6	7.0	6.9	4.1	10.9	4.4	9.8
Store	10.1	5.7	9.4	9.3	6.9	9.7	2.8	8.9	5.7	4.0
Unlicensed	9.8	5.7	10.5	8.0	9.1	7.1	2.2	9.0	3.3	4.8
Indian Reservation	7.1	5.8	6.0	7.8	4.6	8.9	4.3	7.5	1.9	4.3

Source: Gambling Impact and Behavior Survey, Public Use File (weighted RDD–patron sample).

The picture becomes more complicated when we examine the types of gambling that people of different ages are likely to do. As Table 2 shows, with only a few exceptions, past-year gambling participation in specific types of gambling is highest among adults aged thirty to sixty-four and lowest among adults aged sixty-five and over. Adults aged fifty to sixty-four are substantially more likely than individuals in other age groups to have engaged in charitable gambling and to have gambled at an Indian casino or bingo hall. In contrast, adults aged eighteen to twenty-nine are substantially more likely than older adults to have gambled privately. Adults aged sixty-five and over are the group least likely to have gambled privately, at an unlicensed establishment, or at a store, bar, restaurant, truck stop, or similar location. While older adults are less likely than younger adults to have ever gambled and to have gambled in the past year, these individuals are just as likely—if not more likely—to gamble weekly. As Table 1 shows, 12 percent of adults aged eighteen to twenty-nine and 16 percent of adults aged thirty to forty-nine acknowledged gambling weekly; in contrast, 21 percent of adults aged fifty to sixty-four and 19 percent of adults aged sixty-five and over gamble weekly on one or more activities.

Ethnicity and Gambling

While gender and age are the strongest demographic predictors of gambling, ethnicity also plays a role. Table 1 shows that while lifetime and past-year gambling participation are significantly higher for Whites than for other racial and ethnic groups in the United States, weekly gambling participation is actually highest among African Americans. However, there are substantial differences in the proportion of men and women in these ethnic groups who gamble: while 29 percent of Black men and 21 percent of White men gamble weekly, only 17 percent of Black women and 11 percent of White women gamble this frequently.

When it comes to participation in particular types of gambling, Table 2 shows that adults from every ethnic group are just as likely to have gambled in the past year on the lottery, at a casino, or on a horse or dog race. However, White adults are substantially more likely than adults from other ethnic groups to have gambled in the past year on a charitable event, at a store, bar, or restaurant that offered only one gambling activity (usually video poker or some other gaming machine), at an unlicensed establishment, or at a tribal gaming operation. Non-White adults are more likely than Whites to have gambled in the past year on bingo and Black adults are the least likely to have gambled in the past year on private types of wagering, such as card games in someone's home or on games of personal skill.

ATTITUDES TOWARD GAMBLING

Although gambling participation has increased since 1975, attitudes toward gambling have not changed dramatically in the United States. Most Americans hold complex and ambivalent, rather than simple pro- or anti-, attitudes about the effects of gambling on society. A Gallup survey in 1999 found that 29 percent of adults felt that gambling is immoral, compared with 27 percent in 1996 and 32 percent in 1992.[13] The same survey found that only 22 percent of adults favored further expansion of legal gambling while 47 percent favored the status quo and 29 percent wanted legal gambling opportunities reduced or banned outright. The reason for this general disinclination for the expansion of gambling was evidently that, while 67 percent of adults felt that casinos generally help a community's economy, 56 percent believed that casinos damage everyday family and community life.

As with gambling participation, age is the strongest demographic predictor of attitudes toward gambling. On a five-point scale from very good to very bad, only 25 percent of eighteen- to twenty-nine-year-olds considered the overall effects of legalized gambling on society to be bad or very bad, a percentage that rises steadily by age group, reaching 56 percent among those sixty-five and older. There are no significant differences in this attitude by income or ethnicity, and only slight differences by sex and education, with males and those with less than a high school education tending to be slightly more positive about gambling's social effects.[14]

While attitudes toward gambling remain complex, the *reasons* why people gamble have changed in the United States since 1975. The percentage of people who said they gambled in order to win money increased by one-half between 1975 and 1998, from 44 to 66 percent. In contrast, the percentage who said they gambled for excitement or challenge declined by almost one-third, from 70 to 49 percent. The 1998 numbers tell a similar story to those of a 1993 Roper survey, which found that 75 percent of casino patrons said the single primary reason they visit casinos is to win "a really large amount of money," while only 57 percent said that entertainment and recreation were important reasons.[15] Americans in the 1990s and the new millennium appear to gamble less for the sheer joy of it and more as though it were a nonsalaried second job, like day-trading or selling real estate. Furthermore, while people are now more likely to gamble in order to win money, the fact remains that most people who gamble, and especially those who gamble regularly, are most likely to lose money over the long term.

Reasons for gambling, like participation, vary by gender, age and ethnicity. For example, men are more likely than women, and young adults (those aged 18 to 29) are more likely than older adults, to say that they gamble for excitement. Adults under thirty are also much more likely than adults aged sixty-five and older to say that winning money is an important reason to gamble. Among different racial and ethnic groups, Hispanics are more likely than Blacks to say that they gamble in order to socialize while Blacks are more likely than Whites or Hispanics to say that they gamble in order to win money. There are also ethnic differences in the reasons that nongamblers give for *not* gambling: 29 percent of Hispanic nongamblers, versus 49 percent of Black nongamblers and 58 percent of White nongamblers, refrained from gambling for moral reasons, while 72 percent of Black nongamblers and 67 percent of White nongamblers—but only 54 percent of Hispanic nongamblers—refrained for financial reasons. These data suggest that Hispanics tend to approach gambling more as a social activity and Blacks more as a financial proposition.

WHAT IS PROBLEM GAMBLING?

For most people, gambling is an enjoyable, if occasional, experience. Whether it is buying a lottery ticket, placing a bet on a horserace, going to a casino for an evening, or wagering privately with friends, most people gamble for entertainment or for social reasons and typically do not risk more than they can afford to lose. For some people, however, gambling leads to debilitating problems that can also result in harm to people close to them and to the wider community. These are the people we call "problem gamblers."[16]

When they think about problem gamblers, most people have a stereotype in mind—someone like Marty.[17] When Marty was a child, his relatives would take him to the racetrack and place bets for him. His family's social life revolved around bingo, card games with friends, and other gambling activities. Marty started betting heavily in high school on sports and card games after several big wins. Even while winning, Marty had fights with his parents and told numerous lies to get out of paying back friends from whom he had borrowed money to gamble. As an adult, still gambling heavily on sports, card games, and horses, Marty "borrowed" more than $25,000 from several elderly relatives. He planned to pay them back when he finally won "the big one" but instead got further and further into debt with bookmakers and loansharks. Eventually, his wife confronted him, and his family agreed to pay back everything he owed if he would quit gambling. Marty took the money and paid off his debts but kept gambling. Finally, again deep in debt and desperate, Marty went to Las Vegas with $20,000 that he had taken from the company where he worked and lost it all. Marty was eventually arrested and served time in prison.

Until the 1990s, treatment professionals and gambling researchers, as well as journalists and the general public, assumed that this picture of the problem gambler was true for all problem gamblers.[18] But the reality of problem gambling is more complex and diverse than the stereotype that many of us have of problem gamblers. While the story of Patty Van Hooser does not fit the stereotype, she is nevertheless just as much of a problem gambler as Marty.

A single mom at the age of twenty-two Patty worked odd jobs and struggled to bring up two kids. Patty started getting into trouble with her gambling when she won big on bingo, once. Within a few years, she was gambling daily on slot machines at a local casino on the way home from work. It was a way to escape the stress of caring for her elderly parents, her husband, and her troubled children. She began borrowing from friends, cashing bad checks, and using family food money to gamble. After a suicide attempt, Patty joined Gamblers Anonymous. She and her husband had to sell her car, refinance their mortgage, and file for bankruptcy, but Patty's story ends happily—she now works as an administrator for a small, nonprofit group that counsels problem gamblers.[19]

Defining Our Terms

While there is general agreement that some people experience serious problems associated with their gambling, a confusing array of terms has been used to refer to individuals who experience such difficulties. Some of these terms include problem gambling, excessive gambling, disordered gambling, compulsive gambling, addictive gambling, and pathological gambling. Debates about terminology among gambling researchers have centered on two issues:

- the difficulties of comparing data that are based on different definitions and measures of gambling problems, and
- the importance of developing a terminology that represents a dynamic continuum of experiences rather than arbitrary categories.

While "problem gambling" is the term most widely used to refer to individuals who experience difficulties with their gambling, it has been used in a variety of ways. In some situations, it is used to indicate all of the patterns of gambling behavior that compromise, disrupt, or damage personal, family, or vocational pursuits.[20] In these instances, problem gambling refers to a continuum of gambling-related difficulties ranging from mild to extremely severe. In certain situations, such as in reporting the results of epidemiological research, the term "problem gambling" is limited to those who score in a given range on one or another of the accepted screens for problem and pathological gambling.

Problem gamblers, as well as those who score even lower on problem gambling screens (sometimes referred to as "at-risk" gamblers) are of concern because they represent much larger proportions of the population than pathological gamblers alone. Problem gamblers and at-risk gamblers are also of interest because of the possibility that their gambling-related difficulties may become more severe over time. Finally, problem and at-risk gamblers are of interest because of the likelihood that their gambling can be more easily influenced by social attitudes and public awareness.[21]

Although there are numerous historical and fictional references to gambling problems, pathological gambling was not widely recognized as a mental disorder until the final quarter of the twentieth century. The term was first included in the *Diagnostic and Statistical Manual* (DSM) of the American Psychiatric Association in 1980.[22] Each revision of the DSM (in 1987 and 1994) has contained changes in the diagnostic criteria for pathological gambling as research has improved our understanding of the disorder. Presently, the essential features of pathological gambling are

- A continuous or periodic loss of control over gambling;
- A progression, in gambling frequency and amounts wagered, in preoccupation with gambling and in obtaining money with which to gamble; and
- A continuation of gambling despite adverse consequences.[23]

A formal diagnosis of pathological gambling is usually arrived at by a qualified and experienced clinician following a lengthy clinical interview. To make a diagnosis of pathological gambling, the clinician must determine that the patient has met five or more of the ten diagnostic indicators associated with pathological gambling. Table 3 presents the most recent diagnostic criteria for pathological gambling.

Table 3: Diagnostic Criteria for Pathological Gambling

Persistent and recurrent maladaptive gambling behavior as indicated by five (or more) of the following:

Preoccupation	Preoccupied with gambling (e.g., preoccupied with reliving past gambling experiences, handicapping or planning the next venture, or thinking of ways to get money with which to gamble)
Tolerance	Needs to gamble with increasing amounts of money in order to achieve the desired excitement
Withdrawal	Restlessness or irritability when attempting to cut down or stop gambling
Escape	Gambling as a way of escaping from problems or relieving dysphoric mood (e.g., feelings of helplessness, guilt, anxiety, or depression)
Chasing	After losing money gambling, often returns another day in order to get even ("chasing" one's losses)
Lying	Lies to family members, therapists, or others to conceal the extent of involvement with gambling
Loss of Control	Made repeated unsuccessful efforts to control, cut back or stop gambling
Illegal Acts	Committed illegal acts, such as forgery, fraud, theft or embezzlement, in order to finance gambling
Risking Significantnity Relationships	Jeopardized or lost a significant relationship, job, educational or career opportu because of gambling
Bailout	Reliance on others to provide money to relieve a desperate financial situation caused by gambling

The gambling behavior is not better accounted for by a manic episode.

Source: *Diagnostic and Statistical Manual of Mental Disorders*, 4th ed. (Washington, D.C.: American Psychiatric Association, 1944).

PROBLEM GAMBLING IN THE GENERAL POPULATION

Until 1998, only one national prevalence survey had been conducted in the United States.[24] Although the screen used to measure compulsive gambling in this survey has been criticized,[25] it provided the first-ever prevalence estimates of this disorder. The overall prevalence of "probable compulsive gambling" was deemed to be 0.77 percent (1.1 percent for men, 0.5 percent for women). A further 2.3 percent were classified as "potential compulsive gamblers." In Nevada, which was oversampled because of the researchers' interest in comparing states with and without casino gambling, the prevalence of "probable compulsive gambling" was much higher than the national average, namely 2.5 percent (3.3 percent for men, 2.0 percent for women). Based largely on the strong relationship between the availability of gambling and gambling participation and the differences between Nevada and the rest of the country, the researchers concluded that widespread legalization of gambling in the United States was likely to result in a significant increase in problem gambling.

In 1998, the National Gambling Impact Study Commission initiated an extensive research program as part of its charge to conduct "a comprehensive study of the social and economic impacts of gambling in the United States."[27] The national Gambling Impact and Behavior Study (GIBS) was one of several elements in the full program of research. The GIBS, carried out by the National Opinion Research Center (NORC) and its partners, included five separate initiatives: a nationally representative telephone survey of 2,417 adults, a national telephone survey of 534 youths aged sixteen and seventeen; intercept interviews with 530 adult patrons of gaming facilities, a longitudinal data base (1980 to 1997) of social and economic indicators, including gambling revenues, in a random national sample of 100 communities; and case studies in ten communities regarding the effects of large-scale casinos opening in close proximity.[28]

Guidelines from the National Gambling Impact Study Commission specified that the DSM-IV criteria were to be used to identify problem and pathological gamblers in the general population. In constructing the questionnaire for the adult, youth, and patron surveys, the national research team developed a new problem gambling screen. The *NORC Diagnostic Screen* for Gambling Problems (NODS) was tested for its performance in a clinical sample prior to its adoption in the national surveys. In these tests, the screen demonstrated strong internal consistency, high sensitivity, and good specificity and retest reliability. Unfortunately, since there is no information about how the performance of the NODS compares with the problem gambling screen used in the first national survey in 1975, there is no way to compare problem gambling prevalence rates in 1975 and 1998.

Results based on the lifetime NODS and the combined samples of adults and gaming facility patrons showed that the national prevalence of "pathological gambling" (NODS score 5 or more) was 1.2 percent (1.7

percent for men, 0.8 percent for women). A further 1.5 percent of the respondents in the combined sample were classified as "problem gamblers" (NODS score 3 or 4). Based on these figures, the research team estimated that about 2.5 million American adults are pathological gamblers and another 3 million adults should be considered problem gamblers. Extending the criteria more broadly, an additional 7.7 percent of the respondents were classified as "at risk" (NODS score 1 or 2). This represents about 15 million American adults who can be considered at risk for problem gambling.

Also based on the combined sample of adults and gaming facility patrons, the national research team found that men are more likely to be pathological, problem, and at-risk gamblers than women; that pathological, problem, and at-risk gambling are proportionately higher among African Americans than among other ethnic groups; that about one in five of the 1 percent of adults who consider themselves professional gamblers can be classified as "pathological"; and that the availability of a casino within fifty miles (versus 50 to 250 miles) is associated with about double the prevalence of problem and pathological gambling.

PROBLEM GAMBLING AND SPECIFIC GAMBLING ACTIVITIES

Until recently, little notice was taken by gambling researchers or policy makers of particular features of different gambling activities and their likely impact on the prevalence of problem gambling in the general population. While gambling activities can be classified in many ways, several researchers have suggested that "event frequency," or the number of opportunities to wager in a specified period of time, is closely related to the development of gambling problems.[29] Another critical concern related to particular features of gambling activities is the spread of "convenience gambling" outside of venues traditionally reserved for gambling. Convenience gambling is defined by the National Gambling Impact Study Commission as "legal, stand-alone slot machines, video poker, video keno and other EGDs (electronic gaming devices)" available "in bars, truck stops, convenience stores and a variety of other locations."[30]

While there has been little analysis, data relevant to the relationship between specific types of gambling and/or features of gambling games and the prevalence of problem gambling are available. The recent Australian national survey is particularly relevant in this context because of the widespread availability of gaming machines in Australia.[31] Gaming machines in Australia, known as "pokies," are stand-alone machines with keys or touch-sensitive screens that accept coins or bills and offer video poker, video keno, video bingo, and video blackjack, as well as "reel" games. There are thousands of gaming machines located at social clubs, hotels, bars, and restaurants in most of the Australian states. Looking across several different states, the Australian researchers found that as the number of machines increased, both the proportion of the adult population that played gaming machines weekly and the proportion of problem gamblers among weekly players increased.

Findings from recent state-level studies in Louisiana, Montana, New York, and Oregon support the conclusion that greater numbers of machines are associated with higher problem gambling prevalence rates. EGDs in these four states have rather different characteristics. For example, Montana authorized EGDs much earlier than any of the other states. While the EGDs in New York and Oregon are owned and operated by the state lottery, the EGDs in Louisiana and Montana are regulated by the state but are privately owned and operated. Finally, while Louisiana and Oregon have less than one video poker machine per capita, Montana has more than five machines per capita.

There are other features of the games offered on these machines that are important for understanding differences in participation and problem gambling prevalence rates. While keno drawings are broadcast on a single screen that players can watch after purchasing a ticket, video poker is played on stand-alone machines with keys or a touch-sensitive screen into which players feed coins (or bills) directly. Although keno is most often played at bars or restaurants, it is also available in other, more traditional lottery outlets, such as convenience stores. In contrast, video poker is closely linked to licenses to sell and/or serve alcoholic beverages. Since conditions for obtaining such licenses vary across states, EGDs may be located in a variety of settings, including bars, restaurants, hotels, truck stops, racetracks, and off-track betting facilities. A final contrast between video keno and other EGDs is in the frequency of the game.

Keno provides a new game every five minutes in contrast to the fifteen seconds required to play a hand of video poker.

Higher past-year and weekly participation rates are associated with higher numbers of machines per capita as well as with event frequency. In New York and Oregon, only 1 to 3 percent of adults play the slower keno game on a weekly basis. In Louisiana and Oregon, the faster video poker games (on stand-alone machines) is associated with higher rates of past year participation (19 percent in Louisiana and 24 percent in Oregon) although, as with keno, only about 3 percent of the adult population participates in video poker once a week or more often. In Montana, where several video gambling games are available on far more numerous stand-alone machines, 39 percent of the adult population has played on these machines in the past year and 9 percent play these machines once a week or more often.

Problem gambling prevalence rates among weekly EGD players and other weekly gamblers are available in all of these states. These prevalence rates are based on the Fisher Screen (which provides only a past-year measure of problem gambling) rather than the more widely used South Oaks Gambling Screen. While the small sample sizes suggest caution in interpreting these results, the prevalence of problem gambling among EGD players is substantially higher than among other weekly gamblers. Furthermore, problem gambling prevalence rates are higher in Louisiana and Oregon, where video poker has been operating for less than a decade, than in Montana, where gaming machines have been operating for substantially longer or in New York, where only the slower keno game is available.

The potential link between the availability of specific types of gambling and problem gambling prevalence is a critical policy issue. While causation is difficult to prove without longitudinal research, there is a correlation between the availability of EGDs and higher prevalence rates of problem gambling, particularly among women. These links should be a matter of concern to policy makers at all levels of government as they make decisions related to legal gambling in their jurisdictions.

NOTES

1. John Rosecrance, *Gambling without Guilt: The Legitimation of an American Pastime* (Belmont, Calif.: Wadsworth, 1988), pp. 3–6, 161–63.

2. Maureen Kallick et al., *A Survey of American Gambling Attitudes and Behavior* (Research Report series: University of Michigan Press, 1987).

3. Dean R. Gerstein et al., *Gambling Impact and Behavior Study: Report to the National Gambling Impact Study Commission* (Chicago: National Opinion Research Center at the University of Chicago, 1999).

4. Cited in Gallup Organization report, "Gambling in America: Topline and Trends," 1950.

5. Maureen Kallick et al., *Survey of American Gambling Attitudes and Behavior*, table 1.1-1, p. 2; Dean R. Gerstein et al., *Gambling Impact and Behavior Study*, p. 7, fig. 1.

6. Gerstein et al., *Gambling Impact and Behavior Study*, p. 7, fig. 1a.

7. Joseph Hraba and Gang Lee, "Gender, Gambling, and Problem Gambling," *Journal of Gambling Studies* 12 (1996): 83–101; Henry R. Lesieur and Sheila B. Blume, "When Lady Luck Loses: Women and Compulsive Gambling," in *Feminist Perspectives on Addictions*, ed. Nan van den Bergh (New York: Springer, 1991), pp. 181–97.

8. Kallick et al., *Survey of American Gambling Attitudes and Behavior*, table 1.1-1, p. 2.

9. Hraba and Lee, "Gender, Gambling, and Problem Gambling;" table 1, p. 92.

10. Rachel A. Volberg and Steven M. Banks, "A New Approach to Understanding Gambling and Problem Gambling in the General Population" (paper presented at the Ninth International Conference on Gambling and Risk Taking, Las Vegas, June 1994).

11. *Gambling Impact and Behavior Survey*, Public Use File (weighted RDD-patron sample). Available through the Inter-University Consortium for Political and Social Research at the University of Michigan.

12. Waiman P. Mok and Joseph Hraba, "Age and Gambling Behavior: A Declining and Shifting Pattern of Participation," in *Gambling Behavior and Problem Gambling*, ed. William R. Eadington and Judy A. Cornelius (Reno: University of Nevada Press, 1993), pp. 51–74.

13. Gallup Organization, "Gambling in America: Topline and Trends."

14. Rachel A. Volberg, Mariana T. Toce, and Dean R. Gerstein, "From Back Room to Living Room: Changing Attitudes toward Gambling," *Public Perspective* 10, no. 5 (1999): 8–13.

15. Karl Heubusch, "Taking Chances on Casinos," *American Demographics*, April 1997.

16. Max W. Abbott and Rachel A. Volberg, *Gambling and Problem Gambling in the Community: An International Overview and Critique* (Wellington: Department of Internal Affairs, 1999), p. 77.

17. This narrative is a composite from the stories of several Gamblers Anonymous members interviewed for an article in *Sports Illustrated*. The full reference is Clive Gammon, "Tales of Self-Destruction," *Sports Illustrated*, March 10, 1986, 64–72.

18. Rachel A. Volberg and Henry J. Steadman. "Accurately Depicting Pathological Gamblers: Policy and Treatment Implications," *Journal of Gambling Studies* 8, no. 4 (1992): 402.

19. John DiConsiglio, "She Gambled with Her Life," *Redbook*, February 2000, 112–16.

20. Henry R. Lesieur, "Costs and Treatment of Pathological Gambling," *Annals of the American Academy of Political and Social Science* 556 (1998): 154–55. See also Sue Cox et al., *Problem and Pathological Gambling in America: The National Picture* (Columbia, Md.: National Council on Problem Gambling, 1997), pp. 8–10.

21. Howard J. Shaffer, Matthew N. Hall, and Joni Vander Bilt, "Estimating the Prevalence of Disordered Gambling Behavior in the United States and Canada: A Research Synthesis," *American Journal of Public Health* 89, no. 9 (1999): 1369–76. See also Brian Castellani, *Pathological Gambling: The Making of a Medical Problem* (Albany: State University of New York Press, 2000), pp. 197–98.

22. American Psychiatric Association, *Diagnostic and Statistical Manual of Mental Disorders,* 3rd ed. (Washington, D.C.: American Psychiatric Association, 1980). Reprinted in National Research Council, *Pathological Gambling: A Critical Review* (Washington, D.C.: National Academy Press, 1999), pp. 273–75.

23. American Psychiatric Association, *Diagnostic and Statistical Manual of Mental Disorders,* 4th ed. (Washington, D.C.: American Psychiatric Association, 1994). Reprinted in National Research Council, *Pathological Gambling: A Critical Review*, pp. 278–82.

24. Maureen Kallick et al., *Survey of American Gambling Attitudes and Behavior*, Final Report to the Commission on the Review of the National Policy Toward Gambling (Ann Arbor: Survey Research Center, Institute for Social Research, 1976).

25. Lawrence B. Nadler, "The Epidemiology of Pathological Gambling: Critique of Existing Research and Alternative Strategies," *Journal of Gambling Behavior* 1, no. 1 (1985): 35–50.

26. Kallick et al., *Survey of American Attitudes and Behaviors*.

27. Public Law 104–169 (August 3, 1996); *National Gambling Impact Study Commission Act* sec. 2, par. 5.

28. Gerstein et al., *Gambling Impact and Behavior Study*.

29. Mark Griffiths, "Gambling Technologies: Prospects for Problem Gambling," *Journal of Gambling Studies* 15, no. 3 (1999): 265–83.

30. National Gambling Impact Study Commission, *Final Report* (Washington, D.C.: Government Printing Office, 1999), pp. 2–4 [online], http://www.ngisc.gov.

31. Productivity Commission, *Australia's Gambling Industries: Final Report* (Canberra: Commonwealth Government, 1999).

14

YOUTH GAMBLING

Some Social Policy Issues

Jeffrey L. Derevensky, Rina Gupta, Karen Hardoon, Laurie Dickson, and Anne-Elyse Deguire

The history of gambling on an international level has passed through a number of cycles from prohibition to widespread proliferation. Gambling has gone from being associated with sin, crime, and degradation to its current position as a form of socially acceptable entertainment. The vastly changing landscape of gambling throughout the world seems to suggest that the pendulum between abstinence and widespread acceptance that I. Nelson Rose so eloquently describes,[1] may never swing back to prohibition or to a more restrictive position. The prevailing attitudes of governmental legislators and the public at large indicate that new gaming venues (e.g., casinos in jurisdictions currently without such forms of gambling and new technologies in the form of interactive lotteries and Internet gambling) will continue to expand rapidly. This is not to suggest that the antilobbying groups have not succeeded but rather that they have been mere impediments to slowing the growth of specific gambling activities. Gambling, or "gaming" as the industry prefers, is no longer regarded as a vice accompanied with stigmatization but rather as a legitimate form of entertainment. The very fact that some of the best-known educational institutions in the United States, including Harvard, Yale, Princeton, William and Mary, Dartmouth, Rutgers, and the University of Pennsylvania have gained operating funds through lotteries attests to the potential good to be derived from the proceeds of gambling.[2] This tradition continues, with many state lotteries promoting their products by reporting that a proportion of the proceeds are used for educational initiatives and programs.

Our prevailing social policies, often established by default, appear to be predicated upon a model of harm minimization. Yet the development of effective social policy needs to be both reflective and directive of the social context from which it is derived. Good social policies must be reflective of their time while simultaneously projecting the future; they must be attuned to and mindful of history, yet they must exist within the context of the prevailing ideological, social, economic, and political values. They must at least to some degree anticipate the future,[3] and be mindful of broader cultural influences and differences. The escalation of state supported (and owned) gambling is an enormous social experiment for which we currently do not have sufficient data to predict the long-term social costs.

What makes gambling somewhat distinct from other public policy domains is that it cuts across a number of social, economic, public health, and justice policy concerns. Gambling as a public health issue has become increasingly important. David Korn and Howard J. Shaffer make a strong argument for viewing gambling within a public health framework by examining it from a population health and human ecology perspective. They further argue that disordered gambling may not only be a problem in itself but also may be a "gateway" to substance abuse, depression, anxiety, and other significant mental health disorders.[4]

Gambling remains a contentious social policy issue in many countries. While the perspective that gambling is not a harmless, innocuous behavior with few negative consequences is slowly changing, most adults strongly support their continued opportunity to gamble and view it is much less harmful than other potentially additive behaviors and harmful social activities.[5]

Once perceived as an activity primarily relegated to adults, gambling has become a popular form of recreation for adolescents. While in most cases legislative statutes prohibit children and adolescents from participating in legalized forms of gambling, there is little doubt that their resourcefulness enables many children and adolescents to engage in both legal and illegal forms of gambling. Research has revealed that upwards of 80 percent of adolescents engage in some form of gambling,[6] with most best described as social gamblers. Yet, there remains ample evidence that between 4 to 8 percent of adolescents have a very serious gambling problem with another 10 to 15 percent at-risk from the development of a gambling problem.[7] Acknowledging difficulties in comparisons of the data sets, the National Research Council report concluded that "the proportion of pathological gamblers among adolescents in the United States could be more than three times that of adults (5.0 percent versus 1.5 percent)."[8] In the United States and Canada, approximately 15.3 million twelve to seventeen-year-olds have been gambling, while 2.2 million are reported to be experiencing serious gambling related problems. Trends between 1984 and 1999 indicate a significant increase in the proportion of youth who report gambling within the past year and those who report gambling related problems.[9]

Increased child and adolescent gambling is not exclusive to North America. In the United Kingdom, numerous youth studies have been conducted due to children's accessibility to the use of legalized, low-stake slot machines (fruit machines). Fruit machine playing, legalized gambling for children, is widespread among children and adolescents in arcade parlors in England, and their addiction is of serious concern.[10] Large numbers of adolescents report playing fruit machines sometime during their adolescence, with 5 to 18 percent reporting playing weekly[11].

Of equal concern is the age of onset of children's gambling. Adolescents experiencing severe gambling problems report beginning gambling at nine or ten years of age[12] where as adult problem gamblers report that their pathological behaviors began in late childhood and adolescence, often between ten and nineteen years of age.[13] In the United Kingdom, children are reported to have begun playing fruit machines as early as eight to ten years of age.[14] It appears that gambling behavior is established early and begins earlier than other potentially addictive behaviors including tobacco, alcohol, and illicit drug use.[15] Given that there are few observable signs of gambling dependence among children, these problems have not been as readily noticed compared with other addictions (e.g., alcohol or substance abuse).

Gambling is advertised widely, easily accessible to youth, and often housed in places that are perceived to be glamorous and exciting, such as, bars and casinos. Gambling also provides opportunities for socializing, both harmful and beneficial. Although betting in casinos and on lotteries and electronic gaming is generally illegal for adolescents (statutes differ among countries, states, and provinces), the enforcement of such laws, as with underage drinking, is becoming increasingly difficult and almost nonexistent in some states and provinces.

FAMILIAL FACTORS RELATED TO YOUTH GAMBLING

Gambling has also become something of a family affair. Results from several studies suggest that the majority of youth tend to gamble with their family (40 to 68 percent) as well as friends (55 to 82 percent).[16] Equally disturbing are the findings that the majority of parents do not appear to be concerned with their children's gambling behavior. Approximately 80 to 90 percent of parents report that they know their children gamble for money and they do not object.[17] A recent study by Felsher, Derevensky, and Gupta, examining lottery ticket purchases in Canada, found that 77 percent of adolescents reported that their parents purchased scratch lottery tickets and 50 percent purchased lottery draw tickets for their underage children, with 70 percent of adolescents reported having received a lottery ticket as a present (most notably for birthdays, Christmas, or special occasions).[18] Research has also revealed that 78 percent of children gamble in their own homes.[19]

A strong correlation has been found between adolescent gambling and parental gambling involvement.[20] Retrospective studies indicate that 25 to 40 percent of adult pathological gamblers' parents were problem gamblers.[21] Furthermore, the effects of parental gambling have far reaching consequences. For example, children from homes where parental gambling is a problem report feelings of insecurity and a greater need for acceptance.[22]

PEER INFLUENCES

With respect to peer influences, M. D. Griffiths has reported that 44 percent of adolescents participated in gambling activities because their friends were engaged in similar practices.[23] As children get older they tend to gamble less with family members in their own homes and more with friends in their homes.[24] This trend reinforces the notion that for many youth, gambling is perceived as a socially acceptable and entertaining pastime. A recent study by Karen Hardoon and Jeffrey Derevensky reported that children aged ten to twelve who played a computer-simulated game of roulette, individually or in groups, demonstrated changes in their playing behaviors as a result of peer modeling. More specifically, average wagers of female and mixed-gender groupings appeared to be most affected by the group influence, whereby their wagers increased significantly.[25] These findings suggest a strong social learning component involved in the acquisition of such behaviors.

GENDER DIFFERENCES

General findings indicate that gambling is more popular among males than females, with pathological gambling found to be three to four times higher among males than females.[26] Adolescent males have also been found to make higher gross wagers and exhibit greater risk-taking behavior, report initiating gambling at earlier ages, gamble on a larger number and variety of games, gamble more often, spend more time and money when gambling, and experience more gambling-related problems than female adolescents. Also, parents appear to more often encourage gambling in their sons, as more males than females report gambling with their parents.[27] Griffiths has speculated that gambling allows boys to display their masculinity in a social environment by exhibiting "courage and bravery" and thus may be more attractive to them than to girls.[28] With respect to games played, girls seem to prefer scratch tickets and lotteries, whereas boys prefer sports betting and card games.[29]

PHYSIOLOGICAL FACTORS

Adolescent pathological gamblers have been found to have an increased physiological resting state, to have a greater need for sensation seeking, and to be more aroused and excited during gambling than adult gamblers. They have also been found to dissociate more frequently when gambling.[30]

PERSONALITY FACTORS

Youth with serious gambling problems have been found to be greater risk-takers.[31] The literature on risk-taking suggests that males are greater risk-takers than females and that adolescents, in general, tend to be greater risk-takers than adults. Given that gambling activities in and of themselves involve some risk-taking elements, the findings that adolescents take greater risks when gambling and remain at increased risk for the development of addictions are not surprising.

Adolescent problem and pathological gamblers have also been shown to score higher on measures of impulsivity,[32] excitability, extroversion, and anxiety, and lower on conformity and self-discipline than non-problem gamblers.[33] Problem and pathological gamblers have been found to be more self-blaming, guilt prone, anxious, and less emotionally stable.[34] A recent study by Chantal Ste-Marie found that adolescents with significant gambling problems score higher on measures of both trait and state anxiety scales.[35]

EMOTIONAL AND MENTAL STATES

Adolescents with gambling problems have been found to have lower self-esteem and higher rates of depression and to report greater suicide ideation and suicide attempts than other adolescents. They have also been found to have poor or maladaptive general coping skills and tend to use more emotion and avoidant coping styles.[36]

PROBLEM BEHAVIORS ASSOCIATED WITH PATHOLOGICAL GAMBLING

Adolescent problem gamblers have been shown to be prone to engage in multiple, co-morbid addictive behaviors (smoking, drinking, drug use/abuse).[37] They are also more likely to have difficulty in school including increased truancy and poor grades.[38] While adolescents with gambling problems report having a support group, their former friends are often replaced by gambling associates.[39] Problem gambling and pathological gambling have been shown to result in increased delinquency and crime, disruption of familial relationships, and decreased academic performance.[40] Adolescents with gambling problems appear preoccupied with gambling-planning their next gambling activity, lying to their family and friends, and focusing on obtaining money to gamble with.[41]

There is little doubt that even with our increasing knowledge concerning adolescent gambling problems, gambling is largely viewed as a relatively benign activity that is significantly less harmful than alcohol, illegal drugs, or cigarettes. Gambling venues and activities for underage patrons remain easily accessible, with very few children reporting being fearful of getting caught gambling. Not surprisingly, increasing numbers

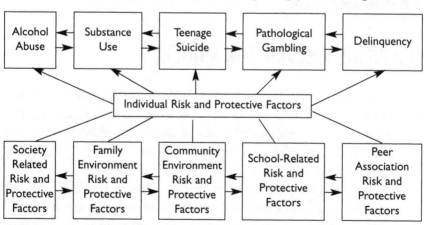

Figure 1. A conceptual model for understanding the domains of risk and protective factors that influence an individual's behavior. Adapted from Paul Brounstein and Janine M. Zweig, *Understanding Substance Abuse Prevention: Toward the Twenty-First Century: A Primer on Effective Programs* (Rockville, Md.: U.S. Department of Health and Human Services, Substance Abuse and Mental Health Services Administration, 1999).

of youth are experiencing gambling problems. There is also evidence that youth move more rapidly from initial gambling experiences to problem gambling than adults.[42]

YOUTH GAMBLING WITHIN THE CONTEXT OF ADOLESCENT RISKY BEHAVIORS

From a developmental perspective, the period of adolescence is marked by significant physiological, cognitive, and emotional changes, feelings of insecurity, an increase in risk-related behaviors, and a desire for greater independence. The Center for Substance Abuse Prevention (CSAP) and the Substance Abuse and Mental Health Services Administration (SAMHSA) have articulated a conceptual model for understanding the domains of risk and protective factors that influence an individual's behavior in which excessive, problematic gambling can be conceptualized (see fig. 1). Given that the prevalence data suggest that 4 to 8 percent of youth currently have serious gambling and gambling-related problems and another 10 to 15 percent are at risk for developing such problems, a better understanding of the risk factors associated with excessive gambling is paramount.

GAMBLING PREVENTION MODELS

Incorporating a harm-reduction approach, recent research has been undertaken to identify the risk factors for adolescent problem gambling. The examination of the commonalities of risk factors for problem gambling and other addictions provides sufficient evidence to suggest that gambling can similarly be incorporated into more general addiction and adolescent risk-behavior-prevention programs. Current research efforts[43] may suggest the utility of a general mental health program that addresses a number of adolescent risky behaviors simultaneously (e.g., substance abuse, gambling, risky driving, truancy, and risky sexual activity).

While adolescent risky behaviors share many common risk factors, the activities themselves can differ on several important dimensions.

Nevertheless, a harm-reduction approach appears appropriate for targeting those risky activities that yield no significant negative consequences when engaged in responsibly and moderately and are socially acceptable. Whether harm-reduction prevention programs are designed specifically for problem gambling or incorporated into a general mental health curriculum targeting multiple high-risk behaviors, the need for merging an abstinence approach with a harm-reduction prevention model is exemplified by the apparent contradiction that arises when the principles of the harm-reduction paradigm are applied to adolescents. Research highlights that early age of onset of gambling represents a significant risk factor for problem gambling.[44] As a result, delaying the age of onset of gambling experiences may be fundamental in a successful prevention paradigm yet is more appropriate to an abstinence model.

On the other hand, teaching "responsible" gambling through enhancement of emotional and cognitive coping skills and by providing cognitive decision-making tools may also be appropriate. School-based programs need to target specific information about gambling to various age groups, educating youth about the forms of gambling they will most likely be exposed at each particular age (e.g., nine-year-olds are likely to be exposed to scratch tickets and bingo). One of the central goals of science-based prevention is to promote resilience. Thus, we need to ensure that harm-reduction programs include components that are specific to the period of adolescent development. Despite the lack of emphasis on promoting resilience in current harm-reduction programs, both resource factors (those operating independent of risk status)[45] and protective factors (those interacting with risk status) contribute to resilience and need to be considered in the design of effective youth-gambling prevention programs.

Although there are currently no studies on protective mechanisms, or more generally on resiliency, for youth with respect to problem gambling, similar protective factors have been found to affect a multiple number of health and developmental outcomes in the presence of various stressors.[46] Thus, it is likely that the common protective factors found for a number of problem behaviors will be operative in promoting resiliency to problem gambling as well. To date, few prevention programs have addressed the issue of problem gambling, and those few have not had widespread dissemination, nor has their effectiveness been empirically validated.

It is clear that more basic, applied and longitudinal research is needed to investigate psychosocial and biological risk factors associated with youth experiencing gambling problems and to incorporate the results in the development of prevention programs. Additional research is also needed to examine the changes in prevalence rates, differences among gambling screens, cultural and/or ethnic differences, and the effects of the availability and accessibility of gambling and advertising on youth-gambling behavior and associated problems.

There remains little doubt that adolescents constitute a particularly high-risk group for acquiring gambling problems given their high rates of risk taking, their perceived invulnerability, their lack of recognition that gambling can lead to serious problems, and the social acceptability and glamorization of gambling throughout the world. It is important to note that gambling issues cut across a number of other public health policy domains—social, economic, health, and justice—and are only beginning to emerge on governmental radar screens as an important issue. Unfortunately, the governments that regulate, control, and in some cases own the gambling sites are also the recipients of the financial benefits, clearly representing a conflict of interest. Given that it takes several years to develop a significant gambling problem (often referred to as "the downward spiral"), the true social impact on youth will likely take years to realize. Our lottery corporations continue to encourage individuals to *buy the dream*. This is particularly troublesome for adolescents as we encourage them to study hard, achieve academically, and go to college because money and success will follow. . . . All their dreams can come true.

Equally important is that under most governmental statutes children and adolescents are prohibited from participating in legalized forms of gambling; yet we know that most young people have little difficulty purchasing lottery tickets and accessing other forms of gambling. A concerted effort must be made to ensure that those statutes are adhered to, with steep fines and penalties for the operators violating such laws. Where such laws are nonexistent, government legislators are strongly urged to initiate strong legislative statutes. Specific licensed products that are particularly attractive to underage populations, including cartoons, such as *South Park* and *Betty Boop*, and World Wrestling Federation products should be prohibited from being associated with games of chance and gambling. Role models should not be used to promote adolescent gambling. For example, Britney Spears, the youthful singing and entertainment phenomenon, was recently solicited by the Las Vegas Convention Bureau to be their official spokesperson. Spears, then twenty years old, was not even old enough to legally gamble in Nevada.

Based on our current knowledge of youth gambling problems, consideration of the following items is regarded as crucial for informing policy development:

Additional Empirical Research. The field of youth gambling is relatively new, and as a result there currently are significant gaps in our knowledge. Much of the research to date has focused on prevalence studies. Unfortunately, no longitudinal research has been conducted focusing on following individual gamblers from youth to adulthood. While there is ample research from the alcohol, drug use, and cigarette-smoking literature to suggest that a risk-resiliency model may have significant benefits for our understanding as to why some individuals are at high risk for developing a significant gambling problem, further research on gambling itself is required. Governmental agencies, private foundations, and the gambling industry would be well advised to support research initiatives in order to better understand this vulnerable population. Much-needed basic and applied research funding is required to help identify common and unique risk and protective factors for gambling problems and other addictive behaviors, including longitudinal research to examine the natural history of pathological gambling from childhood to adolescence through later adulthood; molecular, genetic, and neuropsychological research to help account for changes in gambling progression; research assessing whether certain gambling activities may become a gateway to subsequent gambling problems; and the development and /or refinement of current instruments used to assess adolescent gambling severity.

Emerging Public Health Issues. Given the pervasiveness of the problems associated with youth gambling problems and the concomitant mental health, social, economic, educational and legal problems, there is a need to clearly identify the social, economic, and familial costs and any potential benefits associated with youth gambling. We need a better understanding of the effects of accessibility and availability of gaming venues on future gambling behaviors. Specific research needs to focus on

gambling advertisements and their relationship to the onset and maintenance of adolescent gambling and problem gambling. From a treatment
perspective, adequate funds must be made available to help those youth
currently experiencing severe gambling and gambling-related behaviors
and their families. Along with our current treatment initiatives, we must
begin a thorough exploration of best practices for working with these
youth and ways in which we can encourage youth to seek help for gambling problems. A public health approach that examines the balance
among health, social, and economic costs and benefits is needed to for-
mulate a responsible gambling policy and strategy.[47]

Harm-Minimization Programs. While there is still some controversy
over abstinence versus harm-minimization, there is little doubt that most
youth gamble among themselves and with family members and that most
jurisdictions have multiple forms of legalized gambling for adults or adolescents. Yet a review of the literature revealed that relatively few gambling prevention or sensitization programs exist and those programs lack
empirical evaluation as to their effectiveness.[48] As a consequence, programs incorporating science-based problem gambling prevention need to
be developed and evaluated as to their efficacy in order to help establish
model programs. A substantial infusion of federal and state grants for the
development of school-based and community-based gambling prevention
programs is warranted. Such prevention initiatives must be ongoing from
the elementary school level, should include competency building skills,
enhancement of effective coping and adaptive behaviors, must emphasize
changing attitudes, increase knowledge related to gambling, help modify
erroneous conceptions, strengthen problem-solving skills, and enhance
coping and adaptive skills.

Technological Advances. Gambling has not been immune to technological
advances. On the contrary, technology continues to provide new gambling
opportunities in the form of Internet gambling and more technologically
advanced slot machines, VLTs, interactive lottery games, interactive television games, and telephone wagering.[49] It is predicted that participation
in Internet gambling will increase tenfold in coming years because (1) it
is easy to access and use from home, (2) Internet gambling has the potential to offer visually exciting effects similar to video games, slot machines,

and VLTs, and (3) the event frequency can be very rapid, particularly if the gambler subscribes to multiple sites. Given the increasing popularity, accessibility, and familiarity of the Internet, it represents another venue for potential problems for adolescents. Similarly, technological advances may well enhance innovative ways of educating our youth through Web-based courses, prevention initiatives, and online treatment. As government policy makers move forward, the introduction of Internet gambling should be viewed with extreme caution and safeguards need to be established to prevent problem gambling.

Advertising. There is little doubt that youth are particularly susceptible to advertisements in general and are considered an important target by advertisers. The advertising and glamorization of gambling is of great concern. The Virginia Lottery has advertising campaigns linked with NASCAR racing (a highly popular sport for adolescent and young adult males), several states have used Betty Boop in connection with their lottery, while other promotions include the opportunity to win Harley Davidson motorcycles. Recent data also suggest that young people pay particular attention to lottery advertisements, and like adults, are more likely to purchase scratch tickets when placed on checkout counters of local convenience stores.[50] However, advertising campaigns geared toward informing and sensitizing the public can actually be beneficial.[51] Public policy and advertising designed to enhance awareness of problems related to youth gambling needs to be implemented. Simultaneously, governments should establish strict advertising guidelines to discourage extravagant or misleading claims about gambling and opportunities to win.

Information Dissemination. The use of existing federal agencies to serve as a national clearinghouse for research and materials that will ultimately distribute best practices in the field of gambling prevention and treatment is necessary. Government gaming commissions should produce educational leaflets and brochures, post visible warning signs on gambling machines, and distribute information concerning the odds of winning on different types of gambling activities.

Regulatory Bodies. Regulatory bodies need an arms-length approach to properly monitor gambling. Periodic commissions to review national policies on gambling, while beneficial, are not sufficient. Policies need to be enacted which promote responsible gambling, adopt harm-minimization approaches, govern advertising and dissemination of material, and fund appropriate treatment facilities and prevention activities. Applicants for a gambling license or facility, including governmental agencies, must adopt a clear mission statement as to their policy on pathological or problem gambling. This statement should be accompanied with a tax or other percentage contribution to create a dedicated fund for the development and ongoing support of problem gambling, research, public awareness, prevention, education, and treatment programs. Regulatory bodies need to continue to be sensitive to emerging and social issues related to pathological and problem gambling.

CONCLUSIONS

Many other more visible adolescent problems have prompted significant social policy recommendations (e.g., cigarette smoking, alcohol and substance use and abuse, increased suicide rates). However, issues surrounding youth gambling problems have been largely ignored. Only recently have health professionals, educators, and public policy makers acknowledged the need for the prevention of problem gambling. In light of the scarcity of empirical knowledge about the prevention of this disorder, the similarities between adolescent problem gambling and other risky youth behaviors—particularly alcohol and substance abuse—can be informative in the conceptualization of the future direction of gambling prevention programs and should be made a priority for legislators. Unfortunately, most pathological gambling prevention programs lack a strong theoretical orientation and have been implemented without being empirically evaluated. This deficiency is of serious concern, as such programs may in fact be inciting gambling behavior. Finally, most existing programs are school-based, aimed at children and adolescents, although it should be remembered that adults also remain at risk for the development of serious pathological gambling programs. Such behaviors can occur at any age.

There is a general assumption that individual policies and programs, although helpful, must be nested within a more cohesive policy framework to be maximally effective.[52] Our governments should not take the important social and public health policy issue of gambling lightly. Our youth remain particularly vulnerable to the lure of gambling and require our immediate attention, concern, and efforts.

NOTES

1. I. Nelson Rose, "Legal Gambling's Historic Triumph at the Polls," in *Gambling and the Law* (Hollywood: Gambling Times, 1986).

2. Fred Preston et al., "Gambling as Stigmatized Behavior: Regional Relabeling and the Law," *Annals of the American Academy of Social Scientists* 556 (1998): 186–96.

3. Nancy Hall, Sharon Kagan, and Edward Zigler. "The Changing Nature of Child and Family Policy: An overview," in *Children, Families, and Government: Preparing for the Twenty-First Century*, ed. Edward Zigler, Sharon L. Kagan, and Nancy Hall (Cambridge: Cambridge University Press, 1996).

4. David Korn and Howard Shaffer, "Gambling and the Health of the Public: Adopting a Public Health Perspective," *Journal of Gambling Studies* 15 (1999): 289–365.

5. Jason Azmier, *Gambling in Canada: Triumph, Tragedy, or Tradeoff? Canadian Gambling Behavior and Attitudes* (Calgary, Alta.: Canada West Foundation, 2000).

6. Durand F. Jacobs, "Juvenile Gambling in North America: An Analysis of Long Term Trends and Future Prospects," *Journal of Gambling Studies* 16 (2000): 119–52; National Research Council, *Pathological Gambling: A Critical Review* (Washington, D.C.: National Academy Press, 1999); Howard J. Shaffer and Matthew M. Hall, "Estimating the Prevalence of Adolescent Gambling Disorders: A Quantitative Synthesis and Guide toward Standard Gambling Nomenclature," *Journal of Gambling Studies* 12, no. 2 (1996): 193–214.

7. Jeffrey L. Derevensky and Rina Gupta, "Youth Gambling: A Clinical and Research Perspective," *E-Gambling: Electronic Journal of Gambling Issues* 2 (2000): 1–11.; Rina Gupta and Jeffrey Derevensky, "Adolescent Gambling Behavior: A Prevalence Study and Examination of the Correlates Associated with Excessive Gambling," *Journal of Gambling Studies* 14 (1998): 319–45; Harold Wynne, Garry Smith, and Durand Jacobs, *Adolescent Gambling and Problem Gambling in Alberta* (report prepared for the Alberta Alcohol and Drug Abuse Commission, Edmonton, Alberta: Wynne Resources Ltd., 1996).

8. National Research Council, *Pathological Gambling* (Washington, D.C.: National Academy Press, 1997), p. 89

9. Jacobs, "Juvenile Gambling in North America."

10. Sue Fisher, "The Amusement Arcade as a Social Space for Adolescents: An Empirical Study," *Journal of Adolescence* 18 (1995): 71–86; Mark D. Griffiths, "The Acquisition, Development, and Maintenance of Fruit Machine Gambling in Adolescents," *Journal of Gambling Studies* 6 (1990): 193–204.

11. J. Huxley and Doug Carroll, "A Survey of Fruit Machine Gambling in Adolescents," *Journal of Gambling Studies* 8 (1992): 167–79.

12. Gupta and Derevensky, "Adolescent Gambling Behavior"; Wynne et al., *Adolescent Gambling.*

13. L. J. Dell, E. M. Ruzicka, and A. T. Palisi, "Personality and Other Factors Associated with Gambling Addiction," *International Journal of the Addictions* 16 (1981): 149–56.

14. Griffiths "The Acquisition . . . of Fruit Machine Gambling in Adolescents."

15. Gupta and Derevensky, "Adolescent Gambling Behavior."

16. Rina Gupta and Jeffrey Derevensky, "Familial and Social Influences on Juvenile Gambling Behavior," *Journal of Gambling Studies* 13, no. 3 (1997): 179–92; Huxley and Carroll, "A Survey of Fruit Machine Gambling in Adolescents"; S. M. Moore and K. Otshuka, "Gambling Activities of Young Australians: Developing a Model of Behavior," *Journal of Gambling Studies* 13 (1997): 207–36.

17. Robert Ladouceur et al., "Parents' Attitudes, Knowledge, and Behavior toward Gambling: A Five Year Follow-up" (paper presented at the Annual meeting of the National Council on Problem Gambling, Seattle, Washington, 2001).

18. Jennifer Felsher, Rina Gupta, and Jeffrey Derevensky, "An Examination of Lottery Ticket Purchases by Minors" (paper presented at the annual meeting of the National Council on Problem Gambling, Seattle, Washington, 2001).

19. Gupta and Derevensky, "Familial and Social Influences on Juvenile Gambling Behavior."

20. Robert Wood and Mark D. Griffiths, "The Acquisition, Development, and Maintenance of Lottery and Scratchcard Gambling in Adolescence," *Journal of Adolescence* 21 (1998): 265–72.

21. Durand F. Jacobs, A. Marston, and R. Singer, "Testing a General Theory of Addiction: Similarities and Differences among Alcoholics, Pathological Gamblers, and Overeaters," in *Health and Clinical Psychology*, vol. 4, ed. Janet J. Sanchez-Soza (Amsterdam, Neth.: Elsevier Science, 1985).

22. Henry R. Lesieur and Jerome Rothschild, "Children of Gamblers Anonymous Members," *Journal of Gambling Behavior* 5 (1989): 269–81.

23. Griffiths, "The Acquisition . . . of Fruit Machine Gambling in Adolescents."

24. R. Gupta and J. L. Derevensky, "The Relationship between Gambling and Video-Game Playing Behaviour in Children and Adolescents," *Journal of Gambling Studies* 12, no. 4 (1996): 375–94; Gupta and Derevensky, "Familial and Social Influences on Juvenile Gambling Behavior."

25. Karen Hardoon and Jeffrey Derevensky, "Social Influences Involved in Children's Gambling Behavior," *Journal of Gambling Studies* (in press).

26. J. L. Derevensky and R. Gupta, "Prevalence Estimates of Adolescent Gambling: A Comparison of the SOGS-RA, DSM-IV-J, and the GA Twenty Questions," *Journal of Gambling Studies* 16 (2000): 227–51.; Robert Ladouceur, Dominique Dubé, and Annie Bujold, "Gambling among Primary School Students," *Journal of Gambling Studies* 10, no. 4 (1994): 363–70; Randy Stinchfield, "Gambling and Correlates of Gambling among Minnesota Public School Students," *Journal of Gambling Studies* 16, nos. 2 and 3 (2000): 153–73; Henry R. Lesieur et al., "Gambling and Pathological Gambling among University Students," *Addictive Behaviors* 16 (1991): 517–27; Rachel A. Volberg, "The Prevalence and Demographics of Pathological Gamblers: Implications for Public Health," *American Journal of Public Health* 84 (1994): 237–41.

27. Ladouceur, Dubé, and Bujold, "Gambling among Primary School Students."

28. M. D. Griffiths, "Gambling in Children and Adolescents," *Journal of Gambling Behavior* 5 (1989): 66–83.

29. J. L. Derevensky, R. Gupta, and G. Della-Cioppa, "A Developmental Perspective of Gambling Behavior in Children and Adolescents," *Journal of Gambling Studies* 12, no. 1 (1996): 49–66.; Volberg, "The Prevalence and Demographics of Pathological Gamblers" and "Gambling and Problem Gambling in New York: A Ten-Year Replication Survey, 1986 to 1996" (report to the New York Council on Problem Gambling, Albany: New York Council on Problem Gambling, 1996); Wynne et al., *Adolescent Gambling.*

30. Rina Gupta and Jeffrey Derevensky, "An Empirical Examination of Jacobs' General Theory of Addictions: Do Adolescent Gamblers Fit the Theory?" *Journal of Gambling Studies* 14 (1998): 17–49.; D. F. Jacobs, A. Marston, and R. Singer, "Testing a General Theory of Addiction."

31. Jeffrey Derevensky and Rina Gupta, "Risk Taking and Gambling Behavior among Adolescents: An Empirical Examination" (paper presented at the Tenth National Conference on Gambling Behavior, Chicago, 1996); Marvin Zuckerman, *Behavioral Expressions and Biosocial Bases of Sensation Seeking* (New York: Cambridge University Press, 1994).

32. Gupta and Derevensky, "Familial and Social Influences on Juvenile Gambling Behavior"; M. A. Zimmerman, T. Meeland, and S. E Kru, "Measurement and Structure of Pathological Gambling Behavior," *Journal of Personality Assessment* 49, no. 1 (1985): 76–81.

33. Julian I. Taber et al., "Ego Strength and Achievement Motivation in Pathological Gamblers," *Journal of Gambling Behavior* 2 (1986): 69–80; Frank Vitaro et al., "Gambling, Substance Use, and Impulsivity during Adolescence," *Psychology of Addictive Behaviors* (in press).

34. R. Gupta and J. L. Derevensky, "Adolescents with Gambling Problems: From Research to Treatment," *Journal of Gambling Studies* 16 (2000): 315–42.

35. Chantal Ste-Marie, "Anxiety and Social Stress Related to Adolescent Gambling Behavior" (unpublished master's thesis, McGill University, 2001).

36. N. Marget, Rina Gupta, and Jeffrey L. Derevensky, "The Psychosocial Factors Underlying Adolescent Problem Gambling" (poster presented at the Annual Meeting of the American Psychological Association, Boston, 1999); Lisa Nower, J. L. Derevensky, and R. Gupta, "Youth Gamblers and Substance Abusers: A Comparison of Stress-Coping Styles and Risk-Taking Behavior of Two Addicted Adolescent Populations" (paper presented at the 11th International Conference on Gambling and Risk-Taking, Las Vegas, 2000).

37. Robert Ladouceur, Dominique Dubé, and Annie Bujold, "Prevalence of Pathological Gambling and Related Problems among College Students in the Quebec Metropolitan Area," *Canadian Journal of Psychiatry* 39 (1994): 289–93; Anthony Maden, Mark Swinton, and John Gunn, "Gambling in Young Offenders," *Criminal Behavior and Mental Health* 2 (1992): 300–308; Stinchfield, "Gambling and Correlates of Gambling"; Ken C. Winters and Nikki Anderson, "Gambling Involvement and Drug Use among Adolescents," *Journal of Gambling Studies* 16, nos. 2 and 3 (2000): 175–98.

38. Robert Ladouceur et al., "Pathological Gambling and Related Problems among Adolescents," *Journal of Child & Adolescent Substance Abuse* 8, no. 4 (1999): 55–68; Lesieur et al., "Gambling and Pathological Gambling among University Students."

39. Gupta and Derevensky, "Adolescents with Gambling Problems."

40. Gupta and Derevensky, "Adolescent Gambling Behavior"; Wynne et al., *Adolescent Gambling.*

41. Derevensky and Gupta, "Youth Gambling"; Gupta and Derevensky, "Adolescents with Gambling Problems."

42. Gupta and Derevensky, "Adolescent Gambling Behavior."

43. Jane E. Costello et al., "Development of Psychiatric Comorbidity with Substance Abuse in Adolescents: Effects of Timing and Sex," *Journal of Clinical*

Child Psychology 28, no. 3 (1999): 298–311; Nancy L. Galambos and Lauree C. Tilton-Weaver, "Multiple Risk Behavior in Adolescents and Young Adults," *Health Review* 10 (1998): 9–20; Rolf Loeber et al., "Multiple Risk Factors for Multiproblem Boys: Co-occurrence of Delinquency, Substance Use, Attention Deficit, Conduct Problems, Physical Aggression, Covert Behavior, Depressed Mood, and Shy/Withdrawn Behavior," in *New Perspectives on Adolescent Risk Behavior*, ed. Richard Jessor (Cambridge: Cambridge University Press, 1998).

44. Gupta and Derevensky, "Adolescent Gambling Behavior"; Durand F. Jacobs, "Juvenile Gambling in North America"; National Research Council, *Pathological Gambling: A Critical Review*; Wynne et al., *Adolescent Gambling*.

45. Constance Hammen, "The Family-Environmental Context of Depression: A Perspective on Children's Risk," in *Developmental Perspectives on Depression*, ed. Dante Cicchetti and Sheree L. Toth (Rochester Symposium on Developmental Psychopathology, Rochester: University of Rochester Press, 1992).

46. Michael Rutter, "Psychosocial Resilience and Protective Mechanisms," in *Risk and Protective Factors in the Development of Psychopathology*, ed. Jon and Garzmey Norman (New York: Cambridge University Press, 1990); Emmy E. Werner and Ruth S. Smith, *Vulnerable but Invincible: A Study of Resilient Children* (New York: McGraw-Hill, 1982).

47. Korn and Shaffer, "Gambling and the Health of the Public."

48. Derevensky et al., "Prevention Efforts toward Minimizing Gambling Problems" (paper prepared for the National Council on Problem Gambling, Center for Mental Health Services [CMS] and the Substance Abuse and Mental Health Services Administration [SAMHSA], Washington, D.C., 2001).

49. Mark Griffiths and Richard Wood, "Risk Factors in Adolescence: The Case of Gambling, Videogame Playing, and the Internet," *Journal of Gambling Studies* 16, nos. 2 and 3 (2000): 199–225.

50. J. Derevensky and R. Gupta, "*Le problème de jeu touché aussi les jeunes*," *Psychologie Québec* 18, no. 6 (2001): 23–27.

51. Richard Earle, *The Art of Cause Marketing: How to Use Advertising to Change Personal Behavior and Public Policy* (Chicago: NTC Business Books, 2000).

52. Hall, Kagan, and Zigler, "The Changing Nature of Child and Family Policy."

15

LATE-LIFE GAMBLING

The Attitudes and Behaviors of Older Adults

Dennis P. McNeilly and William J. Burke

This study presents the first detailed profile of the gambling behavior and attitudes of older adults; i.e., those aged sixty-five and over. It examines the extent of both gambling and pathological gambling among this previously underresearched group and highlights the need for an increased awareness of the impact of legalized gambling on older adults in the United States.

Legalized gambling, particularly casino and lottery gambling, has become increasingly available and accessible to those outside of Nevada and Atlantic City within the last ten years. Although raised during the Great Depression, when gambling was commonly regarded as a sin or a vice, many of today's older adults have embraced it as a new form of mainstream entertainment in their retirement years. Promotional programs such

Reprinted with changes from *Journal of Gambling Studies* 16, no. 4 (2000): 393–415.

The authors wish to thank Adrienne Van Winkle for her invaluable assistance throughout this study and Earl Falkner and Daryl Bohac, who provided comments on drafts of this article.

as inexpensive buffet meals, transportation, coupons, slot clubs, dance clubs, and discount prescription offers are tailored to these older adults who still remember their first World War II ration books and help encourage those who might otherwise not normally visit a gambling venue.

Research into the impact of gambling among this group since the emergence of available legalized gambling in the last decade, however, has been lacking. Few studies have directly investigated the gambling behavior of older adults, and, of those, most have been drawn from methodologically weak observational data or conducted prior to the expansion of gambling in this country within the last ten years. Various studies of this group have found that casino gambling increased older adults' self-esteem[1] and also that older adults tended to withdraw from multiple gambling activity to concentrate (with the exception of bingo) on more limited types instead.[2]

When gambling disorders have been examined among adults sampled from the general population, two recent studies have found an increase in gambling disorders throughout the country.[3] It has been suggested that the number of compulsive/problem gamblers will increase at an accelerated rate due to the changing social attitudes toward gambling from negative to positive.[4] One of those studies found that the number of older adults who had ever gambled had increased by 45 percent between 1975 and 1997 and that, in the four-year period between 1994 and 1998, female gamblers in this age group had risen by 20 percent.[5] In addition, a more recent study found gambling to be the most frequently identified social activity among this age group, with bingo the most popular activity, followed by casino gambling.[6]

Though published research on gambling and older adults is very limited, the number of anecdotal reports on the potential public health consequences of problem gambling among older adults is significant. One recent Detroit study found elderly persons twice as likely as others to have a compulsive gambler in their household.[7] Other case reports have stressed the increasing numbers of older adults with problem gambling behaviors[8] while treatment professionals have reported that middle-aged to older women have become the fastest growing group (50 percent) of those presenting in casino gambling treatment programs.[9] These women have been categorized as emotional "relief or escape" gamblers who appear to gamble to relieve their negative feelings of isolation, boredom, and depression, or to avoid difficult situations. From the evidence, the potential for a public health problem of disordered gambling among this age group is clear, and it is equally clear that more research is needed into the area.

METHODS

This study was undertaken with these concerns in mind. It was conducted in a Midwest metropolitan area where casino gambling became locally available four years ago and a state lottery was initiated six years ago. It used cluster sampling to select adults aged sixty-five plus from five different sources: senior centers (N = 44), retirement centers (N = 113), American Association of Retired Persons (AARP) chapter members (N = 67), commercial and charitable bingo parlors (N = 45) (the community group sample), and community-dwelling older adults who had participated in a shuttle bus day-trip to a casino (N = 47) (the gambling patron sample). Comparisons could therefore be made between two separate groups: (1) those who were active patrons of bingo parlors and day bus-trips to a casino and (2) those who were drawn from the community and not actively involved in gambling at the time they were surveyed. A questionnaire was administered to these participants which was designed to obtain a profile of respondents' level of participation in gambling, disordered gambling behavior, levels of depression and life satisfaction, and general background demographics, in order to compare them to what is known about younger problem gamblers.[10]

RESULTS

A total of 315 (69 percent) completed questionnaires were returned by mail out of the 455 sent out. Comparisons were made between the two groups on measures of depression, life satisfaction, gambling behaviors, motivations for gambling, attitudes towards gambling and demographics.[11]

The majority of respondents in each of the two groups were retired female Caucasians with at least a high school education whose average income ranged from $15,000 to $34,999. The groups differed in terms of age, marital status, and current residence. The group sampled from within the community included a larger percentage of women who were older, widowed, and lived in a retirement home, whereas the gambling patron group had higher percentages of women who were married and lived in their own home. No significant differences were found between the two groups on levels of depression or life satisfaction. No significant differences were found within the gambling patron group when subdivided into those respondents from a bingo venue and those from a casino venue.

However, statistically significant differences were found between the two groups in terms of behavioral characteristics. The gambling patron group were more likely to smoke (14.8 percent), drive a car (88.9 percent), eat fewer than two meals a day (15.6 percent) and do volunteer work on an occasional basis (40 percent), while the group sampled from within the community were more likely to report they spent time reading books on a several-times-a-week basis (57.1 percent). When the gambling patron group was further analyzed and subdivided into those respondents from a bingo venue and those from a casino venue, a statistically significant difference found casino patrons more likely to report they spent time reading books on a several-times-a-week basis (27 percent) and attended a church or synagogue on a once-a-week or more basis (69.2 percent) than were the bingo venue patrons.

Significant differences were also found in responses to the SOGS-R questions that were concerned with the type and frequency of gambling. The gambling patron group reported higher frequencies in all types of gambling. They gambled on a "less than once a week" basis in playing cards (24.7 percent), horse races (11.6 percent), dice games (8.1 percent), casino gambling (63.6 percent), the lottery (26.7 percent), bingo (14.9 percent), slot machines (55.2 percent), and pull tabs (29.4 percent). The gambling patron group were also more likely to report gambling on a "once-a-week or more" basis when gambling in a casino (23.9 percent), playing the lottery (17.4 percent), bingo (41.4 percent), slot machines (27.6 percent), shooting pool (11.6 percent), and pull tabs (8.2 percent). The group sampled from within the community of older adults did report a higher frequency of playing cards for money on a "once-a-week-or-more" basis (8.1 percent).

When the gambling patron group was further analyzed and subdivided into those respondents from bingo and casino venues, it was found that bingo patrons were more likely to report they gambled on a "less than once a week" basis in playing pull tabs (20.5 percent) and to report they gambled on a "once-a-week-or-more" basis in playing bingo for money (41.3 percent) than were the casino gambling venue respondents. In terms of average amount spent, it was found that the gambling patron group spent significantly more than the community group on the lottery, bingo, and casino gambling. Consequently, each time they gambled, the gambling patron group was found to have spent on average a total of $2.27 on the lottery, $12.16 on bingo, and $53.12 on casino gambling. Similarly, the gambling patron group reported spending higher amounts per day on their gambling than the group sampled from within the community. When this group was further analyzed and subdivided into those respondents from a bingo venue and those from a casino venue, the bingo venue respondents had a highly statistically significant difference between the amount they spent on average on bingo ($21.32) than the average amount spent by the casino venue respondents ($1.81).

When responses to SOGS-R questions were compared, the gambling patron group were found to differ significantly from the community group. The former were more likely to report they had gambled more than they intended to (46.2 percent), felt guilty about gambling (20.9 percent), argued with others about handling money (19.8 percent), argued over money and gambling (10.9 percent), borrowed money from spouse to gamble (5 percent), borrowed money from credit cards to gamble (11.3 percent), and cashed in bonds to gamble (2.5 percent). When asked if they returned to win back their losses, the gambling patron group were found to return "some of the time (less than half of the times I've lost)." Significant differences were also found between the two groups when they were asked if they considered various types of gambling as harmless entertainment. The gambling patron group were more likely to report they believed that both the lottery and casino gambling were harmless entertainment.

When asked about their motivations for casino gambling, between-group comparisons revealed significant differences. The gambling patron group were more likely to report they engaged in casino gambling to relax and have fun (68.1 percent), get away for the day (43.7 percent), pass the time (42.7 percent), and relieve boredom (30 percent). This group were also more likely to report they went to a casino because of the inexpensive meals (42 percent) while the comparison group were more likely to report they went to a casino to meet new people (11.6 percent). It should also be noted that the two groups were not found to be significantly different in their responses to other motivations for casino gambling. Specifically, they tended not to identify special casino gambling promotions and incentives, such as free transportation and slot-club promotions to a casino, as motivation for their gambling in a casino. They also reported they did not gamble in a casino as a means to socialize with their friends.

A final comparison between the two groups was made on their overall SOGS-R scores. It was found that the gambling patron group had significantly higher scores than did those sampled from within the community, the majority of whom obtained a score of 0 (see fig. 1). While both groups received a SOGS-R score of 0 (84.4 percent of the community group and 45.1 percent of the gambling patron group), there were significant differences between the groups in the higher ranges. A SOGS-R Score = 1–2 was recorded for 38.5 percent of the gambling patron group and 11.6 percent of the community group; the figures for Score = 3–4 were 5.5 percent and 1.3 percent for these groups respectively; while a Score of 5 or more (often considered indicative of probable pathological gambling) was recorded for 11 percent of the gambling group and 2.7 percent of the community group.

CONCLUSIONS

This study investigated older adults' level of participation in gambling and profiled their problematic gambling behavior, levels of depression, life satisfaction, attitudes toward gambling, and motivations for gambling. It was found that respondents who were sampled at gambling venues were more likely to access several different types of gambling with greater frequency and to spend on average more on gambling each time they gambled than the community group. It also found that those participants who were sampled at gambling venues were more likely to report that they gambled more than they had intended, felt guilty about their gambling, argued over money, and borrowed money from a spouse or credit cards to gamble, than those from the community group.

SOGS-R Gambling Scores:
Community and Gambling Patron Groups

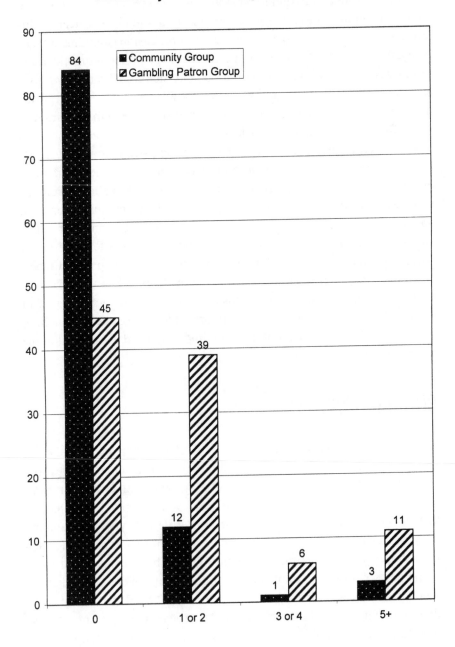

Gambling venue respondents were more likely than community ones to consider that the lottery and casino gambling were harmless entertainment and were also more likely to report that they gambled at a casino in order to relax and have fun, get away for the day, pass the time, enjoy the inexpensive meals, and gamble when they felt bored. The community group were more likely to report that they gambled in a casino to meet new people.

The results of this study also provide an indication of the levels of possible problematic or disordered gambling behavior among these two groups of older adults. Although the majority of both groups scored 0 in the SOGS-R questions, a higher percentage of the gambling patron group was found to have scores in the higher ranges of this instrument, which measure increasing levels of problem behavior.

The results of this study suggest potentially higher levels of disordered gambling behaviors among older adults who were sampled at gambling venues than those previously reported among the general adult population and believed also true for the older adult population. The higher levels of disordered gambling found here may be reflective of a largely unrecognized public health problem of problem gambling among older adults and may also be reflective of what has been observed among gambling treatment professionals as the shortened period of time it takes older adults to reach a crisis stage in their gambling behaviors.[12]

Similar to the types of reported motivations for casino gambling among younger adult pathological gamblers, the older adults who were sampled at gambling venues reported that they gambled as a means to relax, escape boredom, pass the time, and get away for the day. While a majority of the gambling patron group reported they were motivated to gamble in a casino because of the inexpensive meals, it was the only gambling industry-supported promotion (e.g., free transportation, discount coupons, slot clubs, dance clubs, or discount prescription offers, etc.) cited by the older adults as a gambling motivator. This finding is contrary to what has been suggested by numerous anecdotal reports that often associate older adults' predilection for gambling and subsequent problematic gambling behaviors with gambling-industry promotional programs. This finding suggests that older adults may be willing participants of discounted or free promotions for transportation, etc., but with the possible exception of inexpensive meals, they are not necessarily motivated to gamble as a result of such gambling industry promotions.

The results of this study run contrary to what had been previously found to be a decline in the propensity for gambling as one ages,[13] though older adults may continue to gravitate to only a few (one or two) types of gambling.[14] Older adults, not unlike their younger counterparts, have increasingly begun to participate in gambling as it has become more socially accepted and accessible. It is also likely that many engage in more than one type of gambling, some of which they do not consider actual "gambling" (e.g., the lottery, bingo, and pull tabs). They may only think of themselves as gambling when they go to a casino, where the results of this study found they most often tend to play the slot machines.

On a more cautious note, it should be pointed out that the results of this study were drawn from small cross-sectional samples of self-reports from older adults in a metropolitan area close to several casinos, and as a result, the higher levels of possible disordered gambling among those sampled may be due to the immediate geographical availability of casino gambling.

Nevertheless, this research presents an initial picture of the attitudes, beliefs, and behavior of the gambling patterns of a previously "invisible" group. The overall implications of this study highlight the need for a greater awareness of the phenomenal growth that legalized gambling, particularly casino gambling, may have on older adults in this country. This need is all the more pressing as a greater percentage of the population turns retirement age at a time of unparalleled availability and accessibility to commercial gambling as form of mainstream entertainment for one's retirement years.

NOTES

1. Felicia F. Campbell, "The Future of Gambling," *Futurist* 10 (April 1976): 84–90.

2. Waiman P. Mok and Joseph Hraba, "Age and Gambling Behavior: A Declining and Shifting Pattern of Participation," *Journal of Gambling Studies* 7, no. 4 (1991): 313–36.

3. Howard Shaffer, *Estimating the Prevalence of Disordered Gambling Behavior in the United States and Canada: A Meta-analysis* (Boston: Harvard Medical School Division on Addictions, 1997); National Opinion Research

Council, *Gambling Impact and Behavior Study* (Chicago: University of Chicago Press, 1999).

4. Shaffer, *Estimating the Prevalence of Disordered Gambling Behavior.*

5. National Opinion Research Center, *Gambling Impact and Behavior Study* (Chicago: National Opinion Research Center, 1999).

6. Dennis P. McNeilly and William J. Burke, "Disposable Time and Disposable Income: Problem Gambling Behaviors in Older Adults," *Journal of Clinical Geropsychology* (in press).

7. Robin Widgery, *The Effects of Casino Gambling on At-Risk Groups in the City of Detroit* (Detroit: Social Systems Research Institute Report, May 18, 1998).

8. Andrew Glazer, "Pathologic Gambling," *Nurse Practitioner* 23, no. 9 (1998): 74–82.

9. Keith Chrostowski "Compulsive Gamblers Inevitably Crash in Despair," *Kansas City Star*, March 10, 1997.

10. The 103-item questionnaire used in this study was generated from items included in the Geriatric Depression Scale Short Form, Satisfaction With Life Scale, South Oaks Gambling Screen Revised—past-year information, background demographic questions, and items generated by the author to assess attitudes and motivations for gambling.

11. Descriptive frequencies, means, percentages, standard deviations, and 95 percent confidence intervals were computed and compared for the categorical variables. Nonparametric Chi-square, t-test, and one-way ANOVA statistical analyses were utilized for between group comparisons. Group-comparison analyses were made on the basis of respondents' active involvement in gambling when surveyed.

12. Pat Fowler, quoted in "Addiction Crisis Stage Comes Quick for Slot Players" *Mississippi Sun Herald*, November 25, 1997.

13. Maureen Kallick et al., "Gambling Participation," in *A Survey of American Gambling Attitudes and Behavior*, ed. M. Kallick et al. (Ann Arbor: University of Michigan Press, 1979).

14. Mok and Hraba, "Age and Gambling Behavior."

♥ ♠ ♣

16

A PUBLIC POLICY RESPONSE TO PROBLEM GAMBLING

Keith Whyte

The negative effects of gambling, or problem gambling, have been known since ancient times. However, until recently problem gambling has not been seen as a public policy issue but rather as a personal or individual problem. New research has not only increased our understanding of this disorder, but has also revealed the extent of the consequences to our society of problem gambling.

Gambling in the United States is generally prohibited unless affirmatively legalized by government. Therefore, much of the responsibility to address problem gambling is borne by federal, state, tribal, and local government. Gambling, which once may have been seen as aberrant behavior, is now a normative activity in the United States. Over 85 percent of Americans have gambled at least once in their lives, and over 65 percent in the past year.[1] Forty-seven of the 50 states now have some

The views expressed in this paper are those of the author, and do not necessarily represent the views of the National Council on Problem Gambling.

form of legalized gambling. New types of games continue to proliferate and some states have eased regulations or limits on gambling, in response to the increased competition among state and tribal government for gambling revenue.

The primary public policy concern regarding gambling is the addictive disorder known as pathological gambling, best described as "a progressive disorder characterized by a continuous or periodic loss of control over gambling; a preoccupation with gambling or obtaining money for gambling; irrational thinking, and a continuation of the behavior despite adverse consequences."[2] The rate of pathological gambling among adults is estimated at 1 percent in the past year, with an additional 2 to 3 percent of adults considered problem gamblers. The negative impacts of these 9 to 12 million adults have a ripple effect throughout the country.

Problem gambling touches every corner of our society, afflicting inner cities, affluent suburbs, and rural communities. No group, whether rich or poor, educated or uneducated, professional or blue-collar, young or old, is exempt. The vast majority of problem gamblers in America are employed. Some of the elderly suffer from addiction, as do people in the prime of their lives. Gambling and problem gambling are prevalent among the young, often at rates exceeding those of adults.

Numerous anecdotes and other "soft" evidence throughout history and literature relate to individuals with gambling problems, but I would like to focus on a brief review of research-based or "hard" evidence. The recent surge in scientific study of problem gambling has given us new information to examine, but it is important to remember that most current problem gambling research is built upon previous studies. Some of the more relevant findings are highlighted below, but please note this list is not intended to be exhaustive.

The Harvard Medical School Division on Addictions published a landmark meta-analysis of prevalence research in 1997. The authors note, "Disordered gambling is an apparently robust phenomenon that research can identify across a wide range of investigative procedures that vary in quality of method." Furthermore, the researchers found that in the past year, 1.14 percent of adults met criteria for pathological (or level 3) gambling, and another 2.8 percent could be considered problem gamblers.[3]

Research in a number of fields, notably genetics, has produced valuable information on problem gambling. In a recent study of twins, inherited factors explained between 35 and 54 percent of pathological gambling symptoms.[4] Pathological gamblers are more likely than others to carry the D_2A1 allele, which has also been linked to other addictive and impulsive disorders in genetics studies.[5] Adult pathological gamblers are also three to eight times more likely to report at least one parent with a gambling problem than nonproblem gamblers.[6]

A great deal has been learned from evaluating programs in the substance abuse field. Obviously, there is a good deal of overlap between problem gambling and other addictive disorders. In fact, a review of studies found that between 25 and 63 percent of pathological gamblers have a lifetime substance abuse disorder.[7] Not surprisingly, medications such as Naltrexone have proven effective in blocking craving in some pathological gamblers.[8] More evidence comes from the National Problem Gambling Helpline Network. This tollfree and nationwide service received over 115,000 calls in 2000 alone. Call volume increased 25 percent to more than 144,000 calls in 2001. Although not all calls are problem-gambling specific, every call must be treated as a crisis call, and individuals who contact a helpline are often in great distress. An evaluation of a state helpline found that helpline callers had a mean score well above the cutoff rate for pathological gambling, indicating that these callers appear to represent a seriously disordered group.[9]

Further evidence comes from a study produced by the U.S. National Academy of Sciences. The National Research Council (NRC), the principal operating agency of the academy, was commissioned to compile a review of problem gambling research. Its report states:

> The availability of legal gambling has increased sharply in the past twenty years. More people are gambling, and they are wagering more. As a result, there is increased concern about pathological gambling. Clinical evidence suggests that pathological gamblers engage in destructive behaviors: they commit crimes, they run up large debts, they damage relationships with family and friends, and they kill themselves."[10]

CONCLUSIONS

Problem gambling is a robust phenomenon. Research across a wide variety of disciplines, including biology, psychology, and epidemiology has consistently confirmed its presence. The problem demands a comprehensive solution involving not only federal programs but also efforts on the part of states, counties, cities, communities, and families, as well as civic groups, coalitions, and other organizations. This cooperative effort must be guided by a clear and consistent policy approach designed to mitigate the negative impacts of gambling problems on individuals, families, and communities.

The research to date in problem gambling, as well as our experience with substance abuse, confirms that no single approach could adequately address this public health issue. Prevention, education, treatment, and research must be complemented by the commitment to maintain and enforce gambling laws, especially regarding access and participation in gambling by minors. This strategy ties policy to a scientific body of knowledge about the nation's problems with gambling. These goals are useful for state and local governments as well as the private sector.

I have somewhat arbitrarily assembled five essential components of a comprehensive responsible gambling policy: Prevention, Education, Treatment, Enforcement, and Research (PETER). The components must of course be applied across various domains, such as gaming industry employees, customers, and community. Programs must address gender, racial, ethnic, cultural and socioeconomic diversity, and they must be evidence-based. To date, no U.S. jurisdiction has such a comprehensive plan, including adequate resources, to address problem gambling.

Preventing problem gambling in the first place is preferable to addressing the problem later through treatment and law enforcement. Although to date no problem-gambling specific prevention programs have been adequately evaluated, models from other addictive disorders can almost certainly be successfully adapted. In addition, age of onset for gambling precedes use of tobacco, hard liquor, and marijuana.[11] Problem gambling, therefore, may be a gateway to other problems among youth. Prevention also has important benefits to the overall health and welfare of young people by helping them reach maturity without debilitating mental health and/or substance abuse problems.

Americans must be educated about problem gambling as a serious public health issue. If individuals choose to gamble, they should do so with an awareness of the rules of the games and a balanced assessment of the odds. In addition gamblers should receive education on potential consequences, including damage to finances and health. Finally, information must be made available on warning signs of a gambling problem, responsible gaming guidelines for players, and availability of help for problems.

There are approximately three million pathological gamblers who need immediate treatment. Without help, these adults will suffer from poor health, unstable family relations, devastating financial problems, and other negative consequences of this disorder. Such gambling is a chronic, relapsing disorder that exacts an enormous cost on individuals, families, businesses, communities, and nations. Addicted individuals frequently engage in self-destructive and criminal behavior. Treatment programs can reduce the consequences of addiction for the rest of society. The ultimate goal of treatment is to enable a patient to become abstinent and to improve functioning through sustained recovery. On the way to that goal, reduction of problem gambling, improvement of the addict's ability to function in society, and addressing the medical needs of the addicted are useful interim outcomes. Providing treatment for America's problem gamblers is both compassionate public policy and a sound investment.

Enforcement of existing gambling-related laws is an important, if often overlooked, means to combat illegal gambling and underage gambling, both of which breed problem gambling. A comprehensive 1997 study showed that nationwide more than 75 percent of adolescents gambled at least once. At least 30 percent had bet on each of these four forms of gambling in the past year: lottery, sports, games of skill, and non-casino card games.[12] Almost all of these minors were gambling illegally. The industry and government must reduce these opportunities for youth to gamble and must close the loopholes in state and local laws that allow minors to gamble. Unlike controlled and/or addictive substances such as alcohol or tobacco, gambling products are sold without human oversight in some states. Lottery tickets are placed in vending machines, some of which are located in public areas. It is therefore unsurprising that youth are able to easily access both legal and illegal forms of gambling. Betting on sporting events is the most widespread form of illegal gambling despite the fact that it is prohibited in forty-nine of fifty states. However, almost every U.S. newspaper prints the betting line in the sports section.

Adequate research is the key to continually improving the effectiveness of our prevention, education, treatment, and enforcement efforts. I recognize that much of the basic research has not yet been done. For instance, only two nationally representative problem gambling prevalence studies have been conducted in the United States in the last twenty-five years.[13]

In the United States, tribal, state, and local governments have taken the lead in legalizing, regulating, and promoting gambling. However, they have uniformly failed to develop concomitant policy on problem gambling. Without a clear policy, efforts will continue to be piecemeal and of limited effectiveness. Government must dedicate sufficient resources to address problem gambling in order to develop and maintain a comprehensive responsible gambling policy, and every jurisdiction should develop a strategy that incorporates prevention, education, treatment, enforcement, and research.

NOTES

1. National Research Council (NRC), *Pathological Gambling: A Critical Review* (Washington, D.C.: National Academy Press, 1997).

2. Richard J. Rosenthal, "Pathological Gambling," *Psychiatric Annals* 22 (1992): 72–78.

3. Howard Shaffer et al., *Estimating the Prevalence of Disordered Gambling Behavior in the United States and Canada: A Meta-analysis* (Cambridge: Harvard Medical School, Division on Addictions, 1997).

4. Seth Eisen et al., "Obsessive-Compulsive Disorder in Patients with Schizophrenia or Schizoaffective Disorder," *American Journal of Psychiatry* 40 (1997): 2–3

5. David Comings et al., "A Study of the Dopamine D_2 Receptor Gene in Pathological Gambling," *Pharmacogenetics* 6 (1996): 223–34.

6. Blaise Gambino et al., "Perceived Family History of Problem Gambling and Scores on the SOGS," *Journal of Gambling Studies* 9 (1993): 164–84.

7. David N. Crockford and Nady el-Guebaly, "Psychiatric Co-morbidity in Pathological Gambling: A Critical Review," *Canadian Journal of Psychiatry* 43 (1998): 43–50.

8. Suck Won Kim, "Opiod Antagonists in the Treatment of Impulse-Control Disorders," *Journal of Clinical Psychiatry* 59, no. 4 (1998): 159–62.

9. Randy Stinchfield, "Reliability, Validity, and Classification Accuracy of the SOGS" (paper presented at the 12th National Conference on Problem Gambling, Las Vegas, June 18–20, 1998).

10. NRC, *Pathological Gambling: A Critical Review.*

11. David Jacobs, "Juvenile Gambling in North America: An Analysis of Long Term Trends and Future Prospects," *Journal of Gambling Studies* 16, nos. 2 and 3 (2000).

12. Shaffer et al., *Estimating the Prevalence of Disordered Gambling.*

13. National Gambling Impact Study Commission, *Final Report* (Washington, D.C.: Government Printing Office, 1999).

Section 6

PSYCHOLOGICAL AND ENVIRONMENTAL FACTORS

17
THE ENVIRONMENTAL PSYCHOLOGY OF GAMBLING

Mark Griffiths and Jonathan Parke

O ver the last century, the gaming industry has used various induce-
ments and ploys to entice people to gamble. An analysis of gambling
marketing methods mainly falls into two categories: *situational
characteristics*, which bring the potential gamblers into the gambling environment, and *structural characteristics*, which induce the person either to
gamble or to continue gambling.[1] The effectiveness of these methods suggests there is much to be learned about the psychology of gambling from an
analysis of these characteristics.

SITUATIONAL CHARACTERISTICS

Situational characteristics are primarily features of the environment (e.g.,
location of the arcade, the number of arcades in a specified area, possible

membership requirements, etc.) but can also include internal features of the arcade itself (decor, heating, lighting, etc.). These variables may be important in both the initial decision to gamble and the maintenance of the behavior. They may also help clarify why some forms of gambling are more attractive to particular socioeconomic classes. In essence, by identifying particular situational characteristics it may be possible to

- examine how different situations might evoke different levels of gambling in the same individual,
- understand player motivation and what influences how they gamble, bringing us closer to understanding the "player psyche," and
- educate problem gamblers about such warning signs as an ancillary form of prevention and treatment.

This essay therefore, examines the situational characteristics of gambling environments and assesses what impact these may have on the acquisition and, perhaps more important, the development and maintenance of gambling. Most of the information reported in this essay comes from a variety of sources including gambling industry personnel and both participant and nonparticipant observational fieldwork by the authors over a ten-year period. The areas examined include the psychology of familiarity in gambling environments, sensory factors (e.g., sound/noise effects, light/color effects), money access (e.g., lack of change facilities or arcades with cash dispensers), physical comfort determinants (e.g., heating or seating), and proximity to other activities.

SITUATIONAL DETERMINANTS AND SENSORY FACTORS

Sound Effects and Noise

A number of authors have made the point that the sound effects (particularly in slot machines) are gambling inducers. Constant noise gives the impression (1) of a noisy, fun, and exciting environment and (2) fosters the delusion that winning is more common than losing (you can't hear the sound of losing!). However, these are very general effects that merely create an overall impression.

Music

Over the last ten years, we have noticed that music appears to play an increasingly important part of one particular gambling environment—the amusement arcade. Effects of the listening context on responses to music largely have been neglected despite the prevalence of music in our everyday lives. Music can heighten psychological arousal or help listeners relax. In either case, these effects may influence behavior in commercial situations such as shopping or gambling, for example, by making people spend more or less money. Early studies showed that when customers in a supermarket were exposed to loud music, their shopping rate—how much they bought per minute spent in the store—was higher than when quiet music was played. However, people also spent less time in the supermarket, so the end result was the same. Effects on gamblers under similar conditions are likely to be similar.

Studies have demonstrated that music can have reliable effects on atmosphere and purchase intentions in commercial environments. One study examined the effects of different types of music in a university campus cafeteria.[2] The authors found that the type of music affected customers' views of the atmosphere in the cafeteria and influenced their purchase intentions.[2] Pop music made them view the cafeteria as an "optimistic" and "confident" environment but not a peaceful one. Classical music led to a feeling of "elegance" and "high class" but scored lowest on the "optimism" factor. The absence of music resulted in a feeling of "peacefulness" but a lack of customer confidence. Easy listening music led to the most negative feedback. Although there was no statistically significant difference among the amounts customers were prepared to spend when exposed to different types of music, the study showed that customers were willing to pay more for their food when they had been listening to classical or pop music.[3]

Given this small but growing research area, further investigation of background music in gambling environments is much needed to determine whether such music maintains or exacerbates gambling behavior in some individuals. These effects will obviously depend on the musical preferences of the gamblers themselves. Given previous research in other environments, it is likely that pop music will be the most effective in stimulating the impulse to gamble. Empirical research would be useful to determine whether background music will

- Increase confidence in gamblers.
- Increase arousal in gamblers.
- Relax the gambler.
- Help the gambler disregard previous losses.
- Induce a "romantic" affective state, leading the gambler to believe that his or her chances of winning are better than they are.

Light and Color Effects

Light and color can also affect behavioral patterns in a variety of contexts. For instance, there is little doubt about the direct relationship between color stimulation and central nervous system activity although why this should be so is not clear. Lighting levels can affect performance and arousal levels. As light levels increase so does visual acuity, but only up to a critical point. High levels of illumination can actually decrease performance by suppressing some information cues, e.g., visual gradients. Therefore, light levels and performance follow an inverted U shape when plotted. It has also been found that dim lighting or reduced light levels lessen eye contact and increase verbal latency in conversations.[4]

There is also some evidence that color evokes affective states and influences behavior. It has been suggested that some colors are associated with certain moods, e.g., red is "exciting" and "stimulating"; blue is "comfortable," "secure," and "soothing"; orange is "disturbing," and green is "leisurely." In addition, variations in color can affect human physiological reactions such as blood pressure and breathing rate.[5] Some researchers have found that color may affect people's mood, arousal,[6] and attitudes, and it has been speculated that these differences may indirectly affect behavior. By comparing people's galvanic skin responses, it has been shown that red induces higher levels of arousal than green. There is also some speculation that red can sometimes be connected with aggression, with green having a quieting effect, although the indirect effects of color on performance are related to cultural differences in the meaning and conventional uses of various colors.

To date there has been little research into the differential effects of color stimulation on more complex behavior in ecologically valid settings, and only one study has examined the differential effects of red and blue lighting on gambling behavior. In this experiment, Stark and his colleagues hypothesized that if red is arousing, subjects exposed to red light are likely to gamble more frequently, stake more money, and take more risks than subjects exposed to blue light. Their hypothesis was confirmed, with red lighting having less of an inhibitory effect on gambling behavior than blue lighting.[7] Why this should be so was again open to question. The most credible reason put forward was along semiological lines, which stressed the cultural significance of the different colors for participants.

A study by Griffiths and Swift involving five amusement arcades in Plymouth, England, found that the general color of all the arcades' interiors was toward the red end of the spectrum. Furthermore, lighting was very dim and the slot machines relied heavily on flashing lights. Two possible effects of dim lighting that might affect gambling profit were suggested. First, if visual acuity decreases as lighting levels decrease, there is a possibility of poorer performance in slot machine gambling which relies (to some extent) on visual ability. Such an effect over a long period of time will lead to more losing plays in a specified period, thus increasing profit for the management. A second more subtle effect may arise from the tendency of dim lighting to increase verbal latency and reduce eye contact.[8] A number of researchers have reported that playing is peripheral to social interaction for some adolescents, and so if dim lighting reduces social interaction with peers, there will subsequently be more gambling if such individuals stay in the arcade.

Aroma

Olfaction (sense of smell) has also been investigated experimentally in a gambling environment. Hirsch investigated the effect of ambient aromas on gambling behavior in a Las Vegas casino at two slot machine areas odorized with pleasant but distinct aromas and at an unodorized control slot machine area. The amounts of money gambled in the three areas were compared for the weekend of the odorization and for the weekends before and after. The amount of money gambled in the slot machines surrounding the first odorant during the experimental weekend was significantly greater than the amount gambled in the same area during the weekends before and after the experiment, possibly due to olfactory recall. The increase appeared greater on Saturday, when the concentration of odorant was higher. The amounts of money gambled in the slot machines surrounding the second odorant and in the control area did not change significantly compared with the weekends before or after the odorization.[9] Again, although research in the area of olfaction and gambling is limited, it does suggest that smell may influence gambling behavior.

SITUATIONAL DETERMINANTS AND FAMILIARITY

One marketing innovation that gambling establishments are beginning to tap into is the psychology of familiarity. According to Costa, names are important in impression formation.[10] The psychology of gambling advertising and "naming" is also important in attracting customers. Gambling advertising is usually aimed at the social (rather than the pathological) gambler. The imagery in almost all advertisements is designed to make a person spend money, and the word *gambling* is avoided. Instead, guilt-reducing statements referring to leisure are used, for example, "Try your luck," "Test your skill," or "Get into the holiday spirit." More recent studies on the psychology of familiarity point out that many gambling establishments are named after a familiar person, place, or event that potential gamblers might like or affiliate themselves with. The name of a casino or an arcade will often create an attractive image in the gambler's mind. Such names include Sun Valley, Caesars, Ocean Beach, and San Francisco Bay Leisure.

A 1994 study on the marketing strategies of amusement arcades reported that arcade advertisements (which were usually in the form of posters in the arcade window or self-standing boards placed on the pavement outside the arcade) did not use the word gambling in any form.

Many of the signs and slogans in seaside towns were geared specifically toward the young (e.g., "children's entertainment," or "fun for the kids"). Other ads, usually at inland arcades, were designed to attract the "twentieth-century child" with a thirst for technology (e.g., "Come inside—all the latest machines") or a sense of humor (e.g., "Come inside—slots of fun").[11]

SITUATIONAL DETERMINANTS AND MONEY ACCESS

One factor that has changed over the last decade is the installation of automatic telling machines (ATMs) in close proximity to casinos and arcades. If gamblers bring only a limited amount of money into the gambling environment and there is no cash dispenser nearby, they will usually give up and cut their losses. The distance from the ATM to (say) a slot machine may be inversely proportional to how much the gambler might eventually lose.

SITUATIONAL DETERMINANTS AND PHYSICAL COMFORT

If gamblers are physically comfortable, there is more chance that they will stay in the gambling environment. Comfort can be used by management to encourage and prolong gambling, which can be surprisingly tiring, particularly under stressful financial situations such as chasing. Often gamblers will continue to chase their losses for very long periods (e.g., the whole day) or until their money runs out. However, if players get physically and emotionally tired or lose concentration, their gambling session may be prematurely terminated.

Seating

Taking gamblers off their feet enhances physical comfort considerably. Again, some individuals can gamble for very long periods. Common sense dictates that if they can sit down instead of standing up, they will gamble until their desire is satiated rather than allowing fatigue to prematurely terminate a gambling session. It would appear that the lack of seating inhibits prolonged gambling, and vice versa.

Heating

Playing slot machines often results in increased body temperatures for two reasons:

- The emotional effects of gambling often produce an increase in body temperature and perspiration because of the arousing nature of the activity.
- The proximity of the gambler to slot machines can also increase body temperatures because the machine becomes hotter through constant playing.

The combined effect of these temperature increases causes physical discomfort, which discourages prolonged play. Staff members who do not usually spend much time close to a machine often dictate the environment's room temperature. For this reason, room temperatures may be too warm for gamblers even though they may be suitable for staff.

Although no research has been specifically carried out into the relationship between temperature and gambling, there has been some empirical work on temperature in a gaming context. However, this research suggests that increasing temperature may increase gambling rather than decrease it. Anderson, Deuser, and DeNeve manipulated the room temperature while subjects were playing video games and found that raising the temperature consistently increased hostile and competitive affect and cognition in players.[12] It could perhaps be speculated that increased temperatures may increase the amount of gambling because competitiveness appears to be an important factor in gambling maintenance for some people, but empirical evidence is needed to support such an assertion.

Refreshments and Amenities

Yet another obvious customer care tactic is the availability of refreshments and restrooms. These amenities are of particular importance to gamblers because (1) they often gamble for long periods, and (2) they are often reluctant to leave a slot machine or the roulette table to get a drink or food or to use the restroom as they are often chasing losses and/or do not want to lose their lucky seat or favorite machine.

In a New Zealand study, thirty bars that housed slot machines were compared with another thirty that did not. In the bars without slot machines, almost all of the customers drank pints. However, in the bars with slot machines, only 8 percent of the clientele drank pint measures primarily because the slot machine players did not want to leave the machines to use the restroom in case someone "stole" their machine.[13] Gambling treatment specialist Joanna Franklin has also reported that an increasing proportion of her female clients have developed bladder problems as a result of their prolonged slot machine gambling. Again, these gamblers are holding off using the restroom because they do not want to lose "their" machine and unfortunately damaging their bladders in the process.

FLOOR LAYOUT IN GAMBLING ENVIRONMENTS

According to a study by Greenlees, the variables that are crucial to slot machine success are floor location, coin denomination, and pay-off schedules of the machines.[14] In U.S casinos, restaurants are often positioned in the center so that customers have to pass the gaming area before *and* after they have eaten. Another strategy is to use deliberately circuitous paths to keep customers in the casino longer, the assumption being that if the patrons are in the casino longer they will spend more money. It is also worth noting that some forms of gambling machines (e.g., slot machines) are more profitable than others (e.g., video game machines). This difference can have two effects on marketing strategy. The first is that there tend to be far more slot machines than video games in arcades. Second, the less profitable machines tend to be placed at the back of the arcade so that video game players have to walk past the more profitable slot machines to get to their preferred type of game.

Research has also shown that a majority of U.K. arcades offer at least one alternative service (e.g., snack bar) in a bid either to attract new customers or to keep those already in the arcade as long as possible.[15] The majority of arcades with a snack bar or restaurant positioned it at the rear of the arcade, forcing its customers to pass many slot machines to reach it. U.S. casinos used a similar strategy.

ENVIRONMENTAL STIMULATION AND NOVELTY

Another way in which the environment may affect gambling behavior depends on how "stimulating" or novel a particular gambling environment may be for the gambler. Newer, more unusual environments may inhibit high levels of gambling and risk-taking because new environments usually signal uncertainty, making caution an automatic response. Furthermore, arousal theories of gambling assume that excitement and stimulation are primary motivations for gambling. Several studies have shown increased levels of arousal to be the result of gambling. If this is true, it is logical to argue that the need to gamble or to take risks might be lower if the individual is already receiving stimulation from somewhere other than gambling itself. Therefore, a stimulating gambling environment may lower the desire to be aroused from gambling.

Las Vegas is an ideal place to test these speculations empirically. It could be hypothesized that the "Vegas" environment has some inhibiting effects on gambling levels. It is common knowledge that this resort destination is a novel and exciting environment. Becoming aroused or excited by the Vegas experience is possible even without having gambled at all. Live shows, firework displays, and architectural originality may attract a wide range of customers to the resorts but actually lower the drive to gamble.

Admittedly, there are some problems with this speculation. The theory assumes that individuals are motivated only by the need to become aroused, a claim that is empirically unsubstantiated. Second, some researchers claim that increased arousal may lead to an increased desire to gamble. Research is clearly needed in this area to evaluate the effect of environmental stimulation with any precision.

INCENTIVES FOR PROLONGING GAMBLING

Many gambling establishments will offer incentives to get people to gamble on their premises. In the United Kingdom, for instance, many amusement arcades have bonus incentives such as cash prize draws, gift raffles, tokens or credit boosts, and scratch cards (which can only be redeemed in the arcade itself). These ploys have a number of effects. Firstly, they provide incentives for initial exposure to the gambling environment. Secondly, they expose customers to other forms of gambling (e.g., scratchcards and raffles). Thirdly, the prizes awarded are often tokens to play on the machines, which ultimately increases exposure to slot machines.

The frequency of such bonuses varies depending on the establishment, but they can occur hourly, daily, weekly, or seasonally. These are often used to entice the consumer in many retail environments and have the appeal of making gamblers feel they are getting something for nothing.

SOCIAL FACILITATION AND INHIBITION

In gambling environments, the presence of other people appears to affect an individual's gambling behavior. However, to date, there has been no evidence to suggest that social facilitation affects gambling behavior or even risk-taking in general. Our own research has suggested that this social process operates in the gambling environment together with social inhibition.

Preliminary data indicate that the presence of a lively atmosphere may affect performance levels while gambling. For instance, it may encourage a more carefree attitude, further increase arousal, and/or draw and hold social players.

Friends: Our research also indicates that the presence of friends may influence gambling behavior. The specific effects appear to depend on whether the friends are actually gamblers themselves. Based on our initial observation, the presence of gambling friends on gamblers appears to have three main effects:

- *Increased risk taking.* This behavior occurs because there is a need to impress fellow gamblers through "risky but exciting" play (i.e., increased risk taking). Friends who gamble are used to risk taking and, respect a certain "fearless" element in another person's play (in addition to the ability to win). Furthermore, they encourage riskier play since they enjoy a secondary high from watching others gamble and therefore, there is a selfish element to their encouragement.

- *Improved skill level.* Because gamblers want to demonstrate the highest skill levels to fellow gamblers, they are usually very alert and aware of any opportunity to win when friends are present, not only for a profit motive but to ensure a positive evaluation from fellow gamblers.

- *Increased play duration.* A group of friends gambling on slot machines will watch each other and enjoy the "secondary high," thereby staying longer in that environment. However, this dynamic is more complicated than it may first appear. Take the case of three friends who gamble. Friend A begins playing the first slot machine while his two friends observe and encourage him. After a short time, Friend B gets bored as the secondary high is no longer enough, so he begins to play another machine. Meanwhile, Friend A is ready to leave the arcade but Friend B does not want to leave yet as he is still chasing his losses. The effect is a vicious circle in which each of the three friends remains in the arcade until all of them are ready and willing to leave. The implications of this dynamic for prolonged gambling are clear—the longer they observe each other in the gambling environment, the more environmental cues they will experience which have the likely effect of eventually inducing slot-machine gambling.

In contrast to the presence of fellow gamblers, the presence of nongambling friends appears to be primarily inhibitory. Reasons include:

- *Non-gambling friends giving negative appraisals for unnecessary risk taking.* Friends who do not gamble do not understand the motivations for gambling, particularly when the gambler is losing. As a result, it is common for nongambling friends to make negative judgements regarding the gambler's character (e.g., he or she is unwise, impulsive, or weak). For this reason, many gamblers will take fewer risks, play lower-stake machines, and stay in the gambling environment for shorter periods.

- *Nongambling friends wanting to do something else.* Impatient nongambling friends who find gambling "boring" will encourage the gambler to leave the environment to pursue other more "sensible" or "fun" activities with them.

One of the most interesting observations of our research relates to the effect of younger, more susceptible onlookers on gamblers. Essentially, gamblers admit to showing off by (1) increasing concentration on tasks requiring skill, (2) taking higher risks, and (3) playing recklessly. Gamblers who are watched by inexperienced onlookers gain both self-esteem and social approval, both of which can be reinforcing motivations for continued gambling.

PROXIMITY TO OTHER ACTIVITIES AND INTRINSIC ASSOCIATION

Cornish outlined a situational characteristic that, although not given an explicit name, could be described as "intrinsic association."[16] Intrinsic association refers to the degree to which the gambling activity is associated with other interests and attractions, for example, betting at a sporting event that the gambler would normally attend, anyway. In arcade terms, intrinsic association could refer to gambling on a fruit machine as an ancillary activity to being in the arcade for other reasons (e.g., to work of to buy something). Another variation is "proximity play," or participating in an activity as a consequence of its being located next to something else that the person was doing or intended to do (e.g., being in the arcade primarily to play video games but going on to play a fruit machine instead).

CONCLUSIONS

It is clear that situational characteristics of gambling environments have the potential to initiate gambling behavior. Excessive gambling can occur regardless of the gambler's biological and/or psychological constitution. However, there is little evidence to suggest that the gambling industry has used the psychological literature to "exploit" gamblers. The success of the gambling establishment's situational characteristics (where success is defined as an increase in gambling resulting from those characteristics) depends upon the psychosituational interaction between the gambler and the establishment. The importance of a characteristic approach to gambling is the possibility of pinpointing more accurately in what ways an individual's psychological constitution is influencing his or her gambling behavior. Such an approach also allows for psychologically context-specific explanations of gambling behavior rather than global explanations (such as "addictive personality").

The information presented in this essay is intended to demonstrate that gambling behavior is the product of more than simply the interaction between the structural characteristics of the gambling activity and the psychology of the gambler. Furthermore, these situational characteristics do not affect the acquisition stage of gambling behavior but may play an even more important role in the maintenance of gambling. For these reasons, it is fair to argue that inadequate attention has been given to situational variables in gambling.

We acknowledge that many of the ideas presented in this essay have limited empirical support and that more substantial experimental evidence is required before many of the speculations outlined can be confirmed. However, it is worth noting that the essay is only the first stage in examining situational variables in gambling, and we hope that it will alert interested parties to the possibility that they exist and will also act as an impetus for more concrete and definitive research.

It is worth commenting further on the utility of these ideas for the psychology of gambling. Obviously, knowing that situational variables exist gives researchers and treatment professionals a slightly better view of the potentially unclear picture formed by gambling behavior. For example, if treatment professionals know which aspects of the environment are likely to perpetuate gambling behavior, they may be able to train their clients to interpret these aspects and deal with them appropriately. Many problem gamblers who have been only subconsciously aware of situational variables may be better able to control their gambling with such an improved awareness. For example, knowing that they may gamble more or take more risks when in the presence of a group could possibly help them to avoid the situation or at least reduce its influence.

The directions from which to move on from this essay are clear. First, more experimental evidence must be gathered so that these speculations can be considered with greater confidence. For instance, further work is still needed to pinpoint which situational characteristics are most likely to affect initiation of gambling. It may be that light, color, and sound effects are integral to increasing baseline levels of gambling among slot machine players but not among gamblers who prefer lotteries or horse racing. Second, if the environment is important in defining gambling behavior, then this fact clearly has implications for studying gambling in ecologically valid settings. Finally, environmental factors in gambling behavior should be incorporated in the general literature so that researchers and practitioners alike can have a more comprehensive picture of the psychology of gambling.

Much of this essay is deliberately speculative and would greatly be enhanced both by further empirical work and greater cooperation from the gambling industry, which could easily confirm or deny much of what has been written in this essay.

NOTES

1. Mark D. Griffiths, "Fruit Machine Gambling: The Importance of Structural Characteristics," *Journal of Gambling Studies* 9 (1993): 101–20.

2. Adrian C. North, David J. Hargreaves, and Jennifer McKendrick, "The Influence of In-Store Music on Wine Selections," *Journal of Applied Psychology* 84 (1999): 271–76.

3. Adrian C. North and David J. Hargreaves, "The Effect of Music on Atmosphere and Purchase Intentions in a Cafeteria," *Journal of Applied Social Psychology* 28 (1998): 2254–73.

4. Suzanne J. Carr and James M. Dabbs, "The Effects of Lighting, Distance, and Intimacy of Topic on Verbal and Visual Behavior," *Sociometry* 37 (1974): 592–600.

5. C. A. Acking and R. Kuller, "The Perception of an Interior as a Function of Its Color," *Ergonomics* 15 (1972): 645–54.

6. Albert Mehrabian and Jim A. Russell, "The Basic Emotional Impact of Environments," *Perceptual and Motor Skills* 38 (1974): 283–301.

7. G. M. Stark, D. M Saunders, and P. Wookey, "Differential Effects of Red and Blue Lighting on Gambling Behavior," *Current Psychological Research* 2 (1982): 95–100.

8. Mark D. Griffiths and Gill-Helen Swift, "The Use of Light and Color in Gambling Arcades: A Pilot Study," *Society for the Study of Gambling Newsletter* 21 (1992): 16–22.

9. Alan R. Hirsch, "Effects of Ambient Odors on Slot-Machine Usage in a Las Vegas Casino," *Psychology-and-Marketing* 12 (1995): 585–94.

10. Nick Costa, *Automatic Pleasures: The History of the Coin Machine* (London: Kevin Francis Publishing, 1988).

11. Mark D. Griffiths, "The Observational Analysis of Marketing Methods in U.K. Amusement Arcades," *Society for the Study of Gambling Newsletter* 24 (1994): 17–24.

12. C. A. Anderson, W. E. Deuser, and K. M. DeNeve. "Hot Temperatures, Hostile Affect, Hostile Cognition, and Arousal: Tests of a General Model of Affective Aggression," *Personality and Social Psychology Bulletin* 21 (1995): 434–48.

13. Ralph Gerdelan, "Problem Gambling in New Zealand" (paper presented at the Innovation 2001 Conference, Canadian Foundation on Compulsive Gambling, Toronto, Ontario, 2001).

14. Malcolm Greenlees, *Casino Accounting and Financial Management* (Reno: University of Nevada Press, 1988).

15. Griffiths, "The Observational Analysis of Marketing Methods in U.K. Amusement Arcades," pp. 17–24.

16. David B. Cornish, *Gambling: A Review of the Literature and its Implications for Policy and Research.* (London: Stationery Office, 1978).

18

PROBABILITY ON THE CASINO FLOOR

Neil A. Manson

RATIONALITY AND EXPECTED VALUE

Any proper discussion of gambling requires an understanding of the probabilistic features of the games themselves. Only then will be we be able to talk precisely about the cost gamblers pay for their pursuit of the pleasure of gambling. The mathematical theory of probability can lend us a concept—that of expected value—that is particularly apt in creating such an understanding. The expected value (e.v.) of a wager, investment, or other course of action (A) having a number (n) of possible outcomes (O), each outcome having a specific probability of occurrence (P) and a specific value of occurring (R), is the sum of the series of products of the probability of an outcome and the value of that outcome.[1]

Thanks go to Fritz Warfield and Peter Collins for their comments on drafts of this paper.

Suppose there is a raffle, entry into which requires purchase of a $10 ticket. First prize is a car worth $10,000. There are ten second-place prizes, each a gift certificate worth $100. All tickets are redeemable at McDonald's for a Happy Meal worth $3. Two thousand people have entered the lottery. What is the expected value of a ticket? The answer is easy to calculate: {[P(winning first prize) × R(winning first prize)] + [P(winning second prize) × R(winning second prize)] + [P(winning a Happy Meal) × R(winning a Happy Meal)]} = [(1/2,000 × $10,000) + (10/2,000 × $100) + (2,000/2,000 × $3)] = ($5 + 50¢ + $3.00) = $8.50. Another way to look at this is that $20,000 is being brought in by the raffle but only $17,000 is being paid out. If 2,000 tickets are to pay out $17,000 with no remainder, the fair price for each ticket should be $8.50, not $10. A hypothetical deep-pocketed investor would be ill-advised to snatch up all of the lottery tickets. She would be sure to lose $3,000 and that's assuming she'd want to eat 2,000 Happy Meals.

Notice that this does not mean to say that each raffle ticket has an expected value of $8.50. First, it does not mean that there is any partic-ular outcome for which the prize is $8.50. A $10 raffle ticket will get you $10,000, $100, or $3, but never $8.50. Second, it does not mean that if you buy a $10 raffle ticket you should expect to lose money. Suppose we modified the raffle as follows: 1,100 tickets are winners, with the prize being a check for $12; the other 900 tickets are losers. In this case your ticket is more likely than not to be a winner, but the expected value (1,100/2,000 × $12 = $6.60) is only two-thirds the cost of a ticket. Third, the expected value's being less than the cost of the ticket does not mean a ticket-holder is guaranteed to lose. Someone in the first raffle will win a $10,000 car.

Last, it does not mean that if you start with a pot of money (say, $100) that is devoted to repeatedly making that wager (suppose the raffle is a daily event), you should expect to end up with 85 percent of your start-up money. Suppose you buy $100 worth of $10 tickets for the raffle described above (2000 tickets with 900 losers and 1100 winners of $12 checks). After the first day of play you'll likely end up with an amount of money close to $66 ($6.60 for every $10 wagered). You decide to take this money and use it to play the lottery again. After the second day you'll likely end up with approximately two-thirds of two-thirds of $100: that is, four-ninths of $100. And so on. Every day you play you should expect to lose about a third of the amount with which you started the day's wagering. And that means that, in a fairly short time, your initial $100 investment will be whittled down to nothing.

So what does it mean to say the expected value of the first raffle is $8.50? One thing it means is that if the total cash value of the prizes were divided evenly amongst the participants in the raffle, each person would get $8.50. But of course, gamblers rarely behave this way. The more interesting consequence of the calculation of expected value is this: if you enter such a raffle over and over, in the long run you can expect to end up with, on average, $8.50 for every $10 bet. That is, you can expect to lose $1.50 on average for each time you enter such a raffle, and the more often you play, the more strongly inclined you are to converge on this rate of loss. Of course, you may exceed expectations and get a higher return. You may also underachieve, getting a lower-than-expected return. How it turns out for you is a matter of luck.

It is crucial to remember that the expected value calculations apply to the total amount of money wagered and not to the total amount of money invested. In the case above of continually ploughing your daily winnings into the next day's raffle, the money you start with ($100) is considerably less than the total amount of money you wager. The total amount wagered will probably be approximately $100 + ($100 × 66%) + ($100 × 66% × 66%) + ($100 × 66% × 66% × 66%), and so on. If you work this series out to the limit, you will see that you should expect your total amount wagered to be a bit less than $300. Of course, the reason this process grinds your initial $100 down to nothing rather than giving you $200 ($200 is the expected value of $300 worth of wagers on raffle tickets) is that you keep blowing your winnings on raffle tickets, you fool! If you wager this way your behavior is analogous to that of a bank teller. She may have conducted a million dollars worth of cash transactions in a week, even though the amount of cash in her till at any given time is far less than a million dollars. The dollar amount of interest to the bank is not so much the amount of cash in the till at the end of each day, but rather the amount of money transacted. After all, banks make their money from transaction costs. The difference between a gambler and a bank, of course, is that banks generally make money from their transactions, while gamblers generally lose money from theirs.

Let's go back to our original Happy Meal raffle. Since the expected value of a ticket is less than the price paid, the ticket is said to have a "negative expectation." Does this necessarily mean one should not buy a raffle ticket? No. Whether one should or should not buy the ticket depends on one's motivations, one's value assignments, one's pleasures. Some enjoy donating to good causes, some get at least $10 worth of pleasure contemplating the prospect of winning a $10,000 car, some find it worth $10 to get fundraisers off their backs, and so on. While sweeping declarations tying expected value to rationality have surface appeal (e.g., "It is wrong, always, everywhere, and for everyone, to undertake a course of action with a negative expectation"), the reality is that expected values are only numbers. They can be useful tools for deciding what to do—especially when comparing alternative courses of action—but they are hardly sufficient in themselves to dictate an answer. For example, insurance policies and warranties (like raffle tickets) almost always have negative expectations. That fact does not by itself render their purchasers irrational. Indeed, a good case could be made that if consumers never purchased products that had negative expectations, the global economy would grind to a halt.

Nevertheless, knowing the expected value of a particular wager will prove extremely useful when comprehensively assessing that form of gambling. We can say that some wagers are better or worse than others without taking stands on the rationality of gambling as a whole (I'll touch on that issue at the end of this essay). Furthermore, a clear understanding of the expected values of various wagers will allow us to isolate and highlight factors other than expected value that are important in assessing various forms of gambling. And since just about every form of gambling is now offered by most casinos, we can get a representative sample of gambling's possibilities simply by taking a stroll on the floor of an imaginary casino.

ROULETTE

Our first stop is at the roulette table. The standard American roulette wheel consists of thirty-eight evenly spaced slots for the numbers 1 through 36 (half colored black, the other half colored red) along with 0 and 00 (both colored green).[2] The payout scheme is predicated on there being thirty-six slots rather than thirty-eight. For example, suppose you place on the roulette table a "straight up" bet of $1 on the number 7. The wheel is spun, as is the ball, and (luckily for you) the ball lands in the 7 slot. You get to keep your $1 and you are paid an additional $35, as the odds for a straight up bet are 35 to 1. Note that this is equivalent to the casino's taking your $1 bet off the roulette table and paying you $36, because odds of 35 to 1 against mean the probability of winning is 1 to 36. Whether, on winning, you do or don't get back your original wager is important when figuring expected value.

This would be an "even-money" bet if there were only thirty-six slots on the wheel, because (using our second method of calculating expected value) if one were to place a $1 bet on the table for each of those thirty-six numbers (thus covering all of the possibilities) one would lose $35 and gain $35. The expected value of a $1 straight up bet would be $1. Alas, casinos are not so generous. They make their money with the two extra numbers. Though a straight up bet on such a roulette table should pay 37 to 1, the casino will only pay you 35 to 1. As it stands, then, the expected value of a $1 bet is $1/38 \times 36; that is, 94.7 cents. Indeed, every bet on the Roulette wheel (except one) has this very same expected value.

Consider, for example, a "row" bet. The thirty-six nonzero numbers on the roulette table are arranged in a twelve-row, three-column layout, with 0 and 00 tacked on. If a number (e.g., 5) from one's selected row (e.g.r 4-5-6) is spun, you get paid 11 to 1. The expected value of a $1 bet is thus $3/38 \times 12; again, 94.7 cents. The same is true with the bets red, black, even, odd, 1 to 18, and 19 to 36. With all of those bets, winners get paid 1 to 1. The expected value of a $1 bet is $18/38 \times 2; again, the familiar 94.7 cents. The only bet with a different expected value is "five numbers," wherein one gets odds of 6 to 1 that any of the numbers 0-00-1-2-3 are spun. In this case, the expected value of a $1 bet is $5/38 \times 7 –92.1¢, not 94.7¢.

Just because every bet on the roulette wheel has the same expected value, however, does not mean every roulette bet is the same. The odds on a straight up bet are 35 to 1; the odds on a 1–18 bet are 1 to 1. Thus the casino is exposed to far greater risk if it permits, say, $1000 to be placed on a straight up bet than if it permits the same amount to be wagered on a 1–18 bet. Typically, casinos deal with this feature by arranging for the expected value of a wager to be lower the higher the odds paid upon winning (we'll see this more clearly with craps). In the case of roulette, however, the total amount of money risked by the players on straight up and other high-payout bets tends to be evenly distributed across the table, thus dampening the risk run by the casino on any particular spin.

CRAPS

Let us move on to another popular game, craps. In this game two six-sided dice are rolled. Although any of the numbers 2 through 12 can be rolled, not all numbers are equally likely. For example, of the thirty-six possible outcomes, there is only one for which the dice sum to 2 (you need to get one 1, then another 1), whereas there are six outcomes for which the dice sum to 7 (1-6, 2-5, 3-4, 4-3, 5-2, and 6-1).[3]

With these probabilities, the expected values of some craps bets can be easily calculated. For example, a *Place Bet* is a bet that a certain number (selected from the numbers 4, 5, 6, 8, 9, and 10) is rolled before a 7 is rolled. Until either the chooser number or a 7 is rolled, the bet stays on the table. Place bets on 8 pay 7 to 6; that is, for each $6 you bet, you win $7 if an 8 is rolled before a 7. Yet the odds of this happening are 5 to 6. Thus for every eleven times you make a $6 place bet on 8, you should expect to win five (each time retaining your $6 bet while winning $7) and lose six (each time leaving you with no money on the table). To get the expected value of $66 in place bets (eleven $6 bets), multiply the probability of winning (5/11) times the return if you win ($13). You end up with $65. For every $66 in place bets on 8, you should expect to get $65 in return. This works out to 98.5› for every $1 wagered (considerably better than the expected value of any roulette bet).

Other place bets have lower expected values. For example, a place bet on the number 10 pays $9 for every $5 bet. Since the odds of winning are 1 to 2 (for every three times you make a place bet on 10, you'll win once and lose twice), three $5 place bets on 10 will yield, on average, $14. This works out to 93.3 cents for every $1 worth of place bets made on 10. The expected values get even worse when we consider proposition bets; say, that a 12 will be the result of the next roll of the dice. Though the odds of this happening are 35 to 1, the payout on winning is only 30 to 1. For every thirty-six $1 proposition bets you make on 12, you should expect to win once, getting back $31, for an expected value of 86.1 cents for every $1 bet. This feature of craps illustrates the general rule mentioned earlier—the higher the odds paid out upon winning a bet, the lower the expected value of making that bet. From the casino's perspective this makes sense because it runs a greater risk of exhausting its ability to pay out on winning bets if large amounts of money are wagered on high odds than if large amounts of money are wagered on low odds. The price the casino exacts for assuming this risk is that it offers a lower expected value for a high-payout wager such as a proposition bet on 12 than it does for a low-payout wager such as a place bet on 8.

Not all craps wagers are such that their expected values are so easily calculated. For example, the pass line bet has the following structure. If a 7 or 11 is rolled on the initial toss of the dice, the bettors win. If a 2, 3, or 12 is rolled, the bettors lose. If any other number (4, 5, 6, 8, 9, or 10) is rolled, it becomes the pass line "Point," with the shooter continuing to roll the dice until the point is rolled again (in which case the pass line bet is a winner) or a 7 is rolled (in which case the pass line bet is a loser). Arduous calculation shows the expected value of a $1 wager on the pass line is 98.6 cents. Making a pass line bet, however, entitles the bettor to make an "odds" bet. The odds bets are similar to the place bets except that their expected values always equal the amount wagered. For example, if the Point is 8, the casino will pay the bettor $6 if the bettor makes a $5 odds bet and an 8 is rolled before a 7 is rolled. Since the odds of this happening are 5 to 6, the expected value of a $1 odds bet on 8 is exactly $1. In short, the odds bet is an even-money proposition. Since many casinos allow makers of pass line bets to place very large odds bets (say, twenty times what a player wagers on the pass line), the overall expected value of $1 worth of such pass line + odds bets can get extremely close to $1. Unfortunately for most craps players, this fact is of little consolation, because their pockets are far too shallow to afford to place such large odds bets.

Suppose you go to a craps table with $1,000. On every roll of the dice, you make a $10 proposition bet on 12. You aren't paying much attention to the amount of money in your chip rack; you take out $10 every roll and if you win you put $310 back into your rack. Time flies, and the next thing you know you've been gambling at the craps table for five hours. Since you know the expected value of a proposition bet on 12 is 86.1› for every dollar wagered, should you expect to have ended up with approximately $860? Absolutely not. Although you came to the table with $1,000, you likely wagered far more than $1,000. As we saw before when discussing lotteries and bank tellers, what matters is not the amount of money with which you start but the amount of money you wager, not the amount invested but the amount transacted (the "cash flow").

If, for example, the dice were tossed at a rate of once per minute, you likely wagered $3,000, in which case you should expect to have finished with around $575 in your rack. In other words, you lost nearly half of your money, not just 14 percent of it. You should expect to lose approximately $85 per hour under these conditions. Now suppose that, instead of having made $10 proposition bets on 12, you had routinely placed $10 on the pass line and $20 on the odds bet. Suppose, furthermore, that given the rate of play, you would have placed, again, a total of $3,000 in bets. Given that, with this betting strategy, every $1 wagered has an expected value of approximately 99¢, you would have expected to finish with around $970 in your rack. That works out to a loss of $6 per hour, considerably less than the $85 per hour loss rate for making $10 Proposition Bets on 12. The difference is as great as that between paying $30 for greens fees at a municipal golf course and paying $425 for a once-in-a-lifetime round at Pebble Beach. Both will take about five hours, but one round of golf works out to $6 an hour while the other costs $85 an hour.

Notice that in coming up with these numbers we considered a hitherto unmentioned factor: the rate of play. In the above scenario we supposed that the dice were tossed at a rate of once per minute, but this is hardly the only possible rate. Supposing you go to a newly opened craps table and are the only player, you could toss the dice as many as six times a minute. Conversely, for a crowded Craps table on which the players collectively place money on just about every bet on offer, the dice are likely going to be tossed at a rate well below once a minute due to the large number of transactions that the croupiers (table staff) must conduct and monitor. The rate of play on any given table will depend partly on the players and partly on the croupiers. Some players stall over which bets to place; others place their bets quickly. Some shooters simply pick up the dice and toss them; others spin them and flip them in their hands while they give their good-luck incantations. Inexperienced croupiers are often considerably slower than old hands at bringing in losing bets and paying out on winners. One point is undeniable: the faster the rate of play, the better for the casino.

The Even-Money Room

The next stop on our casino tour is the even-money room. In this fabled room wagers are offered such that their expected value is precisely equal to the amount wagered. Zero and 00 have been removed from the Roulette wheel. Craps players can place odds bets without making a pass line bet. They can also make a place bet on 8 and get paid 6 to 5 if they win. Unlike every other game one might play against the casinos of the world, the ones in the even-money room offer wagers that don't have negative expectations.

There is, however, a catch. To enter the even-money room, you must agree to some restrictions. These restrictions are of three sorts: (1) limitations on the amount of money you can bring into the room; (2) impositions of minimum amounts of winnings you must make to exit the room; and (3) limitations on the amount of time you can spend in the room. The casino structures these restrictions into a variety of plans. For example, if you opt for Plan A, then you agree to bring only $100 into the room and to stay no longer than two hours. If you opt for Plan B, then you agree to bring only $100 into the room, but you must continue gambling until you either lose your $100 or win $500.

These may sound like great deals, but despite the fact that all the wagers offered are fair bets, in the even-money room the casino has the advantage over you with respect to time and money. With Plan A, for example, some players will begin with a spate of bad luck. Their $100 will be taken and, because of the type-1 requirement, they will be unable to reach into their wallets to give themselves the opportunity to win their money back. Those who start lucky, however, have every opportunity to give their money back to the casino. With Plan B, the normal fluctuations of chance make it very, very likely that players will run out of money before they reach the $500-profit threshold for leaving, even if none of their particular wagers has a negative expectation.

The even-money room is entirely fictitious, but there is a good reason why. No casino has bothered to set up such games with restrictions of types 1, 2, and 3 because most gamblers impose such restrictions on themselves. They come to the casino with limited resources (compared with the casino) and they don't leave until they either run out of money or make a significant profit, or until they are about to miss their bus rides home. This mindset gives the casino a tremendous edge. The casino is almost certain to outlast any player who is determined to win big or go broke trying. And this advantage to the casino is entirely independent of the fact that all of the bets it offers have a negative expectation.

Slot Machines

On our way out of the even-money room we finally notice those flashy, noisy contraptions that surround us: slot machines. They line every wall of the place. The pace of play is furious: drop in a coin, pull a handle, repeat. There's virtually no speed limit beyond the stamina and dexterity of the player. And the games are very popular; slots players greatly out-number table gamers. We steer well clear of the slots, however, because a precondition for our even considering a wager is that it is within our power to calculate the expected value of it. With slots this cannot be done. We don't have the keys to the machine and cannot inspect the wheels, springs, and levers inside it. Who knows what troublesome mechanisms lurk in the bowels of the one-armed bandits? All the crucial information is inaccessible to us. At best we will have to take the word of the casino (and the gaming commission) as to the expected value ("percentage payout") of a particular machine. It is a rare occasion when even this information is directly provided although sometimes it is touted on bill-boards and brochures. What we do know about slots is that for almost all of them, the expected value of a $1 wager is well below 95 cents. As we have already seen, we can do much better.

The Card Room

Our last stop is the card room. Here the casino operates a variety of card games in which players compete against the house. These games include blackjack, baccarat, pai-gow poker, let it ride, and Caribbean stud poker. In the poker room the casino also runs various games with patrons playing against one another: seven-card stud, Omaha and Texas hold 'em, being some of the most popular. In the latter sort of game, the casino makes money simply by taking a percentage of each pot (say, 10 percent up to $50, with no cut taken for any amount beyond the $50) or by requiring an entrance fee for playing. Calculations of expected value in card games are generally far more difficult than with games such as roulette (and even craps). The number of possible outcomes is vastly greater due to there being fifty-two distinct cards in a deck. Analysis of betting strategies in games such as Blackjack can sometimes require the services of professional statisticians. Nevertheless, the expected values of some particular wagers in some particular card games can be easily calculated.

In blackjack, the object of the game is to get one's collection of cards to achieve a sum larger than that of the dealer's cards but no larger than twenty-one. Cards 2 through 9 are worth their stated value, "face" cards (10, jack, queen, and king) are worth ten, and an ace is worth either one or eleven, depending on the wishes of the player. The suits of the cards are irrelevant in blackjack. The players get two cards shown up while the dealer gets one card down and one up. The players always draw first and always have the option of staying with the cards dealt to them or "hitting" (taking another card). Once the players are done selecting their hands, the dealer flips over her cards. If they do not already sum to seventeen or more, the dealer keeps drawing until they do. If she exceeds twenty-one during this process, she "busts," and any players remaining at the table automatically win. Of course, the players are in just as much danger of busting as the dealers. The players will often draw cards when they are at risk of exceeding twenty-one. For example, if a player is dealt a 9 and a 7 and the dealer is showing a face card, most players will take a hit in hopes of drawing a small card, even though they have a strong chance of drawing a high card and hence busting. They do this because they anticipate that, with a face card showing, the dealer is quite likely to achieve at least a seventeen and therefore beat them.

The casino will offer a variety of bets and options in blackjack (e.g., "doubling down" and "splitting"). Different casinos will tweak the rules and options slightly, thus dictating different strategies by the players. What the proper strategies are, precisely, can be a matter of some dispute, but some decisions are fairly clear. For example, the two-card hand "blackjack" consists of an ace and a face card. A hand of blackjack automatically wins and is paid 3 to 2. Thus if you wagered $10 on the Blackjack table and were dealt a blackjack, you would automatically be paid $15. But there's one caveat. If the dealer also has a blackjack, the hand is a tie and you get no money. So if you are dealt a blackjack and you see that the dealer's up card is an ace, you might worry that you'll miss out on your chance to get paid 3 to 2 on your bet. The casino, however, will offer you a way out in this situation. They will pay you 1 to 1 on your bet if you agree to give up on your hand before the dealer turns over her hidden card. So if you bet $10 at the Blackjack table, are dealt a blackjack, and see that the dealer is showing an ace, you can get paid $10 instead of waiting to see if the dealer isn't hiding a face card (in which case you'd win $15) or is (in which case you'd get nothing). Should you "take even money" in this situation?

You should not (though you'd be tempted to). There are fifty-two cards in a deck. Four are aces, sixteen are face cards, and the remaining thirty-two are cards 2 through 9. If you have an ace and a face card and if the dealer is showing an ace, that means there are forty-nine cards left that you have not seen. Of these, fifteen are face cards and thirty-four are not. To see which is better—taking even money or waiting to see the dealer's down card—compare the two strategies in an idealized, perfectly representative run of forty-nine cases. If you take even money all forty-nine times, you will get $10 every time and end up with $490. If you wait to see the dealer's down card, fifteen times she'll have a face card and you'll get nothing, but thirty-four times she won't and you'll get $15. That means you'll end up with $510 using the "wait-and-see" strategy, making it the superior one in our idealized situation.

But what if there are other players at the blackjack table? What if an additional six cards are exposed on the table, and none of them are face cards? Well, in that case you should take even money. This is because there would now be, not forty-nine cards you haven't seen, but forty-three. Of those, fifteen would be face cards and twenty-eight wouldn't be. Comparing our strategies again, this time over an idealized, perfectly representative run of forty-three cases, you'd win $430 if you always took even money but only $420 if you waited to see the dealer's down card. In this case, the cards of the other players provide you with information that changes the expectation for your hand.

This feature of (some) card games makes them different in a crucial way from all the other games we have discussed. In roulette, craps, and slot machines, the outcomes in any particular case are independent of one another. That is, the occurrence of an outcome in one case does not alter the probability of occurrence of any outcome in the next case. If a 27 is spun on the Roulette wheel, that makes it no more or less likely that a 27 will be spun the next time around. If an 8 is rolled on the Craps table five times in a row, the probability that an 8 will be rolled the next time is still 5/36, the same as it ever was. Of course, lots of gamblers mistakenly think otherwise. In honor of their error we speak of "the gambler's fallacy." But the blackjack players who alter their decisions based on what cards they see dealt to their fellow players do not commit the gambler's fallacy. In the case of Blackjack (and most other card games), the outcomes are dependent, not independent. The exposure of certain cards on the table affects the probabilities regarding what the upcoming cards will be.

Now even if we set the nonindependence of card dealings aside, the general rules of the game and the known strategies of play give blackjack only the slightest negative in expected value: less than 1 cent for every $1 wagered. With careful attention to cards dealt, however, sophisticated gamblers have the opportunity to turn the expectations in their favor. Those adept at counting cards in blackjack can exploit this knowledge so as to make decisions that give them an advantage over the casino. Despite what one might think from watching *Rain Man*, however, counting is not so easy to get away with. First, the casino has the option of simply banning players it feels are engaged in card counting. Second, the casino can manipulate the rules so as to prevent card counting, say, by dealing cards to the players face down. Lastly, the casino can simply use more than one deck of cards when dealing Blackjack. Most casinos shuffle together six or eight decks when making a "shoe" for dealing blackjack; few still offer a single-deck game. Although it is still possible to count cards effectively when a six- or eight-deck shoe is used, the probability is vastly lower that the run of the cards will deviate from the norm enough to make alteration in standard betting strategies profitable.

Because the probability of being dealt a certain card is dependent on the cards that have already been dealt, there is an element of skill in playing card games that is absent with roulette, craps, slot machines, and so forth. In certain circumstances this element can result in players gaining a positive expectation for their bets. This is especially true when the opponent is not the casino but other casino patrons. Skilled poker players can regularly win money against weaker opponents. The trick, of course, is to become a skilled poker player. You won't become one without considerable preparation and lost money, and there's the strong possibility that you won't be as good as you think.

THE RATIONALITY OF GAMBLING

What have we learned on our imaginary casino tour? A crucial lesson is that low-loss betting strategies are possible. That is, casinos offer the disciplined, well-informed bettor the possibility of playing for considerable lengths of time at what amounts to a fairly low hourly rate (say, $10 lost per hour). To do this, a gambler must stick to the best bets (e.g., the pass line bet in craps) and adopt the best strategies (e.g., not taking even money for blackjack when facing a dealer's ace). Gambler's furthermore must come with a good deal of money in order to weather the ups and downs of chance, must not bet large amounts of money, must play at a reasonably slow pace, and must leave after a fixed period of time whether their luck has been good or bad. If a gambler does all these things, he or she can reasonably expect to lose a fairly small amount of money per hour.

If all gamblers behaved this way, casino gambling would have to be regarded as comparable to other socially acceptable leisure activities. There would always be the lingering oddity of frittering away money in the pursuit of money (why not just avoid the casino and keep the money?), but as the glitz of Las Vegas shows, there's more entertainment value involved in gambling than just in winning. There's also the buzz of the crowd, the bright lights, the occasional jump for joy. Those with broadly libertarian leanings will have a hard time seeing why we should frown on a $10-per-hour-activity of the sort ideally rational casino gambling would be when we do not frown on, say, the $10-per-hour pursuit of pars and birdies.

The problem, of course, is that very few gamblers are well-informed and disciplined. Most are poorly informed and impulsive. They know little about probability and expected value, they operate on hunches, and frequently they "go for broke." And so a good case can be made that our imaginary casino tour was a waste of time. It was intended to employ the mathematical theory of probability to tell us what people should believe about various forms of gambling. Plausibly, however, what is relevant (for purposes such as setting public policy) is not what people *should* believe but what they *do* believe. And the latter is a matter for cognitive psychologists, not probability theorists. The news from cognitive psychology is grim. Ordinary people (and even professional statisticians) are often wildly mistaken in their intuitions about chance. It seems that information about probability and expected value in gambling is about as motivating as the surgeon general's warning on cigarette packets.

This leads to the really big question regarding gambling. Given the prevalence of poor decision making when it comes to gambling, should the state regulate it? If so, how, and how extensively? This author sees poor decision making and irrationality as such pervasive features of human existence that attempting to regulate them is about as prone to success as spooning out the sea. But readers can make up their own minds on this issue in light of the other essays in this volume.

NOTES

1. Formally, we get:

$$e.v.(A) = \sum_{i=1}^{n} P(O_i) \times R(O_i)$$

While the formula may be daunting, the concept is simple enough.

2. In Europe the term *American Roulette* describes a similar game but with a wheel having only one zero.

3. Thus $P(2) = 1/36$ [or odds of 35-1], $P(3) = 2/36$ [or 17-1], $P(4) = 3/36$ [or 11-1], $P(5) = 4/36$ [or 8-1], $P(6) = 5/36$, $P(7) = 6/36$ [or 5-1], $P(8) = 5/36$, $P(9) = 4/36$ [or 8-1], $P(10) = 3/36$ [or 11-1], $P(11) = 2/36$ [or 17-1], and $P(12) = 1/36$ [or 35-1].

Section 7

ETHICAL AND PHILOSOPHICAL ISSUES

19
REGULATING VICE

America's Struggle with Wicked Pleasure

Jerome H. Skolnick

In this essay, I will develop the outlines of a sociolegal theory of vice and its control, and also ask what vice is—and how and why attitudes toward some vices have shifted. I will also distinguish between what I shall call "normal" and "deviant" vice, and I shall argue that to reduce social harm, "normal" vices should, where possible, be regulated and taxed but should not be exploited for fiscal needs.

So how should we describe vice, a familiar enough concept? Dictionaries define *vice* as "evil" or "immoral" conduct. But surely the idea of vice connotes pleasure and popularity, as well as wickedness. People engage in classic vices—gambling, drinking, smoking, using drugs, and a variety of sexual activities—because they are drawn to these for personal gratification, even though they may or may not think that what they are doing is wicked or immoral.

This paper, in a slightly different form, was delivered as a Fortunoff Lecture at the New York University School of Law, April 23, 2001.

In criminal law, vice generally falls in the area of what Dean Francis A. Allen called nearly half a century ago "the Borderland of Criminal Justice." Allen considered the borderland to be the most important issue in criminal justice for the second half of the twentieth century. Recently, in law enforcement practice and in criminal procedure doctrine, Allen's borderland essay has become increasingly prophetic.

Our attempt to control drug use through the criminal sanction is, of course, our most extensive, expensive, controversial, and complex borderland issue. Drug laws affect a broad segment of the general population, yet have the largest impact on minorities. Of the nearly two million prisoners in the United States, last year nearly 800,000 were Black men, nearly an eighth of Black males between age twenty and thirty-four. And from 25 to 50 percent of them, depending on jurisdiction, were incarcerated on drug charges.

I don't want to center this essay on drug enforcement, however, but rather on the larger issue of how, if at all, criminal law should be used in the borderland of vice control. In the 1960s it was customary for police to maintain a vice control unit which enforced the laws against illegal drug sale and use, gambling, prostitution and almost exclusively male gay sex.

That last issue was famously debated by Oxford philosopher H. L. A. Hart and law lord Sir Patrick Devlin in the 1960s. The issue was whether consenting adult homosexual sex should continue to be a crime. Sir Patrick Devlin maintained that it should be—arguing that law must reflect traditional Christian morals. Devlin ultimately lost the argument when a prestigious parliamentary Commission—the Wolfendon Commission—recommended decriminalizing. Eventually, even Lord Devlin came to recognize that the mandates of the Church of England could and should no longer automatically serve as the basis for law in an increasingly diverse and urban United Kingdom and affirmed the wisdom of the Wolfendon Commission's recommendation.

Expressive justifications of criminal law are often defended on communitarian grounds. Lord Devlin cited sociological theorist Emile Durkheim—who had written that criminal law represents a collective conscience, a moral consensus—to support his position that private, consenting, adult gay sex should remain criminal.

Was Devlin wrong? Can the criminal law be said to rest on a moral consensus? It can, but that moral consensus rarely extends to crimes of vice. I suggest, as others have, that we *do* share a powerful intuition—as it were, a common conscience, about most crimes, if committed against victims. We also share an *ordinal* cultural intuition. We agree that armed robbers should be punished, and more severely than thieves. Similarly, regardless of our position on capital punishment, we generally agree that those who deliberately murder should be punished with the greatest severity the law allows. In contrast, we share no consensus about the penalties, if any, appropriate to a variety of vices such as making illegal bets on the Super Bowl, engaging in nonmarital sex, or possessing five grams of marijuana.

The expressive nature of the War on Drugs was highlighted by William Bennett in 1991 when he headed the National Drug Control Strategy Office and wrote that the use of any illegal drug, of whatever quantity, "degrades human character." Yet I shall argue that, like alcohol consumption during national prohibition, some drugs, particularly marijuana used in small amounts, have attained the status of what I am going to call "normal vice." "Normal vice," I suggest, is distinguishable from "deviant vice," mostly by the numbers of ordinary persons who engage in it yet persist in breaking the applicable vice law. Insofar as marijuana use has become a rite of passage through early American adulthood, it has evolved into a normal vice. It is worth noting here that, although illegal, marijuana is reportedly the top cash crop of Kentucky, West Virginia, and Tennessee.

So, like drinking alcohol during Prohibition, or betting on the Super Bowl with an illegal bookmaker, or viewing pornography in a Hilton Hotel room, the concept "normal vice" implies widespread participation in the vice activity, coupled with the idea that most participants will maintain a conventional lifestyle. That is what distinguishes marijuana use from heroin use and often, cocaine use. In other words, for most indulgers, normal vice is *not* a central, defining feature of their lives. Deviant vice, I suggest, assumes two familiar structures or forms: one is at the level of the individual who develops an impaired lifestyle, which is commonly denoted as "abuse" or "addiction." The other is at the level of organization when based on providing illegal products or services.

ADDICTION

Let us examine the concept of abuse or addiction with reference to gambling. For this purpose, I refer to the DSM-IV—the scale used by the *Diagnostic and Statistical Manual* of the American Psychiatric Association to measure pathological gambling. The existence of five (or more) criteria, ranging from preoccupation to committing illegal acts to fund gambling, is believed to establish this state. These criteria are set out in full in chapters 11 and 13 table 3 of this volume.

It should be noted that this is a scale of undesirable effects of participation in a vice that is based on a scale originally developed to define and understand problem and pathological drinking. DSM-IV does not distinguish between betting illegally on the Super Bowl in New York or betting legally on the Super Bowl in Nevada. The concept of pathology is constructed around reported failures of social interaction and responsibility. Although gambling does not involve ingestion of a psychoactive substance, a small proportion of gamblers—anywhere from 2 to 7 percent—report *social* effects comparable to those experienced by addicts of drugs like alcohol, marijuana, and cocaine. And clinicians often report that their gambling-addicted patients experience "comorbidity" that is, other behavioral problems, substance abuse, mood disorders, and personality disorders, leading us to speculate about addictive personalities.

So addiction—whether to gambling, alcohol, marijuana, or cocaine—is said to have occurred when the vice activity seriously impairs performance in roles we have chosen to play or have thrust upon us—student, teacher, mother, father, teamster, bank executive. By this definition, addiction is more a social, and less a biochemical, concept.

Note that addiction is not necessarily correlated with quantity or frequency of participation—Winston Churchill is said to have daily drunk up to a liter of brandy, consumed from morning until night. Orthodox Jews may consume whiskey, morning and evening, after reciting appropriate prayers and never show signs of insobriety. Winston Churchill was perhaps *dependent* on alcohol, but since he conducted his prime minister role rationally, if not brilliantly, he would not qualify as a problem or "addicted" drinker.

Nor is legality relevant. Prohibition and legal drinking have each produced normal and addicted drinkers. A normal gambler can make illegal bets without becoming addicted, whereas an addicted gambler can become addicted while making bets in legal casinos or racetracks. Through personal experience with gambling and alcoholic beverages, most of us have come to recognize a distinction between normal and deviant gambling and drinking; between use and abuse.

An argument has been made that the negative effects of drinking— such as hospital admissions for cirrhosis of the liver—were reduced in the 1920s. That appears to be true. Nevertheless, one hears few voices advocating a return to national prohibition of alcohol—although problem drinking and more advanced alcoholism remain significant public health issues. One the whole, most of us would conclude that the cost of alcohol prohibition is greater than its benefits.

CRIMINAL ORGANIZATION

Let's turn to the second and more difficult and dangerous form of deviant vice, criminal organization—coupled with the inevitable corruption of law enforcers—which famously became a by-product of our experiment with national prohibition of alcohol. However hard we try, and however severe our punishments, unlawful commercial vice organizations spring up and are difficult to eradicate. This is true so long as there is a steady demand for illegal products or services. And there can be huge profits, because, especially with hard drugs, demand is relatively ineleastic.

There is another reason, which I called in a lecture a decade or so ago "the Darwinian Trafficker Dilemma." Why Darwinian? And why a dilemma? Darwinian because our escalating international enforcement effort typically succeeds in driving out the *weaker* suppliers. When that occurs the *stronger*, more efficient, suppliers, are competitively advantaged.

There are two hard measures of the success of a drug enforcement regime, measures that are comparable to profit for a business corporation. These are street price and potency. A successful enforcement strategy raises street price and lowers potency.

After more than two decades of warring on drugs, beginning with the Reagan administration, street prices of cocaine and heroin are lower by more than half and potency is higher. How can that be when we have repeatedly been shown huge seizures of cocaine and heroin? The answer must be that seizures we see so proudly publicized mainly undermine weaker drug organizations, leaving the stronger even more robust.

As Steve Schulhofer pointed out in a 1994 article analyzing the economics of narcotics enforcement, top down strategies are a cost-effective loser. Criminal law prohibitions of vice are challenged when there is (1) widespread participation and experience with the vice in question and (2) no consensus as to its harms. When that happens, we see cultural conflict about the vice, or at least cultural ambivalence. My favorite illustration of cultural ambivalence is an observation made by Will Rogers during Prohibition. When asked whether Americans were dry or wet, Rogers replied, "If you want to know whether Americans are dry, just watch 'em VOTE. If you want to know whether Americans are wet, just watch 'em DRINK."

Cultural ambivalence about the moral standing of a vice may well be a precursor leading to legal change and some form of regulation. That has occurred several times in our history. Justice White's target, the Eighteenth Amendment, was transformed in an astonishingly brief period, less than fifteen years. It was ratified on January 16, 1919, and repealed by the twenty-first Amendment on December 5, 1933.

The Hart-Devlin debate about homosexual sex as a crime, which had occupied the interest of countless seminars on criminal law policy in the United States and England during the 1960s, is scarcely an issue in criminal law classes today although it remains a major issue in society. Some religions denounce gay sex as a sin. Gays still cannot serve legally in the military or in the Boy Scouts. But in New York City's universities, businesses, and law enforcement agencies, we now take it for granted that sexual orientation and private behavior should be irrelevant. In some places the issue has even shifted from whether gays should be arrested to whether gays should be allowed to marry.

Historically, our most entrenched cultural taboo was that forbidding interracial marriage—really interracial sex, especially between a Black man and a White woman. So powerful was that cultural taboo that racial intermarriage had once been a felony in thirty-nine of forty-eight states. When the Warren Court declared those laws unconstitutional in 1968, they had remained on the books of thirteen states.

We are beginning to see an antiprohibition movement developing in the United States regarding marijuana. Gary E. Johnson, Republican governor of New Mexico, has called repeatedly for reevaluation of the nation's drug penalties; seven states have passed laws supporting medical marijuana because enforcement seems needlessly harsh; and even Governor Pataki seems to be reconsidering the harsh penalties of this state's [New York's] Rockefeller drug laws.

Cigarette smoking, for years mostly considered a normal practice, scarcely a vice, is morphing into a deviant practice, albeit not an illegal one, depending upon the location of smoking.

Perhaps the most profound and surprising transformation of all is in the laws regarding gambling. Consider that during World War II, when the United States was mobilized for war and when the government was urging its citizens to purchase U.S. Treasury "war bonds," nobody proposed a national lottery to raise funds for the war effort. Why not? Because it was unthinkable that a government should exploit the vice of gambling. For more than a century, lotteries had been regarded as immoral throughout the United States, totally outlawed by the beginning of the twentieth century. When the lottery was introduced in New Hampshire in 1946 it was promoted as "sin" taxation. Sin taxes on horseracing, lotteries, liquor, tobacco, and beer came to constitute 60 percent of New Hampshire's budget—taxing vice is yet another resolution of cultural ambivalence—and of course, such a resolution permits moralists to denounce the sin while profiting from its practice. It is interesting to note how quickly East Coast states and eventually the rest of the nation reprised the New Hampshire lottery lesson. They were, to be sure, faced with a public policy version of the Prisoner's Dilemma. If other states introduce the lottery, and yours does not, your citizens will buy lottery tickets from other states. But if you legalize lotteries, you impose a regressive tax on your poorer citizens. This is a dilemma not easily solved, yet most states opted to resolve it by legalization.

In one of his more accessible works, "Quiddities: An Intermittently Philosophical Dictionary" (1987), the philosopher W. V. Quine commented on the state lottery with tongue in cheek as "a public subsidy of intelligence—it yields public income that is calculated to lighten the tax burden of us prudent abstainers at the expense of the benighted masses of wishful thinkers." In plainer English, the poorer play disproportionately—and cut the taxes of the affluent.

The lottery is attractive to legislators and players because it doesn't *seem* to be a tax, since lottery playing is entirely voluntary. But that is deceptive. From an economic perspective, the lottery is best understood, I suggest, as an entertainment—like movies or sporting events. But its hidden tax is around 40 to 50 percent, which is the percentage states take before calculating the jackpot payoff. Worse yet, the percentage of the state's take is never revealed in advertising promoting the lottery. The same states that maintain consumer protection laws against fraudulent advertising hold no compunction against misleading promotion of betting on the lottery.

Perhaps as astonishing as the growth of the lottery has been the expansion of casino gambling, which has long been considered a vice. Victorian England's aversion to casino gambling found a voice even in John Stuart Mill, who, in his essay "On Liberty," compares running a public gambling house to running a house of prostitution. Movies and books have made most of us familiar with the rise of the Las Vegas casino and its roots in organized crime. As the casino business has moved from mob to corporate control, like the lottery and other forms of gambling, casino gambling has evolved into an American institution. Casinos are legal in twenty-eight states. There are nearly 100 riverboat and dockside casinos (in six states) and around 260 on Indian reservations, with many more slated to be built in California. Thirty-seven states and the District of Columbia have introduced lotteries, with $34 billion in annual sales. Illegal sportsbetting is said to be a $50 billion industry; and the infant Internet-betting industry is said to gross $4 to 5 billion annually, and rising.

Ironically, important as they are, Las Vegas, Atlantic City and other casino gambling sites across the nation threaten to be outdone by Indian-sponsored casinos. Foxwoods, in Connecticut, is now the largest casino complex in the world. The Indian gambling era began on February 25, 1987, when the U.S. Supreme Court decided the case of *Cabazon* v. *California Band of Mission Indians*. The Court, in an opinion by Justice White, and joined by an unusual company of justices (Rehnquist, Brennan, Marshall, Blackmun, and Powell) denied California the right to close down an Indian bingo parlor in Riverside County. Since California permitted charity bingo, the Court said, Indian bingo was not a criminal activity. More than that, the justices recognized gambling as a legitimate economic activity for American Indians, comparing it to hunting and fishing. In footnote 10, the Court contrasted gambling with other vices, writing that "nothing in this opinion suggests that cock-fighting, tattoo parlors, nude dancing, and prostitution are permissible on Indian reservations within California." In effect, the justices recognized that, like the consumption of alcoholic beverages, gambling had become culturally acceptable as a normal vice.

There is one situation, or status, that always renders vice deviant. Most of you will recall John Stuart Mill's famous harm principle: "That the only purpose for which power can be rightfully exercised over any member of a civilized community, against his will, is to prevent harm to others." But Mill quickly qualifies that principle, in the next couple of paragraphs, pointing out that it applies only to "human beings in the maturity of their faculties." That caution, it appears, is generally applicable. The more we perceive the young to be involved with a vice, the more we decry it. The public has learned that tobacco is addictive and that addiction begins in teenage years. Now under the legal gun, Philip Morris has pulled the Joe Camel advertisements that are attractive to children. Beer advertisements are also directed at teenagers, but that industry has so far skilfully managed to avoid serious advertising regulation. As I shall point out later, Mill—who was a legendary proponent of free trade—would be outraged by our beer advertising, especially when directed at the young.

States are able to control legal sales of lottery tickets to youth although there are always some adults who will buy for kids. Casino security guards are usually vigilant in keeping youngsters away from the gaming tables although they occasionally slip into the slot machines. But don't underestimate the casino industry. The more casinos look like Disneyland—as they do in Las Vegas—the more they and the adults who take them there teach kids about the propriety of gambling as a leisure activity. And the future of any industry—beer, baseball, cigarettes, and gambling—is with the next generation.

The gambling industry, however, shares a dilemma with other vice industries. The more successful they are in attracting users, the more likely they are to produce pathological users. A minority proportion of users or players—say, 20 to 30 percent—are responsible for a sizable majority of use or play. These are the profitable ones: the two-pack-a-day smoker, Joe Sixpack, and the multiple betting gambler. The casino gambling industry loves the high rollers, as the beer industry loves Joe Sixpack, but each will proclaim publicly and piously that customers should play and drink moderately. The gambling industry has shrewdly taken the lead in addressing compulsive gambling, supporting therapy programs for problem gamblers. But of course casinos employ various strategies to encourage high betting—the most obvious being the use of chips rather than cash. But, after all, that's where the money is.

Will gambling ever revert to its formerly stigmatized status? Probably not in the foreseeable future, but changes do occur over time. When Native Americans build fifty or sixty casinos in California, will that generate a backlash? What about Internet gambling?

Voters have so far been willing to accept casinos in exchange for promised taxes and job creation, so long as they are segregated in resort areas and riverboats. But as Indian casinos become more proximate to urban areas, as they will be in California, or as cities follow the lead of Detroit, with three casinos in the city proper, a backlash against casino gambling may occur.

Although there is a movement toward some form of legalization of marijuana, supported by some politicians, and some wealthy government backers, notably George Soros, the marijuana legalization movement faces a powerful law enforcement constituency of Federal and local police, prosecutors, and correctional officials.

Nevertheless, suppose we were to think about legalization of marijuana. Are there any principles we would wish to follow? I consider myself a Millian liberal, and thus a subscriber to John Stuart Mill's harm principle. But fashioning policy out of principle is not self-evident. And when applying his principle, Mill himself turns out to be quite circumspect.

In the last chapter of his essay, called "Applications," Mill discusses what he calls the Maine Law, the nineteenth-century law prohibiting use and sale of alcohol in the state of Maine. Mill opposes prohibition but is nevertheless quite sensitive to the potential harms of legalization. As in his harm principle, he distinguishes between individual liberty and public consequences. It is permissible, he says, for someone to be drunk in their own home but not on public highways (and he wrote before there were automobiles). Clearly, drunk driving would be a major offence for Mill.

He writes that "trade is a social act" and advocates tight restrictions on alcohol advertising. "The interest of these dealers in promoting intemperance," he wrote, "is a real evil and justifies the State in imposing restrictions and requiring restrictions which, but for that justification, would be infringements of legitimate liberty."

Ironically, the regulations on alcohol advertising proposed by Mill are largely inapplicable in light of U.S. Supreme Court commercial speech doctrine. Mill never even considers—I think it was beyond his libertarian yet Victorian imaginings—the propriety of governments urging citizens to buy lottery tickets, to bet on horseraces in off-track betting parlors, and to promote and tax casino gambling to subsidize the public treasury. It is not a great leap to apply Mill's ideas regarding alcohol to marijuana. In application, Mill's "libertarianism," tempered as it is by social welfare concerns, suggests that when a vice causes *public* harm, it should be carefully regulated although not prohibited. This seems to me a sensible position regarding what I have described as "normal vice." Moreover, like Mill, I would advocate tight controls on inducing demand for any vice.

As a bumper sticker slogan, "Use Yes—Promotion NO," and as a footnote (only a Professor would be silly enough to footnote a bumper sticker), "especially no promotion by the government."

So my conclusion is this: Our legal vice policies are curiously paradoxical. Either we try to prohibit vice, with unintended consequences especially for the poor and non-whites in our society, or we exploit vice by vastly expanding opportunities to engage in it, as in the case of gambling, cigarettes, and alcohol. There is, I suggest, a Millian regulatory mean that lies somewhere between criminalization and exploitation. The search for that mean is where, I suggest, it would be most sensible to focus the nation's public policy response to control the attractions of wicked pleasures.

♥ ♠ ♣
20
THE MORAL CASE FOR LEGALIZING GAMBLING

Peter Collins

This essay discusses the morality of prohibiting gambling and argues that there are compelling moral reasons for thinking that gambling should be legal. My argument is unusual in that it makes a moral case for legalizing gambling rather than arguing simply that it is too difficult to enforce prohibition or that gambling is a politically effective way for governments to generate funds for the public purse. The argument, instead, claims that using the law to prevent people from gambling is a morally illegitimate use of government power.

I begin by discussing what I take to be the two arguments most commonly deployed in support of prohibition and seek to show why they are unacceptable. I then articulate the moral principles that I believe make the case for legalization irresistible. The first type of argument made against legalizing gambling focuses on the gambler him- or herself. The second type focuses on people other than the gambler who are affected by the gambler's activities.

The first argument is the simplest. It runs as follows:

- Gambling is immoral.
- It is the business of government to try to eradicate immorality.
- Therefore it is the business of government to try to eradicate gambling.

This argument is a valid syllogism, which means that if you accept the premises you are logically obliged to accept the conclusion. In fact, throughout history and in many cultures today, both the premises of this argument and its conclusion have been taken for granted. People have assumed unquestioningly that there are absolute moral laws that govern not only how people should treat one another but also which forms of pleasure may be legitimately indulged in and which forms of pleasure are inherently wicked. Typically, moral laws of this sort are thought to be enshrined in the teachings of the religion of the society in which they are accepted and they thus have the authority that comes from being acknowledged as the revealed will of God. The case for prohibiting pleasures on these grounds combines fundamentalist faith with puritan ethics. The result is that those who oppose gambling on these grounds are often imbued with exceptionally strong moral passion.

However, the view that gambling is immoral is far from universally held. In liberal democracies, most opinion polls show it to be a minority view. But even if the view were very widespread, there would still be an overwhelming reason for rejecting prohibition: that, as most people acknowledge, it is morally wrong for the state to interfere with the essentially private choices of individuals about how they will spend their time and money, providing they are not doing harm to anyone else. In particular, it seems wrong for the state to interfere with choices that do not harm others solely on the grounds that some people—even many people—deem the activities in question to be immoral.

Instead, it seems morally more persuasive to propose that the only justification for interference by the state with the freedom of individuals is when the exercise of this freedom threatens to harm others in ways that violate their legitimate rights. This view of the role of government, which has its origins in the political philosophy of Hobbes and Locke, is fundamental to the beliefs of the Founding Fathers of the American Constitution and, as we shall see, it was very clearly articulated in the nineteenth century in John Stuart Mill's famous and still very influential essay, *On Liberty*.

The central tenet of this political philosophy, which lies at the heart of liberal democratic theory, is the principle of "maximum equal liberty." This principle asserts that in a well-governed society everyone will enjoy the maximum amount of freedom to decide for themselves how to live their lives in a way that is compatible with everyone else's enjoying the same amount of freedom. It is, of course, wholly inconsistent with this principle to claim that some people should be prevented from gambling even though they in no way restrict the freedom of others simply because other people think that gambling is wicked.

Because there is a lack of consensus about the inherent wickedness of gambling, prohibitionists frequently offer a more attractive variant on this argument, which runs as follows:

- Gambling (is wicked because it) is bad for people.
- It is the business of government to prevent people from doing things that are bad for them.
- Therefore government should stop people from gambling.

Again, this is a valid syllogism in which the conclusion follows logically from the premises. The argument is essentially "paternalist" in that it claims that government should treat its subjects as good parents treat their children and protect them from themselves. It does not require government to claim absolute knowledge of what is morally right and wrong for everybody.

The paternalist argument instead depends only on there being widespread agreement about what is bad for people and on acceptance of the view that the state has a duty to secure the best interests of its citizens in cases where these citizens, for whatever reason, are incapable of looking after these interests for themselves.

This paternalist version of the argument for prohibition can, of course, encompass the same material as the first, "enforcement of morals" version. It will do this if it is claimed that all activities pronounced by (typically religious) authority to be immoral are also in fact bad for you because, for example, they imperil the future well-being of your immortal soul. A paternalist might thus prohibit gambling on the grounds that it is immoral and therefore will inevitably lead to your being punished by God. But, of course, the paternalist does not need to appeal to either religion or morality. It is enough to claim, as can indeed very plausibly be claimed, that people who gamble run the risk of ruining their lives. It can then be argued that government should prevent people from incurring this risk.

Paternalist arguments for prohibition are much more acceptable in plural societies than arguments that appear to violate the principle that Church and State should be separate. One strong moral argument against paternalism, however, is that it violates the principle of equality. In a version of the paternalist argument applied to gambling, people on both the Right and the Left in politics stress that gambling mainly exploits the poor, who consequently need to be protected by law from the consequences of their own potential folly. But this denies to the poor not only equality of opportunity but also equality of respect. It requires that the state patronize the poor by telling them that they are too irresponsible to gamble.

A more obvious reason why paternalist arguments against gambling are generally repudiated is empirical. It is plausible (though not indisputable) to say that most people who take heroin—or who smoke cigarettes—do themselves significant harm. It is not plausible to make this claim about most people who gamble—or who drink alcohol. As a matter of fact, it seems that the vast majority of people who gamble—who buy lottery tickets, place bets on horse races and other sporting events, or gamble on cards, dice, or slot machines—do so without causing themselves any harm. Certainly, they lose money for the most part and in the long run, but that is simply the price that they knowingly and willingly pay for the pleasure they get from gambling. If this is so, then to ban gambling because a small minority of gamblers are reckless would be as unjustifiable as banning cars because a minority of drivers are reckless. If governments claim that gambling is bad for you they will, therefore, be wrong in most cases.

Even if this were not so, however, prohibiting gambling because it is bad for people still violates the fundamental commitment to individual freedom that is basic to liberal democracy. This principle entails that people must be allowed to decide for themselves how to live their lives even if many of them will in fact choose badly. The principle is very forcibly articulated by John Stuart Mill in the *Essay on Liberty*. Mill writes:

The sole end for which mankind are warranted, individually or collectively, in interfering with the liberty of action of any of their number is
. . . to prevent harm to others. His own good, either physical or moral,
is not a sufficient warrant. He cannot rightly be compelled to do or for-
bear because it will be better for him to do so, because it will make him
happier, or in the opinion of others, to do so would be wise, or even
right. There are good reasons for . . . persuading him . . . but not for
compelling him. . . . Over himself, over his own body and mind, the
individual is sovereign.[1]

Mill's view is widely endorsed in the culture of modern, developed,
secular, and pluralistic societies such as that of the United States. For this
reason, contemporary arguments in favor of prohibiting gambling
increasingly rely on the second kind of claim that needs to be considered:
that gamblers do in fact cause unjustifiable harm to people other than
those who gamble. There are two main versions of this argument. The
first appeals to what I call the "human costs" of gambling; the second to
what are usually called the "social costs" or "externalities." Both versions
rely heavily on alleged facts about "problem gambling."

The first claims that problem gamblers inevitably cause harm to a large
number of people whose lives and well-being are closely bound up with
theirs. The most plausible category of people allegedly so harmed are those
whose lives are emotionally as well as materially bound up with problem
gamblers: their partners, children, parents, and all those who are in any way
dependent on a problem gambler. The types of harm that problem gamblers
inflict on these people include impoverishment, insecurity, humiliation,
depression, domestic distress of all sorts, and perhaps particular emotional
devastation if the gambler goes to prison or commits suicide.

The second version of the "harm to others" argument claims that
legalized gambling has unacceptable economic costs as a result of which
society is overall poorer in material terms than it would be if there were
no legal gambling. One of the most important differences between human
costs and social costs is that the latter are thought to be quantifiable while
the former are not. Mainly for this reason, the human costs argument and
the social costs argument are very different, the former appealing to subjective feelings of compassion, the latter to allegedly objective economic
calculations.

The logic of the human costs argument is more complex than the arguments we have considered so far. It runs as follows:

- Addictive gambling (like any other addiction) causes extreme distress to the family of the addict and others close to him or her.
- These human costs outweigh any benefits that legalizing gambling might bring—pleasure for nonaddictive players, jobs for employees of gambling companies, taxes for governments, etc.
- Legalized gambling inevitably increases the prevalence of gambling addiction.
- It is the duty of governments to protect families and other innocent parties from potential damage by gambling addicts when the human costs outweigh the benefits.
- Therefore, it is the duty of government to prevent increases in the prevalence of addictive gambling by prohibiting gambling itself.

The first premise of this argument is unexceptionable. Gambling addiction is as real as drug addiction and alcoholism. It has the same claim to be thought of and treated as a psychological illness as these other more familiar conditions, and it certainly has very horrible consequences for the loved ones and dependents of gambling addicts, who, in extreme cases, kill not only themselves but their families as well and regard that killing as the only escape from the living hell that life has become for all concerned.

Given these facts, it is easy to see why people are intuitively inclined to accept the second premise as well: that no relatively trivial benefits for the many could possibly justify these appalling sufferings of the few. To compel nonaddictive gamblers to find other pleasures, employees to find other jobs, and governments to find other sources of revenue seems a small price to pay for saving the loved ones of gambling addicts from the extreme suffering that otherwise faces them.

There is no question that if gambling were as addictive as, say, smoking and the vast majority of regular gamblers became addicts, and if prohibition were clearly the best way of drastically reducing the number of such addicts, then the case for prohibiting gambling to protect the innocent victims of the addictive gambler's behavior would be irresistible. The trouble is that the first of these conditions is not met—the vast majority of regular gamblers do not become addicts—and there is some reason for thinking that prohibition would merely result—as with the prohibition of drugs—in people becoming addicted through the underground market.

In other words, the second premise may not be as acceptable as at first appears. It may be that the evils of prohibition—of having gambling services supplied, like drugs, by organized crime—will be worse, not merely adding massive law-enforcement costs but actually making it harder to provide help to addictive gamblers and their families. Moreover, the third premise of the human costs argument is also far from self-evident: it may not be inevitable that legalized gambling increases the incidence of addictive gambling. Legalized gambling may only increase the visibility rather than the prevalence of addictive gambling. It may also be that there are ways of regulating gambling so that the incidence of addictive gambling in a legal environment is less than it would be if gambling were illegal. What is certain is that we do not know enough about how the provision of legal gambling affects the incidence of addictive gambling and how prohibition would alter the picture. Neither advocates of legal gambling nor their opponents should pretend that we do.

There is also an issue of proportionality, which relates to the fourth premise, i.e., the supposed duty of government to minimize harm for the families of addicts. Because the "human costs" argument appeals to widespread feelings of horror and compassion at the plight of the families of addictive gamblers, it is easy to represent those who do not accept it as being callous in respect of the sufferings of gambling addicts and their families. However, the question needs to be asked: How much can government do and how much ought government to try to stop its citizens causing each other distress? The law forbids spouses to hit each other. Should it try—can it reasonably hope—to stop spouses from shouting at one another, especially, say, in front of their children? If it could do so easily and without unacceptable side effects, no doubt the answer would be "yes." But the truth is that to enforce such a prohibition would be accounted an intolerable intrusion into people's private lives. It would have thoroughly undesirable consequences, such as encouraging or requiring neighbors to report on each other. And probably the harm done is comparatively small given all the other evils to which government (and its police) have to attend. In other words, a law to prevent members of families from verbally abusing one another would be accounted overall disproportionate.

Given that addictive gamblers are a small minority even of regular gamblers and the damage they do to others is almost certainly considerably less than that caused by, for example, people who drink too much, it may be thought that it would be disproportionate to take away the freedom of the vast majority of people who gamble harmlessly to pursue pleasure in order to pursue a policy which will have substantial social costs and be of dubious effectiveness in minimizing the suffering of those whom the policy is designed to help.

Given the uncertainties that surround prohibitionist arguments based on the human costs of problem gambling, some advocates of prohibition prefer to point to the "social costs," that is the measurable money costs that are picked up throughout society as a result of legalizing gambling. The claim is then made that these costs outweigh the measurable benefits that the legalization of gambling brings.

To establish whether this claim is true or not, we would need to have an agreed procedure for measuring and comparing costs and benefits. At best we have the beginnings of such a procedure. We can identify the benefits of legalizing gambling as accruing most obviously to people who like gambling. They are now able to indulge their taste without incurring the cost of breaking the law or paying the additional price charged by (usually monopolistic) illegal operators. If the costs of gambling include the risk of going to prison or being compelled to pay a large fine, then these costs will for many prove to be what they are intended to be: literally prohibitive. With legalization gamblers are richer because they can obtain pleasure more cheaply and have more money left over to spend on other things.

The social costs of legalizing gambling are the costs that are incurred mainly by nongamblers and most commonly by taxpayers and that would not have arisen if gambling had not been legalized. These costs, consequently, make those who bear them poorer than they would otherwise have been. Suppose that legalization brings an increase in crime, as might happen if legalization meant that more gamblers engage in embezzlement to finance their gambling or if gamblers prove to be an exceptionally easy target for muggers. Under these circumstances, there would be a demand for additional resources for law enforcement; that is more policing costs, more trial costs and more imprisonment costs which would lead in turn to new demands on the public purse that taxpayers would have to meet. The same is true if it is found that the legalization of gambling leads to an increase in the amount of disease that needs to be treated at the taxpayer's expense, a claim made by people who say that legalization leads to a substantial increase in pathological gambling.

In principle, it should be possible to work out what the total increased costs to the taxpayer will be, as well as how much money will be saved by gamblers, who can now purchase more cheaply the same quantity of pleasure as they could obtain previously through illegal gambling or through more expensive substitute activities. When these two sums are compared, one can say whether there is overall more or less wealth in society.

Unfortunately in practice, economists are not yet in a position to make this calculation. The relevant data are unavailable. Moreover, because too little is known about the causes and consequences of problem gambling, we cannot be sure how many of the social costs would remain the same or even increase under prohibition. It should also be noted that the obvious thing to do in a situation in which an economic activity such as commercial gambling has social costs (or "externalities") is what almost all jurisdictions in fact try to do, namely, to tax the activities of gamblers to ensure that gambling taxes at least cover the social costs that the availability of legal gambling generates.

Most important of all, even if the dollar cost-benefit ratio of legalization proves to be unfavorable, this circumstances would still need to be set against the moral cost of infringing people's liberty of choice. By the same token, even if the dollar benefits of legalization were shown to outweigh the dollar costs, this financial benefit would have to be set against the nondollar human costs we have already mentioned in terms of ruined lives.

Ultimately then, the argument about legalizing gambling is about social and political values. If I reflect on what is most important in my conviction that gambling should not be prohibited by law, it comes down to a set of judgments about the moral principles that I believe guide the conduct of government. Thus I disapprove on moral grounds of highly puritanical societies that frown on pleasure generally and on many largely harmless pleasures in particular. I also disapprove of highly authoritarian societies that arrogate to themselves the right to prescribe which pleasures people may and may not indulge in. Nor do I think it right for societies to make it difficult to be adventurous in the pursuit of pleasure or to inhibit economic creativity by restricting the forms of entertainment that people may provide on a commercial basis. Above all, I believe that the most admirable kind of society from a moral point of view is one in which citizens are allowed to think for themselves and make up their own minds about how they wish to spend their time, money, talents, and energy without being bossed about and frustrated in their designs by the agents of an impersonal government. Of course I recognize that people will make some foolish choices in such a society, but for government to prevent them from making those choices to spare them some possible unhappiness is also to rob them of dignity.

Not to accord to adults the maximum possible freedom to decide for themselves how to live their own lives is to violate their dignity as autonomous moral agents and to reduce citizens to a condition of permanent infantility. This argument differs from Mill's in that it does not require us to claim that government interference might not in fact result in greater happiness for most of its citizens. It is quite clear that people in government do sometimes know what is in the interests of its citizens better than the citizens themselves, just as parents are often right in judging that their children are forming romantic attachments that will cause them great unhappiness. But freedom consists in the right to make bad choices as well as good ones, and a society that seeks to protect people from the consequences of bad choices in matters of lifestyle by taking away their freedom to choose violates their fundamental rights and assaults their dignity as persons no less surely than a society that denies them the freedom to worship or to love as seems best to them.

If it is pointed out to me that people's overindulgences may lead to ill health or destitution that society, through its taxpayers, has to try to alleviate, my response is that, of course, we could have a society in which sufferers from, say, smoking-related diseases were not eligible for state subsidized heath care. However, from considerations of compassion, I believe that society ought to look after not only the undeserving poor but also the sick who are entirely responsible for their own diseases. If that means a higher tax burden, so be it.

These value judgments are not unchallengeable. If I became convinced that legalizing any gambling at all would really create extreme and widespread misery and that prohibition would prevent this, then my commitment to liberty might be trumped in this case. Moreover, if I became convinced that all gambling is as highly dangerous as drinking absinthe or smoking crack cocaine or driving without a seat belt are alleged to be, then I would probably reluctantly support prohibition. In fact, I consider the harm caused by excessive gambling to be relatively small compared with the damage caused by *inter alia* alcohol, drugs, and overeating. In general, I consider the arguments made against legal gambling that emphasize the evils of "problem gambling" to lack a sense of proportion and perspective.

All of this is also quite compatible with thinking that nothing serious is lost in terms of individual freedom when commercial gambling is made subject to some special regulations and its availability limited. It might be thought that gambling, like many other forms of pleasure, should be available only to adults, though this proposition is not as self-evident as it is generally assumed to be. It might be thought that gambling presents special opportunities for various kinds of fraud and that therefore competitive market forces alone will not ensure honest commercial transactions. It might also be thought that gambling should be run as a state monopoly or be otherwise restricted and taxed so as to ensure the maximum benefits for nongamblers (or for gamblers in their capacity not as consumers of gambling services but as member of the general public). Other special regulations might be justified if gambling is integral to a collective strategy to attract tourists. My view that gambling should not be prohibited is also entirely compatible with the view that the world would be a better place if gambling had never been invented or if gambling were to fall into desuetude as people become educated to enjoy many other pleasures that are richer and subtler.

More important, my arguments show that, contrary to what is commonly assumed, there is a strong *moral* case for not prohibiting gambling and that the antigambling lobby has no right to assume that it owns the moral high ground or has a monopoly on commitment to doing what morality requires. Quite apart from the enormous practical and political difficulties that are endemic to it, the position of prohibitionists is vulnerable to powerful moral objections.

NOTE

1. John Stuart Mill, *On Liberty*, 1869, ed. Stefan Collini (Cambridge: Cambridge University Press, 1989), p. 13.

21

PLAYING THE GODS

Gambling and Spirituality, a New Anthropological Perspective

Kathryn Gabriel

Gambling in America, via pari-mutuel betting, the lottery, Indian reservation casinos, or luxury resorts, is now an acceptable form of recreation, but it is still embroiled in controversy. Promoters argue that gambling stimulates the economy while opponents can show hard numbers of its destruction to the community and the individual. The dominant religions of the world judge gambling on a moral basis, but where is the sin? Truth is what the opposite sides of an argument have in common, and the middle ground in this conundrum is not sin; it is spirituality.

Although the idea may seem contradictory, from an anthropological perspective, gambling is as spiritual as praying. Both gambling and praying seek divine affirmation and reversal of fortune. We can look to the Native American tribes as a case in point: For three decades they have struggled to develop casinos on their lands, citing the drastic need for self-sufficiency and autonomy, and this late twentieth- and early twenty-first-century gold rush has indeed resurrected some tribes while others have gone belly up. The tribes themselves will argue that economics and spirituality are separate issues and that the real issue is sovereignty, but they will credit their rituals for the turn of the tables. A large body of ethnological evidence demonstrates that gambling on many reservations has been intricately connected with religious rite and festival for at least five hundred years, and prehistoric sites reveal that gambling existed before Western encroachment on this continent. Sacred gaming, however, is not limited to Native Americans; it lies at the root of most cultures in the world, as if it were an evolutionary phase of human development, the origin myth of our existence.

DICE AND THE CYCLE OF DEATH AND REBIRTH

We can safely assume that gambling, particularly sacred gambling, is almost as old as humankind, and it has known no social or geographic boundaries. Prehistoric gambling was often associated with death and rebirth. One Egyptian tomb painting (c. 3500 B.C.E.), for instance, depicts a nobleman in his afterlife playing a dice-board game of hounds and jackals. Antelope ankle bones, presumed to have been used as dice, are often found in prehistoric tombs and burial caves around the world, perhaps to provide the dead with afterlife recreation or the means by which they could "re-create" life. Icelandic and Hindu mythology mirror many Native American myths that claim that the gods destroy and recreate the world on a dice board.

Game boards and playing fields can themselves be considered altars of the sacred. Magicians, priests, and gamblers all begin their work by circumscribing the consecrated spot.[1] There is little distinction between marking out a space for a sacred purpose and marking it out for purposes of sheer play. The turf, the tennis court, the chessboard, and the pavement hopscotch cannot formally be distinguished from the temple or the magic circle. Game diagrams were built into roofing slabs of a temple in ancient Thebes, carved into the cloister seats of medieval English churches, and pecked into survey markers for the grid underlying the pyramid city of Teotihuacán.

WHICH CAME FIRST: GAME PLAYING OR GAMBLING?

It is difficult to prove which came first, game playing or gambling. Far back in prehistory idle humans began carving and painting bits of bone, shell, stick, arrow, or halved reed, inventing a little game around the number of two-sided dice falling solid-side, black-side, or convex-side up. The binary quality of these pieces began to be associated with "yes" or "no." Before long, players attempted to appropriate the future by risking something of value against it. The ancients might have noticed a pattern to winning and losing, and that certain rituals seemed to affect this pattern, thus surmising that some invisible force controlled the outcome of the game. This same force, perhaps, also controlled the weather, famine, fertility, or the celestial bodies. They personified the forces as superdeities, and gambled to control or appease them.

CONSULTING THE GODS THROUGH GAMING PIECES

In some parts of the globe the gaming pieces were associated with the gods and were consulted for advice. In ancient Chinese temples, for example, the patterns made by a handful of tossed reeds corresponded to the intricate diagrams in the *I Ching*, a Chinese book of ancient origin consisting of sixty-four interrelated hexagrams, which in turn correspond with Taoist philosophical commentaries describing all nature and human endeavor in terms of the interaction between *yin* and *yang*. From Greek historians we know that Zeus and Aphrodite, among others, were consulted with the toss of dice, and the Iliad describes how the Olympian gods were beseeched in lotteries held by soldiers to select a battle champion.

BIBLICAL REFERENCES TO THE CASTING OF LOTS

The Bible tells us that a pair of stone dice was used to determine the will of God. In Isa. 34:17, for instance, dice were cast in order to determine land allotments given to each family to pass on from one generation to the next. The word *lottery* is derived from this practice, referring also to one's destiny. Translators of the Bible may have substituted the familiar word for the more obscure biblical terms, *Urim* and *Thummim*. What the Urim and Thummim were and how they were used remains lost to antiquity, though scholars speculate that they were the names of two divining stones employed by priests in an unknown fashion as a channel for the will of God—one stating the affirmative and the other the negative, the yang and the yin. In Exod. 28:30, for example, God tells Moses that whenever Aaron comes into His presence in holy places, he must carry the Urim and Thummim in his breastpiece (*ephod*) engraved with the names of the tribes of Israel. If he does so, God will always remember His people, and Aaron can determine His will for Israel.

F. N. David, a mathematician philosopher, suggests that gambling was a development of the board game in which the random element of chance was retained and the board dispensed with: "It is, however, equally likely that gaming developed from the wager and the wager from the drawing of lots, the interrogation of the oracles, and so on, which have their roots deep in religious ritual."[2] Gambling, then, was originally entangled in the rudimentary forms of spirituality.

This is not to say that gambling evolved from spirituality or vice versa; the subject is too complex to extract such a simple notion. Rather gambling as sacred play shares features with praying and divining. Those who engage in any of these activities long for the same outcome, that of divine intervention.

EARLY AMERICAN ATTITUDES TOWARD GAMBLING

With lotteries and Indian gaming revenues supplementing education and scholarships, America has returned to its fundraising roots. Although early explorers to America expressed disapproval of the indigenous population for its gambling obsessions and associated "heathen practices," games of hazard were rampant in the New World. Lotteries were critical to funding the colonization of America, the Revolutionary War, and even such universities as Harvard and Princeton. Southerners wagered slaves, plantations, and fortunes at horse racing, cribbage, cards, and dominoes.

New Englanders were split: Some aligned with the British economist Sir William Petty, who called gambling a "tax upon unfortunate self-conceited fools."[3] Others quoted the casting of lots in the Bible as sanction for their backroom betting.

The moral judgment of gambling as a sin in Western thinking may have begun in Roman times when citizens bet future wages, homes, wives, and children at the gaming tables, prompting legislators to establish antigambling laws. Throughout the Dark Ages, the Church vigorously and unsuccessfully blasted against gambling as a vice or because it was too closely woven to the gods of the pagan religions. Sir William, in the seventeenth century, argued that "the Sovereign" should guard "gamblers, lunatics, and idiots" from their own worst instincts. At about the same time, Pascal worked out the mathematical probability of the fall of the dice. This theory promoted a new confidence in gamblers, as if reason could override chance—as if the mind could override spirit—of particular interest to insurance underwriters. Thus, gambling and spirituality were severed in Western thought.

GAMBLING PREVALENT IN NEW WORLD A THOUSAND YEARS BEFORE EUROPEAN CONTACT

The very fact that the United States Congress had to separately classify and distinguish traditional ritual gambling from reservation casino operations under the Indian Gaming Regulatory Act of 1987 suggests that ritual gambling is still prevalent among tribal nations. Gambling existed in this hemisphere at least a thousand years before European contact, as witnessed in the Hohokam and Mesoamerican ball courts of Arizona and Mexico, the bone dice in Anasazi great houses in New Mexico, and the stone discs and playing fields of the Eastern Woodland Mound Builders.[4] Ethnological records dating as far back as the fifteenth century testify to widespread gambling across the continent as a means of earning a living, far less expensive than raiding and warfare. Nineteenth-century pioneer ethnologist Stewart Culin gathered evidence of gaming from 229 North American and Mexican tribes, in his book *Games of the North American Indians*, identifying thirty-six different kinds of games of chance and dexterity that were played, with side bets, at fixed times of the year during festivals and religious rites.

On the surface it would appear that the Native American view of gambling is diametrically opposed to the moral view of gambling adhered to by the major world religions, but the farther back in time one goes, the more the Native American and the Old World views toward gambling converges.[5] Gambling was considered to be a means by which devotees could contact the cosmos, with one overriding exception in approach: Whereas gamblers in the Old World cast lots to divine the will of the gods and to forecast the future, Native Americans played gambling games to come into harmony with their universe. In his 846-page report for the Bureau of American Ethnology, *Games of the North American Indians*, Culin concluded, "In general, games appear to be played ceremonially, as pleasing to the gods, with the object of securing fertility, causing rain, giving and prolonging life, expelling demons, or curing sickness."[6]

GAMBLING AS REVITALIZATION

Among Southwestern and Mexican tribes, gaming rituals were performed to assist the change of seasons from winter to summer and back or, as in the indigenous moccasin game, to divide the day between light and darkness. In short, the act of ceremonial gambling symbolized the continuous cycle of birth, death, and rebirth. This theme was carried over into the American Great Plains, where the Pawnee hand game and its attending gambling myths synchronized the movements of that tribe with the movements of the sun, moon, and morning star. The hand game was also played as a rite of spring before a hunt or to drive a rival tribe into economic ruin. When the Pawnees became nearly depopulated with the diminishing buffalo herds early in the twentieth century, they turned to the Ghost Dance to revive the culture. The Ghost Dance was associated with a messianic religious movement among Southwestern and Great Plains tribes in the late nineteenth century, in which Ghost Dance prophets foretold the imminent disappearance of Whites, the restoration of traditional lands and ways of life, and the resurrection of dead ancestors. When the American government outlawed the Ghost Dance, Pawnees blended parts of the dance with the old hand game ceremony.

This converted ritual was played to ensure reunion with the ancestors and the buffalo in an afterlife that included no White people. Gaming was considered to be a means of revitalizing the tribe, much as it is on many reservations today.

This is not to say that all tribes or individual tribal members favor modern casino gambling on their reservations, and some will go so far as to say it is taboo—an attitude not based on Christian missionary influence but on long experience. Indeed, historical documents report that gambling in earlier centuries had its devastating effects on members of many tribes. Culin's study of Native American games included numerous accounts by early chroniclers who observed, sometimes with shock and moral indignation, the intensity and obsession with which players gambled away their high stakes, with dreadful consequences to the losers. Anthropologists noted that they had seen groups of men and women wagering their ornaments and all their personal goods, even their clothing, until their bodies were nude. The governor of the Washington Territory reported that tribes of the upper Missouri Valley devoted all their leisure time, both day and night, to gambling, to the distress and poverty of their families. These are still serious concerns on and off reservations today.[7]

RITUAL GAMBLING TO BRING HARMONY TO THE COSMOS

A survey of more than a hundred gambling myths, originating from the Subarctic igloos to the ballcourts of the Quiché Maya, reveals the extent to which gambling played a metaphoric role in Native spiritual thought and beliefs.[8] The overwhelming evidence of the myths demonstrates that gambling (within a traditional context) was sanctioned for such purposes as controlling weather or bringing back the sun, the plants, the buffalo, or the health of an individual or group. Equally significant, the myths emphasize that gambling outside of the spiritual context is dangerous for the well-being of the gambler, the community, and, most important, the cosmos. When humans go up against the superbeings in these myths, the stakes include possible enslavement and all of one's possessions—arms, legs, eyes, and heads—usually in that order. Whole tribes and even worlds are often destroyed, and it is up to the hero gambler to restore them. The following Paviotso myth demonstrates the point:

> While hunting one day, a boy is told by a little bird that Centipede has killed all of his people through gambling, cut out and dried their hearts, and strung up all their hands together, burning the rest of their bodies. The bird instructs the youth in how to beat the gambler. With the help of Owl and Gopher, the youth wins. He throws Centipede into the fire and plants the dried hearts in the damp earth. His people are restored on the third sunrise.[9]

Sometimes the gambler myth centers on a youth, who is often the half-human, half-divine offspring of such spirits as Sun, Thunder, or Bear. The youth is exiled from the tribe for excessive gambling or for not attending to his spiritual duties. Before defeating the supergambler, the hero must undergo some sort of vision, quest, or ritual, during which time he is taught the magic components of gambling by a spirit guide or deity.

The following myth told by the Lillooet of British Columbia illustrates this key point:

> An old woman tells a bankrupt gambler to go to the mountains and train for four years. At the end of that period, he goes to a lake where, on the other side, are two underground houses; good people live in one house, cannibals in the other. He enters the house of the good people, whereupon the chief readies him for gambling by whipping him four times, washing him, and giving him his two daughters. The gambler then enters the other house, where he stakes his two wives against the two daughters and the property of the bad chief, and wins. The gambler returns the property to the bad chief but keeps the daughters as wives. Now he has four women, each of whom bears him a daughter. He returns home and enjoys infamy as a great gambler. When another man asks the gambler his secrets, he sends the man directly to the cannibal people. And since this man has not prepared himself, he is eaten.[10]

GAMBLING MYTHS IN THE ANCIENT HINDU MAHABHARATA

Analogous to such "test theme" gambling myths of the Americas is a lengthy gambling sequence in the ancient Hindu text called the Mahabharata, written sometime between 400 B.C.E. and 400 C.E. In this story, which appears in *The Book of the Assembly Hall*, two cousins play dice to determine the rightful heir to the throne.[11] The initial loser, Yudhisthira, is the son of Dharma, the god of Universal Law. Yudhisthira undergoes a thirteen-year sojourn through the forest, during which time he learns volumes of spiritual principles. Only after he passes certain tests presented by deities can he return to take his rightful place as ruler of the universe. This dharmic gambling action is analogous to "right gambling" as described in certain extensive Navajo chantways, in which the hero is exiled as a gambling or sexual zealot for a number of years while he undergoes intense purification and religious training. He, too, returns to beat the Great Gambler.[12]

GAMBLING AS METAPHOR FOR BALANCE

It is common for many figures in Native American mythology to play alternate roles as a good gambler or a bad. Gambling stories are not about good versus evil but about good and evil as part of a continuum that must stay in balance, much like the Taoist yin and yang. In fact, the bad gambler is not always killed but is whittled down to a more manageable force or shot into the air, where he is transfigured from an enemy into a god of a whole new race of people. Nature's continuous flow between birth, death, and rebirth is mimicked in the constant ebb and flow of game playing between two sides.

The key to gambling mythology is that it is universally a metaphor for both the crucifixion and the resurrection. This is true even in Western literature, as anticipated by a bankrupt roulette player in Dostoyevsky's novel, *The Gambler*: "One turn of the wheel, and everything changes. . . . What am I today? Zero. What can I be tomorrow? Tomorrow I may rise from the dead and start to live again!" But be warned: Whatever goes up, must also come down. The spinning wheel of fortune gives the illusion that life is either constantly evolving or devolving. The truth, as the gambling myths illustrate, is that it is a never-ending cycle.

The great spiritual masters of India use the board game of pachisi to illustrate the point that all of life is constantly being shuffled through the revolving door of birth, death, and rebirth. Remember pachisi? We played it as children. Two to four people can play at a time, and their positions are marked by four pieces represented by one of four colors. The goal is to move the pieces all around the spaces of the board, as determined by the roll of the dice, until the markers finally reach "home," or the kingdom of heaven. In the *Puranas* mythology of India, the pair of gods known as Shiva and Shakti create and destroy the worlds through pachisi, using humans as pawns and night and day as dice.

In a spiritual text of India called the Sar Bachan, pachisi's four groups of variant-colored markers are said to represent the four stages of life through which all souls must rotate: vegetation, insect, bird or fish, and mammal.[13] After each form of life is experienced, the soul then revolves through all forms of human experience; the dice of cause and effect determines their "lot" in each experience; in other words, the "karma" of how they played the game in one incarnation determines the circumstances in their next life.

In the game of pachisi, each color group has its own "home path" to heaven. Similarly, in the game of life as depicted in the San Bachan, each soul rushes the gates of heaven by traveling every imaginable path of religious endeavor. Upon death, the soul exits the game through that particular path's version of heaven only to find itself back on the board in a subsequent life. Finally, after the soul has had millions of chances on the dice board, it meets a *Sat Guru* or True Master, who escorts the soul off the board's cycle or birth and rebirth once and for all, and into the imperishable region known as *Sach Khand.*

Consider the gambler as mystic in this poem by the fourteenth-century poet Hafiz,[14] called "Tripping over Joy":

> What is the difference
> Between your Existence
> And that of a Saint?

The Saint knows
That the spiritual path
Is a sublime chess game with God
And that the Beloved
Has just made such a Fantastic Move
That the Saint is now continually
Tripping over joy
And Bursting out in Laughter
And saying, "I Surrender!"

Whereas, my dear,
I am afraid you still think
You have a thousand serious moves

GAMBLING AS SPIRITUAL SEEKING

What the ancient myths in both hemispheres seem to be saying is that gamblers, and especially so-called compulsive gamblers, are, in a manner of speaking, spiritual seekers. In the words of James Mooney, gambling is rooted in the "universal longing of mankind to know the cause of things and how effects may be controlled."[15] True, on the surface, gamblers seek economic fortune, but they are also seeking a personal transformation, a feeling of invincibility and liberation, even if only in the moment of exhilaration. The moment is transitory, and the seeking of further moments is what can sometimes throw the individual out of integrity, causing the effect of addictive cycles.[16]

Critics of this theory may argue that gambling in and of itself cannot be addicting, as alcohol is, and that the "passion for play" may be symptomatic of depression, mania, schizophrenia, and other mental pathology often associated with drug and alcohol abuse. Although the superstition, ritual, and paraphernalia that gamblers use to enhance their luck are all part of the game, when these behaviors excessively cross over into the irrational, particularly when the gambler begins to feel all-powerful and all-knowing, observers should indeed become alarmed.[17] There is an underlying sense of mental illness surrounding the compulsive gamblers in many of the Native American gambling myths, which were probably intended as healing stories for those who harbored such symptoms. Again, in these myths, the antidote is spiritual introspection.

Mental illness aside, gambling should not be viewed as inherently evil or immoral but as a disease of the spirit that uses pleasure to avoid pain. It is not that gamblers are weaker than others—we are all caught in the cycle of pleasure and pain—but that their pain, though no less acute, is veiled. In many Eastern philosophies this dilemma is known as divine discontent, and as the native gambling myths show, such malaise is a necessary step in the process of becoming spiritual. Such gambling cannot be healed by abstention or by the threat of an eternity in hell; it can only be exhausted and surrendered in a moment of epiphany when one can imagine life without gambling but not without spirituality. Where is the sin in that?

Whatever forces the gambler believes is causing him or her to win or to lose, they can never sustain or nurture him or her indefinitely. In fact, the Native American myths show that the effects of gambling in the extreme can be cataclysmic, yet even disaster can catapult the gambler's spiritual development. Of course, these forces do not exist outside of the self but lie within one's own actions. Society can try to exile or reform compulsive gamblers but, ultimately, the gamblers must embark on their own quest that takes them deeper into their traditional beliefs, and beyond. This is not to say that gamblers should not suffer the consequences of their actions. After all, these consequences are part of the experiment to know the cause of things and how effects can be controlled.

Where is the sin in gambling?" Oscar asks Lucinda:

> Our whole faith is a wager. . . . We bet—it is all in Pascal and very wise it is too—we bet that there is a God. We bet our life on it. We calculate the odds, the return, that we shall sit with the saints in paradise. Our anxiety about our bet will wake us before dawn in a cold sweat. . . . And God sees us, sees us suffer. . . . I cannot see . . . that such a God, whose fundamental requirement of us is that we gamble our mortal souls, every second of our temporal existence. . . . It is true! We must gamble every instant of our allotted span. We must stake everything on the unprovable fact of His existence. [I cannot see] that such a God . . . knowing the anguish and trembling hope with which we wager. . . . That such a God can look unkindly on a chap wagering a few quid on

the likelihood of a dumb animal crossing a line first, unless . . . it might be considered blasphemy to apply to common pleasure that which is by its very nature divine.[18]

NOTES

1. Johann Huizinga, *Homo Ludens: A Study of the Play Element in Culture* (Boston: Beacon Press/Huizinga, 1950), pp. 1–27.

2. Florence N. David, *Games, Gods and Gambling: The Origins and History of Probability and Statistical Ideas from the Earliest Times to the Newtonian Era* (New York: Hafner, 1962), pp. 6–7.

3. Neil Petty, *The Petty Papers*, ed. the Marquis of Landsdowne (London: Constable & Co., 1927).

4. Kathryn Gabriel, *Gambler Way: Indian Gaming in Mythology, History, and Archaeology in North America* (Boulder: Johnson Books, 1996), pp. 87–124.

5. Kathryn Gabriel, "The Navajo Great Gambler Legend: A Cultural Phenomenon," in *Diné Hané Bi Naaltsoos: Collected Papers from the Seventh through Tenth Navajo Studies Conferences*, ed. June-el Piper (published on behalf of the Navajo Studies Conference by the Navajo Historic Preservation Department, Window Rock, Arizona: 1999), pp. 239–30.

6. Stewart Culin, *Games of the North American Indians*, reprint, 2 vols., (Lincoln: University of Nebraska Press, 1992). (Originally published in 1902–1903 as *Report of the Bureau of American Ethnology* 24, Washington, D.C.: Smithsonian Institution.)

7. Culin, *Games of the North American Indians*, pp. 174–75, 486.

8. Gabriel, *Gambler Way: Indian Gaming in Mythology*.

9. Robert H. Lowie, "Centipede," in "Shoshonean Tales," *Journal of American Folk-Lore* 37, no. 1 (1912): 229–32.

10. James A. Teit "The Gambler," in "Traditions of the Lillooet Indians of British Columbia," *Journal of American Folk-Lore* 25 (1912): 117.

11. Johannes Adrianus Bernandus Van Buitenen, ed. and trans., *The Mahabharata: The Book of the Assembly Hall.* (Chicago: University of Chicago Press, 1975).

12. Gabriel, *Gambler Way: Indian Gaming in Mythology*, pp. 168–74.

13. Rai Munshi Ram, *With the Three Masters in India*, 3d ed., vol. 3 (Punjab, India: Radha Soami Satsang Beas, 1987), pp. 23–24.

14. Hafiz, "Tripping over Joy," in *I Heard God Laughing: Renderings of Hafiz*, ed. D. Landinsky (Oakland: Mobius Press, 1996), p. 127.

15. James Mooney, *Myths of the Cherokee* Report of the Bureau of American Ethnology 19 (Washington, D.C.: Smithsonian Institution, 1897–1898).

16. Kathryn Gabriel, "Gambling and Spirituality, A New Anthropological Perspective" [online], http://www.nmia.com/~kgabriel/myths.html [1998–2000].

17. Neil D. Isaacs, *You Bet Your Life: The Burdens of Gambling* (Lexington: University Press of Kentucky, 2000).

18. Peter Carey, *Oscar and Lucinda* (New York: Harper & Row, 1988), pp. 218–19.

22

COMBUSTION

An Essay on the Value of Gambling

John Scanlan

The notion of a culture implies a certain degree of refinement; it suggests the working out of a system, perhaps in the founding of institutions or the acceptance of a symbolic language, and so on. Yet, more loosely, we may say that a culture is a convergence of values that, in sorting out what is in from what is out, establishes stability among potentially divergent interests. Implicit in the idea of "combustion," by contrast, is the suggestion of a destructive capacity that blows things up—specifically, in terms of culture, things (like beliefs and practices) that may be valuable.

Whatever the controversies surrounding the growth of gambling in recent years—the variety of political imperatives and business interests at work, moral or medical concerns over the consequences of liberalization on an apparently vulnerable gambling public, and so on—we must not lose sight of the fact that what a culture does in terms of working itself out (that is, in resolving these controversies) may not always stand in accordance with the grounds of that very culture. In other words, it is important to divorce a sociological understanding of gambling from "politics" (a term that I use to mean the various debates just mentioned).

If we consider for a moment gambling as a 'pure' form: as an engagement with uncontrollable chance—we can see that, in reaching beyond bounds of expectation, it strives to clarify the very notion of culturally accepted values. In this sense the gambling impulse (which we may equally call "adventure," "curiosity," etc.) is a foundation for all that we value in Western culture generally.

How can this be? In short, it is because the "combustible" tendency of an activity like gambling is what provokes the withdrawal and consolidation that marks cultural refinement. In other words, it is by disconnecting experience from a universe of chance that social and cultural bonds originate as an inward withdrawal (and meaningful connection) to a domain of bounded rational freedom. With this in mind, gambling as a combustible element then threatens varieties of catastrophe on a number of levels, which correspond principally to the potential impact the activity may have on culturally given attitudes in respect of the human body, our capacity for reason, and the status of nonhuman nature in modernity. In each instance, however, the convergence of cultural meanings that gives form to these three categories (body, reason, nature) would be impossible without the implicit acceptance that value (culture), quite fundamentally, is built upon fragility.[1]

BODY: A FEVER OF INSTABILITY

Gambling provokes a physiological response in the player that upsets a steady and tightly wound equilibrium (control of bodily responses, emissions, and so on) that modern society continues to advocate as a primary condition of "normality."[2] Gambling is "loose" and, at worst, uncontrollable; hence, the representation of the excessive gambler in terms of a total extremity of physical experience:

"Blood rushes to your head, a sensation like a sudden rise in pressure. Your head is going to explode."[3]

"The nerves may stand on end and scream to themselves."[4]

"I drew a deep breath. Fiery ants were crawling all over my body."[5]

Thus the plunge from an ordered condition (bodily composure) into a state of disorder (loosening of self-control) marks at the least a fever of instability and at the most a point of overheating so intense that it threatens to expand from the one to the several, and from the individual to society. In short, the engagement with chance represents the potential cauterization of the body social.

This point is implicit in the work that constitutes the earliest examples of the modern study of gambling as illness. For example, it is found in Freud's influential essay on Dostoevsky (identifying the impulse to gamble as a desire for destabilization and punishment) but equally so in various memoirs and histories of gambling (Henry Chafetz's history of gambling cites a denunciation of 1787 bemoaning the spread of the "contagious distemper" in the United States).[6] The idea of a bodily instability, of a fever or contagion, extends to the present day—and sustains the contemporary psychiatric classification of gambling (in the DSM-IV) as, for example, an "impulse control disorder."[7]

There is, nevertheless, a paradox in this view: impulses can be kept in control only under conditions in which experience never alters from one day to the next. It should be clear, then, that a condition of stability is not valuable in and of itself because—to put it bluntly—if living is a process of movement and change, and if the exploration of "territory" beyond the self is a condition of human development, then varieties in (bodily) experience become an inevitable part of life. In other words, no "equitable" distribution of impulses can be effectively managed as is implied by the normative character of an "impulse control" definition of disorder. And whatever the background to the choices that produce a gambling moment, it nevertheless remains—regardless of the gambler's misguided belief in absolute freedom—a fundamental aspect of free action. In the context of this discussion, freedom is a constituent of the act of wagering which emanates (as a choice to bet) from a period of indecision (to bet or not to bet). The free act derives from the undifferentiated flux of causes and effects that dominates the gambling situation. In deciding to wager, the gambler interrupts a motiveless cycle (possible outcomes) and thus attempts to suspend, and overcome, chance—that is, to reach a determined outcome. The act of gambling is then somewhat analogous to the creation of a culture, which is to say it is a primary act of differentiation: an attempt to force a conjunction between self and the world.[8]

REASON: WHAM . . . JUST LIKE THAT!

The necessity of establishing control over oneself in an effort to guard against falling under the control of forces one doesn't understand (for example, in exercising restraint over one's impulses) finds analogy in the rational explanation of the unpredictable nature of physical phenomena that constitutes the domain of science. Thus, in confronting inexplicable nature (accidents, strange phenomena, etc.), humankind is thrown sideways from a battle with self (characteristic of a later stage in modern development) into an apparently continuous struggle against a motiveless and potentially explosive causality. The impulse to control the body reflects a historically prior "contest" between reason and chance, of which it is merely a further development.

But to get back to reason: the potential impact of unpredictable phenomena on reasonable expectations is illustrated to good effect in a scene from Paul Thomas Anderson's film *Hard Eight*, which establishes the relative ease with which the two main characters regard the unpredictable and chancy. By simply demonstrating the disproportionate influence that unforeseeable phenomena can have on human understanding, the scene reminds us of the close proximity of reason and disorder at all times. Traveling through the Nevada desert with his new acquaintance, Sydney, John—a hopeless and inexperienced gambler who has just lost all his money in Las Vegas—attempts to light a cigarette using the lighter on the dashboard of Sydney's car:

> "The lighter here—it doesn't work," says Sydney. "Here." He hands John a matchbook.
>
> "No thanks," says John, who repeats tries once again to use the car lighter.
>
> "The lighter doesn't work," repeats Sydney.

"I heard you, I . . . I just don't use matches."

"Want to hold the wheel while I light mine?" Sydney says. "You going to smoke then?"

"No," says John.

"So why don't you use these matches?"

"It's just a rule with me, okay? I just don't use matches."

"Why not?"

"I had a really bad experience once and I promised I'd never use them again."

"Tell me?"

John begins: "You know these big, monster books of matches? Those big daddy ones with, like, forty matches in them? I had one of those in my pocket once and they just lit on fire—just exploded."

"Yeah?" asks Sydney. "The matches just went off?".

"Yeah, it had something to do with friction, I guess. Spontaneous friction—I mean, they just went off. . . . I mean, I'm standing in line for a movie and all of a sudden just WHAM!"

As the film proceeds, we see that Sydney has clearly learned how to adapt to chance: that is to say, he knows that chance cannot be beaten, so he lives out his life in a way that demonstrates a degree of control over his own limitations, and this lesson he then teaches John. The moral of this tale is that "things" can just happen—blow up out of nowhere—but rather than being a cause for grave concern, such incidents just remind us that the accidents, exceptions, and anomalies in experience provide the basis for a rational understanding of how phenomena might be related.

NONHUMAN NATURE: ABUNDANCE

Gambling in its "pure" form is, when all is said and done, the corollary of an unruly nature that humankind, in its never ceasing expansion into previously uncontrolled domains, seeks to bring under the control of reason. In Western culture, where a notion of identity-as-sameness is of fundamental importance in philosophically working out meaning (and where the convergence of differences is the paradoxical condition of free society), the combustible promise of gambling presents itself as the expression of a potent and rebellious element that may always be present, but that pushes difference beyond an acceptable expression of refusal, and thus beyond stability toward destruction.

Nature is just the absence of (rational) limits, and gambling likewise explores the unlimited and unknown "motives" in nature. In archaic societies, indeed, divination (practiced, for example, through the casting of lots) was the mode of understanding nature (constituted as the will of the gods), and so the premodern experience of nature was of a "divine lottery . . . where Zeus scatters good and evil fates or lots among men not according to any principle of fair play, let alone divine justice, but according to his own whims."[9] In modern terms, such views simply indicate an acceptance of the abundance of nature and of the power of unseen forces that unleash phenomena (or situations or conditions) that can be interpreted only as examples of a willful natural disorder. Similarly, the gambling act can be seen as a practical engagement with disorder, in which the gratuitousness of nature can be matched only by a wasteful gesture and the purposeless flux of events only by an activity with no end beyond itself, namely, the splurge.[10] By contrast, in modern society the transformation of the abundance of nature into use-values is part of the great attempt to dominate the 'inefficiency' of such a combustible world.

The problem with the gambler, precisely, is that the renunciation of means to control bodily impulses reflects not only an abandonment of reason but also of accepted ways of confronting nature (potentially at the expense of culture). The maverick gesture engages the unpredictable and disposes of practicality in favor of transcendence. Gambling "blows up" the limits that separate human culture from nonhuman nature and becomes (for a moment at least) at one with immediate nature.

There is an understandable tendency to stamp out this combustible, rebellious element—yet if ever this attempt succeeded, it would be disastrous for society because it would deny the place of nonhuman nature in providing the ground for the edification of human culture. As Odo Marquard notes, "*Sense is just the nonsense that we throw away.*"[11] The point should not be missed. To derive meaning and establish value (culture), we must first know and make use of nonsense or disorder, and this, too, is the value of gambling.

NOTES

1. The idea that what is good, or valuable, in humankind must be seen to emanate from a rational element rather than from luck is as old as Western civilization. See, for example, Martha Nussbaum, *The Fragility of Goodness: Luck and Ethics in Greek Tragedy and Philosophy* (Cambridge: Cambridge University Press, 1986).

2. See, for example, Eve Kosofsky Sedgewick, "Epidemics of the Will," in *Zone 6: Incorporations*, ed. Jonathan Crary and Stanford Kwinter (New York: Zone Books, 1992).

3. Frederick Barthelme and Steven Barthelme, *Double Down: Reflections on Gambling and Loss* (Boston and New York: Houghton Mifflin, 1999), p. 118.

4. Stephen Crane, *Last Words* (London: Digby and Long, 1902), p. 263.

5. Fyodor Dostoevsky, *The Gambler* 1866 (New York and London: Norton, 1981), p. 144.

6. Henry Chafetz, *Play the Devil: A History of Gambling in the United States* (New York: Bonanza Books, 1960), p. 38.

7. See Sigmund Freud, "Dostoevsky and Parricide," in *The Standard Edition of the Complete Psychological Works of Sigmund Freud*, vol. 5, ed. James Strachey (London: Hogarth Press, 1953). The most sustained and eloquent descriptions of the physical disordering produced by gambling to excess can be found in the recent memoir of the Barthelme brothers, *Double Down: Reflections on Gambling and Loss*. (See note 3.) On the development of gambling taxonomies, see Allen Collins, "The Pathological Gambler and the Government of Gambling," *History of the Human Sciences* 9, no. 3 (1996): 69–100.

8. Compare Slavoj Zizek, *The Indivisible Remainder: An Essay on Schelling and Related Matters* (London and New York: Verso, 1996).

9. Mihai I. Spariosu, *Dionysus Reborn* (Ithaca: Cornell University Press, 1989), p. 15.

10. Compare Georges Bataille, *The Accursed Share,* vol. 1, *An Essay on General Economy* (New York: Zone Books, 1989).

11. Odo Marquard, *In Defense of the Accidental: Philosophical Studies* (New York and Oxford: Oxford University/Odéon, 1991), pp. 38–39.

LIST OF CONTRIBUTORS

JAY ALBANESE is professor and chair of the Department of Criminal Justice, Virginia Commonwealth University.

WILLIAM J. BURKE is professor and vice-chair of psychiatry at the University of Nebraska Medical Center.

PETER COLLINS is professor and director of the Center for the Study of Gambling and Commercial Gaming at the University of Salford, United Kingdom, and executive director of the South African National Responsible Gambling Program.

ANNE-ELYSE DEGUIRE is the prevention specialist at the International Center for Youth Gambling Problems and High-Risk Behaviors, McGill University, Montreal.

JEFFREY L. DEREVENSKY is professor in the School of Applied Child Psychology; co-director of the Youth Gambling Research and Treatment Clinic and of the International Center for Youth Gambling Problems and High Risk Behaviors at McGill University, Montreal. He is also associate editor of the *Journal of Gambling Studies*.

MARK DICKERSON holds the Tattersall's Chair for Research into Problem Gambling, School of Psychology, University of Western Sydney, Australia.

LAURIE DICKSON is a Ph.D. student in the School of Applied Child Psychology at McGill University, Montreal.

WILLIAM R. EADINGTON is professor of economics and director of the Institute for the Study of Gambling and Commercial Gaming at the University of Nevada, Reno.

KATHRYN GABRIEL is an independent author of books on anthropology, history, and spirituality.

DAVID GIACOPASSI is professor in the Department of Criminology and Criminal Justice, University of Memphis.

ROBERT GOODMAN is professor of environmental design at Hampshire College and former director of the United States Gambling Research Institute.

MARK GRIFFITHS is professor of psychology at the Nottingham Trent University, United Kingdom.

EARL L. GRINOLS is professor of economics at the University of Illinois at Urbana-Champaign and former senior economist on the Council of Economic Advisers.

RINA GUPTA is assistant professor in the School of Applied Child Psychology and co-director of both the Youth Gambling Research and Treatment Clinic and the International Center for Youth Gambling Problems and High-Risk Behaviors at McGill University, Montreal. She is a member of the editorial board of the *Journal of Gambling Studies*.

MICHAEL E. HAMMOND is an associate attorney at Landrum & Shouse, LLP in Lexington, Kentucky, who focuses on civil defense litigation and Internet-related issues.

KAREN HARDOON is a doctoral student in the School of Applied Child Psychology at McGill University, Montreal.

NEIL A. MANSON, is assistant professor of philosophy at Virginia Commonwealth University, Richmond, Virginia.

JAN MCMILLEN is director of the Centre for Gambling Research at the Australian National University, Canberra.

DENNIS P. MCNEILLY is a clinical psychologist and assistant professor of psychiatry at the University of Nebraska Medical Center.

DAVID MIERS is professor of law at Cardiff Law School, Cardiff University, United Kingdom.

MARK NICHOLS is associate professor in the Department of Economics at the University of Nevada, Reno.

JONATHAN PARKE is a psychologist completing his doctorate at the Nottingham Trent University, United Kingdom.

STANTON PEELE, PhD, is a fellow of the Lindesmith Center Drug Policy Foundation.

GERDA REITH, is assistant professor of sociology at the University of Glasgow, United Kingdom.

I. NELSON ROSE is professor of law at Whittier Law School, Costa Mesa, California. He is recognized as a leading authority on gambling laws and is a consultant to governments and industry.

JOHN SCANLAN, is assistant professor of sociology at the University of Paisley, United Kingdom.

HOWARD J. SHAFFER is associate professor of psychology and director in the Division on Addictions, Harvard Medical School and Department of Psychiatry at the Cambridge Hospital. He is also editor of the *Journal of Gambling Studies*.

JEROME H. SKOLNICK is a professor at the NYU School of Law, New York, where he teaches a seminar on the regulation of vice.

B. GRANT STITT is professor and chair of the Department of Criminal Justice, University of Nevada, Reno.

RACHEL A. VOLBERG, a sociologist, is president of Gemini Research, Ltd., the only international organization that specializes in studies of gambling and problem gambling in the general population.

KEITH S. WHYTE is executive director (U.S.) of the National Council on Problem Gambling.